Mobilizing a Great Commission Church for Harvest

Mobilizing a Great Commission Church for Harvest

Voices and Views from the Southern Baptist Professors of Evangelism Fellowship

EDITED BY THOMAS P. JOHNSTON

Foreword by R. Philip Roberts

WIPF & STOCK · Eugene, Oregon

MOBILIZING A GREAT COMMISSION CHURCH FOR HARVEST
Voices and Views from the Southern Baptist Professors of Evangelism Fellowship

Scripture quotations marked (ESV) are from the Holy Bible, English Standard
Version (ESV), © 2001 by Crossway, a publishing ministry of Good News Publishers.
Used by permission. All rights reserved.

Scripture quotations marked (HCSB) taken from the Holman Christian Standard
Bible, © 2003, 2002, 2000, 1999 by Holman Bible Publishers. All rights reserved.

Scripture quotations marked (NAS, NASB) taken from the New American Standard
Bible, © 1960, 1962, 1963, 1968, 1971, 1972, 1973, 1975, 1977, 1995 by The Lockman
Foundation. Used by permission. www.Lockman.org.

Scripture quotations marked (NIV) are taken from the Holy Bible, New
International Version, © 1973, 1978, 1984 by Biblica, Inc. Used by permission of
Zondervan. All rights reserved worldwide. www.zondervan.com.

Much of chapter 17, "Get Real: Mobilizing Students to Witness," is taken from
Raising the Bar: Ministry to Youth in the New Millennium, © 2004 by Alvin L. Reid,
published by Kregel Publications, Grand Rapids, Michigan. Used by permission of
the publisher. All rights reserved.

Wipf & Stock
An Imprint of Wipf and Stock Publishers
199 W. 8th Ave., Suite 3
Eugene, OR 97401

www.wipfandstock.com

ISBN 13: 978-1-61097-264-2

Manufactured in the U.S.A.

This book is dedicated to my late father,

Arthur P. Johnston, PhD (1922–2009);

veteran missionary to France; Professor of Missions and Evangelism, Trinity Evangelical Divinity School; theological advisor on the Board of Trustees of the Billy Graham Evangelistic Association; and founding president of Tyndale Theological Seminary, Badhoevedorp, The Netherlands. I was blessed by his example, loving mentorship, and theological insight.

Contents

Foreword

EVANGELISM IS THE PRISTINE and primary responsibility of the church of Jesus Christ. A quick perusal of the last and commissioning words of Jesus himself, such as the Great Commission in Matthew 28:18–20 or the exhortation of Acts 1:8, makes this duty and its great responsibility crystal clear. Therefore, there can be no more important or vital topic, in terms of ministry, to be addressed than the one highlighted in this volume—evangelism!

If the church goes silent on this one assignment—the proclamation and dissemination of the gospel of Jesus Christ—then Christianity and the possibility of salvation for any and every person on this earth dies with the silence of God's chosen instrument of evangelism: his church. Rather it should, and indeed must, be the case that every Christian lives as if the hope of the world rested on their shoulders. Charles Spurgeon framed in his tome, *The Soul Winner*,[1] this thought well: "That man lives grandly who is as earnest as if the very existence of Christianity depended upon himself, and is determined that to all men within his reach shall be made known the unsearchable riches of Christ."

If this impulse was true for Spurgeon, it ought to be true for all Christians in every age.

Evangelism is the theme of *Mobilizing a Great Commission Church for Harvest*. And that is why this volume is so vitally important. It addresses the concept of how the entire people of God can be involved in sharing the great news of God's gift of eternal life offered to all. Addressing topics such as the pastor's role, every-member mobilization, and developing a

---

1. Charles H. Spurgeon, *The Soul Winner* (New York: Revell, 1895; Reprints, Grand Rapids: Zondervan, 1947; Grand Rapids: Eerdmans, 1963, 1964, 1995).

Great Commission church, the reader will find not only a great deal of information in these pages but a constant challenge to evangelize.

It is my privilege and joy to know personally most of the contributors to this volume. They are men who walk the walk and talk the talk, literally, when it comes to the task of sharing Jesus with others. Because of this fact, I deeply respect and appreciate each one of them. The lives they live lend credence and authenticity to all that they write. Tom Johnston, the book's editor, has served as professor of evangelism at Midwestern Baptist Theological Seminary since the autumn of 2001. He was my first faculty hire after I became president. Dr. Johnston exemplifies the principle that "Evangelism is better caught than taught." His ability and gift to impart to his students the passion to share the good news is extraordinary. He is helped, I realize, by a faculty largely and exceptionally evangelistic. Consequently, I've seen a number of students graduate from seminary with a greater commitment to evangelize than when they arrived. As far as seminary experience is concerned, this phenomenon is, sadly in the history of many seminaries, phenomenal. The same could surely be said of all this volume's writers and their respective institutions. Therefore this work, I believe, along with the ongoing service of its editor and contributors will continue to build and lead churches and their ministers to take the gospel of Jesus to all the world.

—R. Philip Roberts,
President, Midwestern Baptist Theological Seminary

Contributors

Timothy K. Beougher, Billy Graham Professor of Evangelism and Church Growth, Associate Dean and Director of Research Doctoral Studies, Billy Graham School of Missions and Evangelism, Southern Baptist Theological Seminary.

Paul H. Chitwood, Assistant Professor of Evangelism and Church Growth, Billy Graham School of Missions and Evangelism, Southern Baptist Theological Seminary.

Adam W. Greenway, Senior Associate Dean; Associate Vice President for Extension Education; Assistant Professor of Evangelism and Applied Apologetics, Billy Graham School of Missions and Evangelism, Southern Baptist Theological Seminary.

Kenneth S. Hemphill, Founding Director, Center for Church Planting and Revitalization, North Greenville University; Distinguished Professor of Evangelism and Church Growth, Billy Graham School of Missions and Evangelism, Southern Baptist Theological Seminary.

William D. Henard III, Assistant Professor of Evangelism and Church Growth, Billy Graham School of Missions and Evangelism, Southern Baptist Theological Seminary.

Thomas P. Johnston, Associate Professor of Evangelism, Midwestern Baptist Theological Seminary; Director, Midwestern Evangelistic Teams; President, Evangelism Unlimited, Inc.

Charles E. Lawless Jr., Dean, Billy Graham School of Missions and Evangelism; Vice President for Academic Programming; Director of Professional Doctoral Studies; Professor of Evangelism and Church Growth, Billy Graham School of Missions and Evangelism, Southern Baptist Theological Seminary.

Will H. McRaney Jr., Director, Evangelism Strategy Department, Florida Baptist Convention; Adjunct Instructor of Evangelism, New Orleans Baptist Theological Seminary and Liberty Baptist Theological Seminary.

L. David Mills, Assistant Professor of Evangelism and Associate Dean for Applied Ministries, Roy J. Fish School of Evangelism and Missions, Southwestern Baptist Theological Seminary.

Preston L. Nix, Professor of Evangelism and Evangelistic Preaching, occupying the Roland Q. Leavell Chair of Evangelism; Director of the Leavell Center for Evangelism and Church Health; Chairman of the Pastoral Ministries Division, New Orleans Baptist Theological Seminary.

Edsel D. Pate Jr., Chair, Intercultural Studies Department; Director, Kim School of Global Missions; Associate Professor of Missions, Golden Gate Baptist Theological Seminary.

J. D. Payne, Associate Professor of Church Planting and Evangelism; Director of the Center for North American Missions and Church Planting, Southern Baptist Theological Seminary.

Edward Pearson, Baptist Collegiate Minister, University of Arizona; Discipleship Facilitator, Arizona Southern Baptist Convention; Adjunct Evangelism Professor, Golden Gate Baptist Theological Seminary.

Alvin L. Reid, Professor of Evangelism and Student Ministry, Bailey Smith Chair of Evangelism; Southeastern Baptist Theological Seminary.

Darrell W. Robinson, President, Total Church Life Ministries; Distinguished Professor of Evangelism, Midwestern Baptist Theological Seminary.

Jake Roudkovski, Director of Supervised Ministry; Assistant Professor of Evangelism occupying the Max and Bonnie Thornhill Chair of Evangelism; New Orleans Baptist Theological Seminary.

Josef Solc, Professor of Evangelism and Missions, Southeastern Baptist Theological Seminary.

Mark Tolbert, Associate Professor of Evangelism and Pastoral Ministry; Director, Doctor of Ministry Program, New Orleans Baptist Theological Seminary.

David Wheeler, Professor of Evangelism, Liberty Baptist Theological Seminary and Liberty University; Associate Director, Church Planting and Ministry Training Center; Director of Applied Evangelism/Servant Ministries.

1

Unleashing the Power of Matthew's Great Commission

Thomas P. Johnston

FOR NEW TESTAMENT CHRISTIANS, the Great Commission provides the spiritual engine, the driving force, and the forward thrust of their lives. The Great Commission encapsulates Christ's marching orders to his Church. Chuck Kelley reminded members of the Southern Baptist Convention (SBC) that ours is a "Great Commission Hermeneutic."[1] In other words, we ought to read, interpret, and apply the Bible in light of the Great Commission. The Anabaptist Michael Sattler saw in both the Great Commissions of Matthew and Mark reasons why believers and only believers ought to be baptized. This belief he transcribed into the *Schleitheim Confession* in 1527,[2] only to be martyred later that same year.

---

1 .Charles Kelley, *How Did They Do It? The Story of Southern Baptist Evangelism* (New Orleans: Insight, 1993), 119–31.

2. "First. Observe concerning baptism: Baptism shall be given to all those who have learned repentance and amendment of life, and who believe truly that their sins are taken away by Christ, and to all who walk in the resurrection of Jesus Christ, and wish to be buried with him in death, so that they may be resurrected with him, and to all those who with this significance request it [baptism] of us and demand it for themselves. This excludes all infant baptism, the highest and chief abominations of the pope. In this you have the foundation and testimony of the apostles. Mt. 28, Mk. 16, Acts 2, 8, 16, 19. This we wish to hold simply, yet firmly and with assurance." "The Schleitheim Confession," in *Baptist Confessions of Faith*, William L. Lumpkin, ed. (Valley Forge: Judson, 1969), 25.

Yes, and because of its prominence, the Great Commission provides both a meeting place and battleground for a discussion of evangelism, biblical interpretation, and the doctrines of salvation and the church.

In fact, the interpretation and application of Christ's Great Commission, especially in Matthew 28, provides a unique biblical focal point for the multi-disciplinary study of the Bible. Interestingly, one's interpretation and application of this Great Commission passage link together (1) one's view of conversion and salvation (systematic theology), (2) one's view of evangelism and the mission of the church (ecclesiology and missions), and (3) one's approach to spiritual growth and discipleship (practical theology). The study of Matthew's Great Commission passage, therefore, while linking all these concepts together, provides both a crossroads and a battleground for an evaluation of Christ's thoughts on these ideas.

That one can take the words of Jesus in two or three verses as normative must be understood as part of plenary inspiration. One might say, "Two or three verses do not suffice to understand or interpret the thinking of Jesus on any topic!" To this I reply that, if these two or three verses do speak of a topic, then these verses have as much weight as any other words of Jesus on that topic (*sensus plenior*). However, before entering into this discussion please allow me to divulge several presuppositions. First, on the inspiration of Scripture: I believe that God the Holy Spirit exhaled every word of the original languages of the Bible (2 Tim 3:16). Second, on the inerrancy of Scripture: I believe that the Bible is wholly true in all it affirms, and likewise there are not at all any errors in any of the Bible's affirmations. And third, following from point one, on the unity of Scripture: I believe that God the Holy Spirit does not contradict himself, but rather he speaks with one voice throughout all of sacred Scripture and through its multiple authors and genres. Therefore, with these presuppositions in mind, when looking at Matthew 28:19–20, it must be assumed that the teachings of Jesus in this passage do not contradict his teachings in other biblical passages. If anything, the teachings of Jesus in this passage conform to and confirm all his other teachings in the Gospels, as well as to all that is taught in the remainder of Holy Writ, as rightly interpreted.

So, what does Jesus teach in Matthew 28:19–20? In this commissioning Jesus commanded his disciples to win disciples from among all the nations of the earth. In this command, we have the earthly mission of

Christ's disciples, which is in perfect sync with Christ's atonement on the cross for sin, the conversion of those who hear the gospel with a hearing of faith, along with the practical outworking of this mission in individual New Testament churches.

First of all, let us note that when Christ commanded his disciples to go, specifically to all nations, he took language from the cursing portion in Deuteronomy 28 and made it into a command in Matthew 28. For example:

- Deut 28:64–65: "Moreover, the LORD will scatter you among all peoples, from one end of the earth to the other end of the earth; and there you shall serve other gods, wood and stone, which you or your fathers have not known. And among those nations you shall find no rest, and there shall be no resting place for the sole of your foot; but there the LORD will give you a trembling heart, failing of eyes, and despair of soul."

- Deut 28:37: "And you shall become a horror, a proverb, and a taunt among all the people where the LORD will drive you."

Being driven, scattered, and sent to the nations was not necessarily a good thing in the Old Testament; rather it was the language of the curse. Perhaps this is why the Jews in Jerusalem reacted so vehemently and interrupted Paul's testimony in Acts 22. Paul had just told them that God had said to him, "Go! For I will send you far away to the Gentiles" (Acts 22:21). Luke explained their interruption:

- Acts 22:22–24: "And they listened to him up to this statement, and *then* they raised their voices and said, 'Away with such a fellow from the earth, for he should not be allowed to live!' And as they were crying out and throwing off their cloaks and tossing dust into the air, the commander ordered him to be brought into the barracks . . ."

Can such vehement antagonism be understood? Yes, they were acknowledging the blessing of the promised land, as well as the curse of being "diaspora-ed" (driven out) of that land to go forth unto the nations. Yes, it is always a struggle for anyone to be exiled from their own land.

Paul himself faced this contradictory idea in his use of the words hungry, thirsty, and naked (or exposure). These three words in this exact order come from Deuteronomy 28:

- Deut 28:47–48: "Because you did not serve the LORD your God with joy and a glad heart, for the abundance of all things; therefore you shall serve your enemies whom the LORD shall send against you, in hunger, in thirst, in nakedness, and in the lack of all things; and He will put an iron yoke on your neck until He has destroyed you."

Notice how Paul refers to these three occurrences happening to him, using the same order as Deuteronomy 28 (not including his imprisonment):

- 1 Cor 4:11: "To this present hour we are both hungry and thirsty, and are poorly clothed, and are roughly treated, and are homeless."
- 2 Cor 11:27: "*I have been* in labor and hardship, through many sleepless nights, in hunger and thirst, often without food, in cold and exposure."

How did Paul deal with these difficulties in his ministry? He gloried in them (Rom 5:3–5), and he learned to give thanks in all circumstances (Phil 4:11–12).

We as New Testament Christians may try to sugarcoat the Great Commission. Either we relegate it to some overarching mission of the universal church, that has no direct application to our everyday lives, or we ignore that it will cost us dearly. Jesus, however, knew the language that he had borrowed from Deuteronomy 28. He knew that it would not be easy for the disciples. Note, for example, how he prepared his followers for difficult times in Matthew 10 and John 15–16. Therefore, the "Go" in the Great Commission ought not be philosophized into "stay where you are, and do as you please." Jesus said, "Go!"

"Go," Jesus said, "and win disciples." But, you may ask, do not most or all contemporary English Bibles say "m-m-make disciples"? Then, from the word *make* is posited a long-term process of some type of Christian catechetic (or education). Yes, some churches insert multiple sacraments (or "means of grace/holiness") into the word *make*. Others place a two or three year commitment of discipleship meant to "m-m-make" the convert into a true disciple of Jesus. However, exegetically and contextually, it would appear otherwise.

Two contextual arguments bring consternation to this long-term approach to "make." First, the disciple is already "made" or "won" before he should be baptized. The key word for interpretation is the word *them* in verse 19. To whom does the "them" refer in verse 19? In the Greek, the form of this word does not agree with the form of the words *of all nations.* Jesus did not call for the baptism of every baby in a certain country (as territorial churches often teach and practice), nor did he even mean the baptism of every baby of all true believers (as most non-territorial Reformation churches practice). Rather using the aorist of the verb phrase "win disciples," Jesus communicated its point-in-time emphasis. Once a disciple was won, then and only then, was he to be baptized!

Second, Matthew used the word "win disciples," often translated "make disciples," twenty-eight verses prior in Matthew 27:57, speaking of the secret commitment of Joseph of Arimathea:

- Matt 27:57–58: "And when it was evening, there came a rich man from Arimathea, named Joseph, who himself *had* also *become a disciple* of Jesus. This man went to Pilate and asked for the body of Jesus. Then Pilate ordered *it* to be given over *to him.*" [italics mine]

The use of this same verb phrase, "had become a disciple," in Matthew 27:57 (*matheteuo* also found in Matt 13:52 and Acts 14:21) provides several further insights. Matheteuo cannot refer to the long-term relationship Jesus had with the twelve disciples. First of all, the word was never used to describe his relationship with the twelve disciples. Second, Joseph of Arimathea, of whom the verb was used, had not walked with Jesus for two or three years. In fact, John 19:38 stated that Joseph was a secret disciple, something decried in John 12:42–43! Somehow, Joseph seemed to be one of those rulers condemned in John 12:42, who after the crucifixion, decided to take a stand for Jesus. Notice also that, by the tense of the verb, Joseph was already won as a disciple of Jesus. Any true Christian is therefore a disciple of Jesus immediately upon conversion (Acts 11:26), even before receiving water baptism! There is no need, therefore, for multiple levels of spiritual relationship: level one, convert; level two, a baptized convert; level three, a Christian; level four, a disciple. All true Christians are also true disciples, and are so upon conversion.

Therefore, it follows also that the word *matheteuo* in Matthew 28:19 does not, dare I say it, cannot, speak of the continuation of salvation but rather of the beginning of salvation. That is, it speaks of conversion, not of discipleship. There is no distinction between a convert and a disciple as is made by some.[3] Is this not why it is paired up with the verb "evangelize" in Acts 14:21?

- Acts 14:21 (HCSB): "After they had *evangelized* that town and made many disciples, they returned to Lystra, to Iconium, and to Antioch." [italics mine]

- Acts 14:21 (NIV): "They preached the good news in that city and *won* a large number of *disciples*. Then they returned to Lystra, Iconium and Antioch." [italics mine]

- Acts 14:21 (my synthesis of the two): "After they had *evangelized* that city and *won* many *disciples*, they returned to Lystra, Iconium, and Antioch." [italics mine]

When one preaches the gospel or evangelizes, some, and sometimes many, are won as disciples. Notice that the NIV linked "disciple" with the auxiliary, periphrastic, or interpretive verbal phrase "win disciples" rather than "make disciples" in its translation of matheteuo in Acts 14:21. Interesting. Perhaps the translation team felt that contextually, because Paul was in Derbe for only a short time, that all he had the time to do was to "win" some disciples—exactly! Whatever the case, not only is it likely in Acts 14:21 that matheteuo speaks of the beginning of salvation, the same is true in Matthew 28:19, where a disciple must be won *before* he is baptized!

Now, if the NIV translation of *matheteuo* using "win" was valid for Acts 14:21, how about also using the word *win* in Matthew 28:19–20?

- Matt 28:19–20 (my translation): "Go therefore and *win disciples* of all the nations, baptizing them in the name of the Father and of the Son and of the Holy Spirit, teaching them to observe all that I have commanded you; and lo, I am with you always, even to the end of the age."

3. "'Make disciples' is the mandate of the Master (Matthew 28:19–20). We may ignore it, but we cannot evade it.

"Our risen Christ left this legacy—the magna charta of the church. He provided both the model and the method. His life—and death—recast the lives of men. He demonstrated that you have not done anything until you have changed the lives of men.

"'Follow Me,' He urged His men. And then that staggering assurance: 'Lo, I am with you *always* . . .' Somehow we have forgotten that this promise is linked to a process. We cannot embrace the *promise* and ignore the *process*." Howard Hendricks, "Foreword," in *Disciples Are Made—Not Born: Making Disciples Out of Christians*, Walter A. Hendrichsen, (Wheaton, IL: Victor, 1974; 23rd printing, 1985), 5. Italics from original.

The evangelistic power of this translation is amazing! Could it really be that this was what Jesus actually meant when he sent out his disciples to evangelize the world? Doesn't this translation fit perfectly with the words of Jesus when he first called his disciples: "Follow me, and I will make you fishers of men." (Matt 4:19).

The translation "win disciples" also coincides with the aorist tense of the verb *matheteuo* in Matthew 28:19. J. W. Wenham explained the point-in-time emphasis of the aorist tense:

> "In the aorist the action is thought of in its simplest form. In contrast with the linear tenses (Present and Imperfect), which can be thought of as a line or a line of dots:
>
> ————————— or ························
>
> the aorist is a *punctiliar* (or point) tense, which can be thought of as a single dot:
>
> .
>
> The action of the verb is thought of as simply happening, without any regard to its continuance or frequency."[4]

Likewise, the point-in-time use of "win" was also emphasized by Paul when he actually used the Greek word for "win" (*kerdaino*) five times in 1 Corinthians 9:19–22 while speaking of winning the lost to salvation in Christ through conversion. So, translating the verb *matheteuo* as "win disciples" in Matthew 28:19 is contextually consistent within the book of Matthew, is grammatically consistent with the tense of the verb, and is consistent with Paul's methodology as explained in 1 Corinthians 9.

Furthermore, the translation of *matheteuo* as "m-m-make disciples" is rather late in English Bibles. It was first translated this way by John Nelson Darby in his 1884 New Testament. In fact, Darby merely borrowed the term from his French translation of the New Testament in 1859! After Darby translated *matheteuo* as "make disciples" in Matthew 28, virtually all major English Bibles followed suit, up to the present day.

Darby's translation moves us to consider the following: how was it translated prior to Darby? As it turns out, the [second edition] Wycliffe Bible (1388), the Tyndale Bible (1534), the English Geneva (1560), and

4. J. W. Wenham, *The Elements of New Testament Greek* (Cambridge: University Press, 1965), 96.

the King James (1611) all translated *matheteuo* as "teach". In this way they followed the precedent of the Church of Rome's Vulgate which used, and uses, the verb *doceo* (teach) both in Matthew 28:19 and 20. One must remember that Jerome's Vulgate was translated in around AD 404 when the sacramental side of the Church of Rome had gained the upper hand over the evangelical side of the Latin-speaking church (largely comprised of Donatists at that time). Furthermore, the word source for "teach" in verse 19 comes from the Greek word *matheteuo* and the word source for "teach" in verse 20 comes from the Greek word *didasko*. If my earlier premise is true (that a person should not be baptized until they are old enough to become a disciple of Jesus) then it follows that using the same English word *teach* in verses 19 and 20 for two different Greek words (with two different tenses) merely confuses Matthew's Great Commission.

Thus we find that Matthew 28 does step on toes. Sacramental churches do not, cannot, and will not agree with the translation "win disciples" before "baptizing them." Their theology does not allow them to maintain the biblical order of verbs. By baptizing infants, they confuse the order. Furthermore, to them, the phrase "win disciples" smacks of proselytism, a term and concept strongly decried in the past forty years of ecumenical dialogue.[5]

---

5. For example, the 1973 Orthodox and Catholic Common Declaration: "In the name of Christian charity, we reject all forms of proselytism, in the sense of acts by which persons seek to disturb each other's communities by recruiting members from each other through methods, or because of attitudes of mind, which are opposed to Christian love or to what should characterize the relationships between Churches. Let it cease where it may exist." "1973 Common Declaration," in *Doing the Truth in Charity: Statements of Pope Paul VI, Popes John Paul I, John Paul II, and the Secretariat for the Promoting of Christian Unity,* Ecumenical Documents I, Thomas B. Stransky and John B. Sheerin, eds., (Maryknoll, NY: Paulist, 1982), 248.

The 1980 Lutheran-Catholic Conversation: "Naturally *discrimination* must cease if ministers are to cooperate on all levels. Partners cannot cast aspersions on each other and must renounce every form of proselytism (though not mutual criticisms or requests for change)." "Ways to Community, 1980," in *Growth in Agreement: Reports and Agreed Statements of Ecumenical Conversations on a World Level,* Ecumenical Documents II, Harding Meyer and Lukas Vischer (Maryknoll, NY: Paulist, 1984), 235.

The 1982 World Council of Churches Committee on World Mission and Evangelism: "Surely, many ambiguities have accompanied this development and are present even today, not the least of which is the sin of proselytism among other Christian confessions." "Mission and Evangelism—An Ecumenical Affirmation," WCC Commission on World Mission and Evangelism, 1982; in *The Ecumenical Movement: An Anthology of Key Texts and Voices,* Michael Kinnamon and Brian Cope, eds., (Geneva: World Council of Churches, 1997; Grand Rapids: Eerdmans, 1997), 373.

Now if "them" in verse 19 relates only to those who are won as disciples, and only disciples ought to be baptized, then what about the second "them" in verse 20? Herein we have the purpose of the New Testament church. The second "them" refers to those who ought to be taught: "teaching *them* to observe whatsoever I have commanded you." Therefore, only those who are won and baptized ought to be taught to observe all that Christ commanded. Thus the New Testament church's primary responsibility is to teach and train baptized disciples. The church is primarily for believers. The church is not God's sophisticated public relations instrument to woo society into an existential relationship with Christ.

However, when a church believes in works-salvation (such as through sacraments), then church leaders merely have to teach people what to do, and if church members obey what they are told to do, they will be saved. The order of verbs in Matthew 28 is completely mixed up. For example, here is the Church of Rome and the mainstream Protestant view of Matthew 28:

- (Verb 3) Baptize them—Who? Everyone! When? Infancy will do!
- (Verb 4) Teach them to observe—Who? Everyone!

The 1994 Evangelicals and Catholics Together Statement: "At the same time, our commitment to full religious freedom compels us to defend the legal freedom to proselytize even as we call upon Christians to refrain from such activity." "Evangelicals and Catholic Together: The Christian Mission in the Third Millennium," in *A House United? Evangelicals and Catholics Together: A Winning Alliance for the 21st Century*, Keith A. Fournier, with William D. Watkins (Colorado Springs: NavPress, 1994), 346.

The 1994 Colson-Neuhaus Declaration: "There is a necessary distinction between evangelizing [non-Christians] and what is today commonly called proselytizing or 'sheep stealing.'" For "in view of the large number of non-Christians in the world and the enormous challenge of the common evangelistic task, it is neither theologically legitimate nor a prudent use of resources for one Christian community to proselytize among active adherents of another Christian community." Thus, "We condemn the practice of recruiting people from another community for the purposes of denominational or institutional aggrandizement." "Colson-Neuhaus Declaration" in *Roman Catholics and Evangelicals: Agreements and Differences*, Norman L. Geisler and Ralph E. MacKenzie (Grand Rapids: Baker, 1995), 493.

And finally, Point 3 of the 2006 Vatican and World Council of Churches Statement (consisting of 10 points): "3. We affirm that while everyone has a right to invite others to an understanding of their faith, it should not be exercised by violating other's rights and religious sensibilities. At the same time, all should heal themselves from the obsession of converting others." "Report from inter-religious consultation on 'Conversion—assessing the reality'"; accessed November 2, 2007, http://www.oikoumene.org/index.php?id=2252&L=0.

- (Verb 2) M-m-m-make them into disciples—How? Stretched over a lifetime of repentance, obedience of the teachings of Christ, or submission to the sacraments of a church!
- (Verb 1) Go—This command is only for ordained clergy!

See how the verbal order of Matthew 28 is completely reversed by infant baptism? Likewise, use of the word *teach* in verses 19 and 20 confuses the meaning of this commissioning. The clear baptistic progression simply affirms that a person ought to be won as a disciple before he is baptized. Therefore, in this light, using the word *teach* in verse 19, as the King James Version does, is in reality a non-conversionistic translation, and, furthermore, it is possibly anti-conversionistic! Again, sacramental and territorial churches will appreciate the equivocal nature of the use of the word *teach* (it may mean this, it may mean that), as it confirms their wrongful practice of infant baptism. So translating *matheteuo* as *teach* in verse 19 is not only problematic methodologically, it is problematic theologically. Translating *matheteuo* in Matthew 28:19 as *teach* stifles the need for conversion prior to baptism. However, translating *win disciples* confirms, affirms, and reaffirms the importance of conversion prior to baptism!

Notice also that verse 20 refers to sanctification, "teaching them to observe." Whereas, verse 19 speaks of conversion, "Go, win disciples of all nations." Baptism is not salvific, but rather professes to all who see it (or learn of it) that the person baptized has already received the washing of regeneration by the Holy Spirit and is now confessing it in public. Both becoming a disciple (conversion or the new birth) and baptism are instantaneous activities. Just as one does not baptize another person over a period of two years nor does one win a disciple over a period of two years. However, "teaching to observe all that I have commanded you" (in verse 20) takes a lifetime and provides the New Testament church its divine duty towards its own. Interestingly, this Greek verb for *teaching* is in the present tense, which emphasizes linear or prolonged action.

Is discipleship important? Absolutely! In fact, it is not only important, but the essential duty of the New Testament church! Once a disciple has been won through conversion, once he has been baptized, then he enters into a lifetime of learning from and service to his Master, Jesus Christ, in a New Testament church.

Therefore the chronological and logical interpretation of Matthew 28:19–20 follows Baptist practice!

- (Verb 1) Go!
- (Verb 2) Win disciples to and for Christ!
- (Verb 3) Baptize those who are won!
- (Verb 4) Teach to obey (disciple) those who are won and baptized!

Placing infant baptism into the mix confuses the whole verse, as does downgrading matheteuo to mean a prolonged period of discipleship (as is done by churches that baptize infants). Rather, Christ commissioned his disciples to win others as disciples to him, then to baptize those who are won, and then to organize into fellowships those who are won and baptized, so that they may learn to observe all that he commanded them (including the further winning of disciples).

Notice also that the respective order of the verbs as displayed above have further implications. The Roman or mainstream Protestant order generalizes the particularity of baptism, while reversing the emphasis of those who should evangelize. The Roman or mainstream Protestant view is as follows:

- Baptism of all infants (generalized).
- Evangelizing is only for ordained clergy (particularized).

However, the Baptist view opposes this understanding:

- Baptism is only for professing disciples (particularized).
- Evangelizing is for all professing disciples (generalized, among the saved).

The impact of the translation of *matheteuo* does make a difference, as does who is baptized.

With this foundation we can add further lessons from the prior context of Matthew 28. Unto whom are people discipled in Matthew 28:19? The answer is found in Matthew 27:57. People are discipled to Jesus! It clearly states in Matthew 27:57, "And when it was evening, there came a rich man from Arimathea, named Joseph, who himself had also become a disciple of Jesus." Joseph had been won as a disciple of Jesus. Therefore, Christians do not make disciples or clones themselves; rather they win disciples of Jesus, and that through the work of the Holy Spirit by the Word of God!

Also, while the message is not directly stated in Matthew's Great Commission as in those of Mark and Luke, the message of salvation is implied through context. You see, Matthew 28 was not the first time that Jesus had sent out his disciples as recounted by Matthew. He had also sent them out in Matthew 10. Likewise, John the Baptist and Jesus had also gone forth preaching the same message. Notice the obvious parallelism:

- John the Baptist (Matthew 3:1–2): "Now in those days John the Baptist came, preaching in the wilderness of Judea, saying, 'Repent, for the kingdom of heaven is at hand.'"
- Jesus (Matthew 4:17): "From that time Jesus began to preach and say, 'Repent, for the kingdom of heaven is at hand.'"
- Disciples (Matthew 10:7): "And as you go, preach, saying, 'The kingdom of heaven is at hand.'"

John the Baptist was sent to preach a message. Jesus was sent to preach a message. And the disciples were sent out to preach a message. It clearly follows then that when Jesus said, "Go," in Matthew 28:19, that he did not only mean mere geographic displacement. Rather they were to: (1) Go; (2) Preach; and (3) Preach a Message; with the goal of (4) Winning Disciples. And that message had to do with the nearness of the kingdom of God:

- Zeph 1:14: "Near is the great day of the LORD, Near and coming very quickly; Listen, the day of the LORD! In it the warrior cries out bitterly."
- Deut 32:35: "Vengeance is Mine, and retribution, In due time their foot will slip; For the day of their calamity is near, And the impending things are hastening upon them."

The Deuteronomy verse is reminiscent of the powerful sermon of Jonathan Edwards during the First Great Awakening (circa 1740), "Sinners in the Hands of an Angry God"!

Furthermore, the "all nations" ought not to be misapplied in a triumphalist sense, as if Jesus was going to redeem everyone in a nation! This teaching completely contradicts Matthew 7 where Jesus clearly stated:

- Matt 7:13: "Enter by the narrow gate; for the gate is wide, and the way is broad that leads to destruction, and many are those who enter by it."

Rather, the "of all nations" should be understood as stated in Revelation 5:9, "from every tribe and tongue and people and nation." Thus, "of all nations" may be better understood using the particularized, "from all nations."

So, in conclusion, Matthew 28:19–20's commissioning is not really all that different from Mark 16:15, Luke 24:46–47, or Acts 1:8. Mark and Luke emphasized the proclamation of a certain message to the world. Acts emphasized the proclamational aspect, "Be my testifiers." And Matthew emphasized the result of proclaiming the message, the winning of disciples, along with the need to baptize and nurture disciples!

So there we have it. There is no need to use the Great Commission passages to divide the church into numerous splits, as was likely done in Corinth: "I am of Paul, I am of Cephas, I am of Christ" (1 Cor 1:12). We don't need a segmented New Testament church:

- I am for Matthew's Great Commission; I am a disciplemaker!
- I am for Mark's Great Commission; I am an evangelist!
- I am for John's Great Commission; I am into Incarnation Evangelism!
- I am for Luke's Great Commission in Acts 1:8; I am a witness by my lifestyle!

While Christ gave his people multiple gifts and multiple personality traits, he did not segment his church into competing factions. The one voice of the Holy Spirit left us five testimonies of the Great Commission that dovetail in perfect harmony so that we could see and understand its fullness!

So let's go do it! Let's mobilize our congregations to fulfill the Great Commission by proclaiming repentance for the forgiveness of sins, winning disciples from among all nations, baptizing them in the name of the Father and of the Son and of the Holy Spirit, and teaching them to obey all that Christ commanded. Let's stoke the engines of the Great Commission and return to our evangelistic mandate!

2

The Pastor as Key to a Great Commission Church

Edsel D. Pate Jr.

"T HE GREAT COMMISSION IS not just built into everything we do, it is everything we do. As a pastor it's my job to help people look beyond themselves to what God can do through them," said Pastor Bill Langley of the Severns Valley Baptist Church. In 1791, eighteen believers committed to fulfilling the Great Commission met under a sugar maple tree in Elizabethtown, Kentucky and formed the Severns Valley Baptist Church. Today, the church of over three thousand continues to make a difference in Elizabethtown and throughout Kentucky. Besides being a leader in global missions giving, Severns Valley is also committed to reaching their community. According to Langley, they "trotline fish," doing a number of intentional things that are related to evangelism. As pastor, he "defines the waters and calls out the congregation to be fishers of men!"

This is what Jeff Covington, Associate Pastor at Oakwood Park Baptist Church in New Braunfels and Golden Gate Baptist Theological Seminary DMin candidate, describes as Intentional Engagement (I.E.). Oakwood's pastoral team follows Jesus' missionary model of seeking and saving the lost. I.E. is in the DNA of the church from small groups to off-campus ministry sites. Led by Senior Pastor Ray Still, being involved in the Great Commission to reach the local community and the world is simply why the church exists.

Churches that are fulfilling the Great Commission have one thing in common—whether they are historic churches like Severns Valley, contemporary churches like Oakwood Park or Saddleback Church in Lake Forest, California, or trendsetting groups like Mosaic in Los Angeles: they are led by pastors committed to the mission of seeing people transformed by Jesus Christ. Great Commission values are preached, taught, and caught at these places. Like their pastors, believers take the responsibility to share genuine stories across the street and around the world of what Jesus has done in their life. In these churches, Holy Spirit-led pastors have developed a passion to reach those who have never heard. There is a spiritual momentum that's contagious.

WHAT'S A GREAT COMMISSION CHURCH?

Years ago, a Great Commission church might have been defined by how much funding that church gave to missions. The Great Commission was all about doing something "over there." More recently, churches have been challenged to be missional. This term has come to mean a church that is "on mission" in the context that surrounds them as well as the remote corners of the earth. Missionary reports now might come just as easily from a member involved in the local community as overseas. Churches have a renewed sense of ownership and responsibility for the community and city in which they live. Part of this shift has come as we have begun to figure out that the nations have come to us. The world is a smaller place and now Somalia, Vietnam, Afghanistan, and China are no longer "over there" but across the street. According to Fermin Whittaker, executive director of the California Southern Baptist Convention, California Southern Baptists worship in seventy-seven languages each week. But it's not only the world that is across the street from us, but also an evolving Western culture that is vastly different from that which is inside the church. People drive past our churches on Sunday going to the beach, the mountains, the lake, or sporting tournaments. As the culture has changed so has the need for our strategy and methods. What worked in 1960 might work for those people who were born in 1960 but what about those people born in the 1980s or 90s who have no memory of church? Great Commission pastors lead their churches to confront culture with the Gospel—whether that culture is post-Christian Western or post-Saddam Iraqi, both of which are living next door or around the world.

A Great Commission church is more about *being* than doing. While there are some similarities, Great Commission churches don't tend to *do a program*, but instead they seem to possess a spiritual momentum that can be sensed, observed, and measured. You can't read the book of Acts without seeing that a church on mission has a contagious spiritual energy. People are being saved, sharing their faith, responding to God's call, and taking their faith into the workplace, the neighborhood and the world. The Great Commission isn't a particular curriculum, it's a passion and that passion starts with the pastor. The pastor of a Great Commission church leads that church to sacrifice its own culture in order to present the gospel of Christ. This mindset guides the pastor to re-evaluate the use of musical instruments, mode of dress, the use of technology, sermon illustrations, architecture, and so on. He leads the church to abandon everything for the gospel.

Local pastors share much in common with missionary strategy coordinators. The local pastor must understand the unique context and culture of his mission field, and then lead and create strategy to bring light into the darkness. The pastor learns about the community, assesses the field and the church, and then leads. He creates strategy based on the scriptural command to reach the nations and the glory of God. As the pastor shares his faith; teaches and preaches evangelism and missions; and engages the community, God transforms the church and the transformed people of the church transform their community. *How does that happen?*

THE PASTOR MODELS GREAT COMMISSION VALUES

When my family and I lived in Jordan, there were billboards of King Abdullah around the city of Amman and throughout the country. The billboards depicted him with his wife and kids to model what a family in Jordan ought to look like. Those billboards communicated a message and were intentional; the Jordanian family looked like this. In this same way the pastor ought to model what evangelism should look like. Mark Mittelberg, in *Becoming a Contagious Church,* says "the congregation needs to see that we genuinely live out our evangelistic mission, values and strategy. If we want to build contagious churches, we as leaders must first become contagious Christians. There is no dodging the truth in the saying, 'speed of the leader, speed of the team.'"[1]

1. Mark Mittelberg, *Becoming a Contagious Church* (Grand Rapids: Zondervan, 2002), 92.

Prayer for the Lost

I'm not sure why it takes us so long to begin to pray for the lost. Sometimes it seems that prayer is a 911 call—a last resort. We know that God desires people to come to know him. Second Peter 3:9 says that "the Lord is not slow about His promise as some count slowness, but is patient toward you, not wishing for any to come to perish but for all to come to repentance" (all biblical quotes in this chapter are NASB). Jesus also told us to pray (Mark 11:24) for things in faith believing and we'd receive them. Still for some reason we often move ahead in evangelism in our own strength and effort only to be frustrated. Evangelism without prayer is like trying to hit a baseball over the fence in a big league park with a Wiffle bat—it becomes frustrating and futile very quickly! The process of people coming to know Christ is a spiritual event, and inviting the Lord to enter into it is a good idea.

There was a time when I made a list of the names of seven men whom I wanted to see get saved. These were people I had met in the community who had become friends. I just liked being around them and wanted to see them come to the Lord. I tried everything. I went to lunch, played sports, attended their parties and hung out. As I shared Christ with them, using multiple plans and strategies, nothing seemed to work. My Wiffle bat was making contact, but I could manage nothing more than a bunt. I then tried something in desperation—I began to plead to God for these men's souls. While nobody was around, I'd actually go into the place where our church met, kneel at the altar, and pray for these men by name. Within six months, one by one, six of the seven came to know Christ. They came in various ways—some through small groups, some through a regular worship service, a couple from praying at home, some from the result of an evangelistic visit, and so on. The seventh man, however, had yet to respond. He was a realtor in town, had a great car, an athletic-cut physique, and jet black hair. When I looked into the mirror, I wanted to look like him! In the time that we had known each other, and through my sharing Christ with him (and his subsequent refusals), we had become good friends. He was determined that he would not "get saved," as he had too much to give up.

One morning, however, he called me at the church office and said, "Preacher, last night I got saved." I asked him, "How did that happen since I was not there?" Mark proceeded to tell me that a bed salesman had made a call on their house the night before. While at a fair, his wife had filled out a card requesting information for a designer bed and this salesman followed up. After a few minutes of his introductory spiel, the wife excused herself and went to bed, leaving my friend alone with the bed salesman. The bed salesman continued his sales pitch for a few more minutes, then finally said, "Mark, I can tell you are not interested in buying a bed, but let me share with you something you might be interested in." Mark then explained how he had knelt on the floor of his living room and prayed to receive Christ with a *bed salesman*!

I do not understand everything about what happens when people pray, but God moves, the Holy Spirit gets involved, and people come to know Jesus. People ought to know the pastor is praying for the lost. They should hear and see him pray. A Great Commission pastor leads the church in praying for the lost. Be creative and be intentional. Set aside a prayer room for prayer and make it tactile. The idea of a fishing net on the wall of the prayer room where people can write the first names of those they are praying for on small pieces of paper (like key tags) and then tie them onto the net makes for a good image in prayer.

The Pastor Does Personal Evangelism

The pastor ought to be an evangelist. Jesus modeled the Great Commission for the disciples. Jesus came to seek and save the lost (Luke 19:10). He took the disciples along on his evangelistic outreaches. "*Soon afterwards, He began going around from one city and village to another, proclaiming and preaching the kingdom of God. The twelve were with Him.*" There was intentionality to the mission and preaching of Jesus. Paul told Timothy to "*be sober in all things, endure hardship, do the work of an evangelist, fulfill your ministry*" (2 Timothy 4:5). The pastor should model relational and small group evangelism, share his story or testimony, lead out in planned visitation, and even use scripted or "canned" evangelistic presentations.

As a young pastor, I knew that my church would never be more evangelistic than I would be. I also realized that I had not always been good at it! My personal history with one-to-one evangelism had not been altogether pleasant or successful. In fact, instead of "hearing" Paul tell Timothy to endure hardship and do the work of an evangelist, I equated hardship with evangelism! Weekend evangelism schools and retreats where participants went door-to-door are a part of my "evangelistic" past.

Most of those experiences were not too encouraging but I did it because I felt like I should. I remember a youth retreat in the southern California mountains where we spent the morning learning from "The Four Spiritual Laws" booklet. Participants were dropped off later that afternoon at Lake Arrowhead Village and told to go witness and be ready to report later that day on those who had been saved. I looked around and decided I would zero in on the Ferris wheel operator who was not busy and was just standing around. I mustered up the courage to go over and talk to him. I kept hoping customers would come—but they didn't, so I approached him and asked if I could share with him the Four Spiritual Laws. He agreed! I went through the whole presentation and when I asked if he wanted to be saved he said, "I work for Campus Crusade for Christ and just wanted to see if you could get through the presentation!" As hard as it is to admit, leading people to Christ on airplanes, in line at the store, and at restaurants as I paid the bill were not regular occurrences in my life. Not that I didn't try, it just did not seem to work! Maybe it was me, maybe it was the lack of the "gift," or maybe it was the method. Still, I loved people, believed that people needed Jesus, enjoyed building relationships, and wanted to model the Great Commission.

Other pastors may have similar stories. Still, the pastor leads. He visits people, learns evangelistic presentations, develops relationships, and takes church members with him when talking to people about Jesus. When the pastor does this, the church as a whole responds. He might actually find people in the church who have more of a natural gifting in evangelism than he does. That's a good thing, and it shouldn't intimidate him. Sometimes Christians think "shouldn't the pastor personally lead more people to Jesus than anyone else in the church?" It may be that the pastor does not lead more people to Christ, but he can lead more people to lead more people to Christ. As a personal evangelist, the pastor models evangelism as a priority. When he does, the church takes notice and some will follow his example.

The Pastor Gets Involved in the Community

The pastor models community outreach. Growing up at the Euclid Street Baptist Church in Anaheim, California, my pastor Bryan Crow taught me the value of having relationships outside the church in the community. Upon arriving as a new pastor in the desert town of Barstow, California, I joined a service club, met community leaders and had continual opportunities to share the gospel. People were saved and people came to church. I became the town pastor and prayed at park openings, city events, and Kiwanis Club meetings. When someone in the community died, and did not have a pastor, I was called on by the local funeral director to preach the funeral. We had dozens of people visit our church whose first contact with me was a funeral sermon!

As a pastor gets involved as an agent to transform the community, regular church people are inspired to do likewise. When the pastor sees the community as "distressed and dispirited, lost like sheep without a shepherd" (Matthew 9:36), the church *and* community recognize that. Too often pastors live in the town without ever becoming vested in the community. The only time some community leaders see the pastor or church members is when there are problems. They show up when they are against something or need a zoning variance. Those with stock in the community, such as community leaders and businessmen, know whether or not the pastor and/or church care about making an investment in the community. Is the church contributing to the community or is it just a parasitic presence? By engaging the community, the pastor models having a heart for people and a compassion for the lost. When the pastor models love and compassion for the community and shows that he cares and embraces his community, the people in the church will began to see their neighborhood, workplace, school, or community center as their mission field. The pastor should get involved in service clubs, the school district, law enforcement, or other organizations that add value to the community. By doing so he extends his mission field away from the walls of the church. Church members watch and catch this vision.

The Pastor Empowers the Church

The pastor empowers the church to see that following Christ isn't for spectators but for participants. He opens the gate for them to participate. Just as Jesus released people for ministry and evangelism so must the pastor. In Luke 10, Jesus sent out the seventy disciples in pairs. They didn't have all the answers, but he sent them out with the tools that they had. They returned from their mission with joy! Jesus was excited about their enthusiasm; speaking about Satan falling, and marveling in prayer that the "infants" had gotten it! Wise pastors follow this model and release and empower their people for ministry. When the pastor leads his people to see the field where God has placed them (their neighborhood, workplace, school, gym, and so on) as their mission field, and frees them to go, they will begin to fulfill the Great Commission.

The pastor creates a culture in the church that values and empowers evangelism. There is a momentum that comes from this. It's contagious and can't be controlled! Start preaching on how people are to use the gifts and talents God has given them in the community around them and see what happens! The Holy Spirit might actually begin to stir in the hearts of people.

When I started preaching on evangelism, I was surprised when one of the first people to come and talk with me was Robert. Robert told me that he thought God wanted him to stretch a bit in his Christian walk and be involved in ministry. His wife, Marianne, was already involved in traditional ministry programs of the church such as Vacation Bible School, kid's ministry, and more. But Robert was like many men in the church who just attended. Robert was a mechanic at the local Toyota dealership. As he spoke about this desire to get more connected in ministry and evangelism, I found myself wondering—what can this guy do? What box do I have in the church that fits him? I figured out quickly that I did not have nearly as many boxes as God did! Robert suggested that he begin a ministry maintaining and fixing the cars of widows and singles and the poor in the church. He thought he had some friends who could help and he wondered what I thought. Robert had "gotten it" long before I did. He started a small group of mechanics—some believers and some who would later become believers—that met at his house every Tuesday. That group became the image of what the Great Commission was about in our church: people using the gifts that God had given them to reach their neighbors and friends.

After that, we did not have to take any surveys or inventories. The Holy Spirit began to call people right where they were into ministry and evangelism. We didn't buy a program, hold a campaign, or try something new. What we tried was something as old as the Four Gospels! Soon, Elizabeth, a sweet woman in our church, began to share a constant, sincere witness at work and over a short period, several coworkers accepted Christ. Ron and Robbie (who'd been living together) got saved, got married, got off drugs, and started working with drug abusers in recovery. Linda wanted to work with mothers of young children, and Dennis started working with BMX and kids, and the Holy Spirit added to the church. I could have never imagined, and thought up as many ways for the church to be the church and spread light in the community, but once the people were empowered to do the work of the ministry, it happened.

The Pastor Promotes and Advocates for Evangelism

The pastor sounds the call and promotes outreach in the church and around the world. He keeps the message hot. Everything that happens has an evangelistic element. Whether it's the Mother and Daughter Banquet or the Aspiring Artist Retreat or the Senior Adult Music presentation, the pastor makes sure that evangelism is a part of those events. The pastor further promotes evangelism through small groups, special events, and even by old-fashioned revival meetings. Every semester I learn something new in our evangelism classes at Golden Gate. While all of our Golden Gate evangelism students were connected in some way to a local church small group, not one student over the last three semesters had been in-volved in a church that had held a revival meeting. This is disturbing. Revival meetings, when done right, can be a significant event in the life of the church. Believers connect with their non-believing friends and invite them to an evangelistic meeting. There's nothing wrong with that. The pastor sets the tone as to whether the church views a revival meeting and evangelism as an essential permeating element of the church—or just something to be tolerated!

He promotes it in a tangible way through the budget of the church. Sure, Great Commission churches cooperate with other churches to do missions and evangelism, but they also fund evangelism in the areas in which they live. The pastor leads out by leading the budget process to consider spending resources for events, training, revivals, materials, small group curriculum, and all kinds of media related to evangelism. The pastor resists the temptation to work under the "everything in the budget is evangelism" mantra and leads in finding ways and means to reach the community and the world with the Gospel.

Promotion from the Pulpit

The pastor promotes evangelism from the pulpit through teaching and preaching. Preaching through the "evangelism styles" talked about by Bill Hybels in *Becoming a Contagious Christian* is a good way to help regular church folk see that they can do evangelism without having to be an expert. New Christians can invite people to church, serve, have a Matthew Party, or give a testimony—and all of those ways ought to be validated.[2]

As part of the message or worship service, the pastor can recognize new believers by having them share their testimony live or through a video. The church is encouraged by real stories of how Jesus has changed the lives of ordinary, real people. Encouraging a new believer to prepare a written testimony for inclusion in a video program that will be shown in a worship service will also involve others in the church, as members connected to the evangelism program help to video or fine-tune written testimonies.

Celebrating baptism is another way evangelism is highlighted in a worship service: making baptism an occasion where the gospel is proclaimed through the event and making sure that the message of the gospel is clear. A number of churches are also calling for people to respond to the gospel and be baptized immediately. Why not also have the baptism waters ready and call for people to be baptized right away at the end of an evangelistic message? For instance, preaching on Philip and the Ethiopian eunuch and then extending an invitation for those who receive Christ to immediately be baptized can be effective.

SUMMARY

In 2008, LifeWay Resources published a short booklet of just over sixty pages called *Great Commission Resurgence*. Several Southern Baptist denominational leaders wrote with regard to the Great Commission in the local church, North America, and around the world. In writing about the Great Commission in the local church, Chuck Lawless said: "In all of our studies at the Graham School (Billy Graham School of Missions Evangelism and Church Growth, The Southern Baptist Theological Seminary) we have never studied a strong Great Commission minded church led by a pastor who is unconcerned about evangelism and discipleship. Rather, pastors who are fervent about the Great Commission produce congregations that share that passion."[3]

---

2. Bill Hybels and Mark Mittelberg, *Becoming a Contagious Christian* (Grand Rapids: Zondervan, 1994).

3. Chuck Lawless, *Great Commission Resurgence* (Nashville: LifeWay Resources, 2008), 28.

In Matthew 28:19–20 Jesus gave us our final instructions. Evangelism ought to permeate everything that we do. He promised to be faithful, to never leave or forsake us! In Luke 18 Jesus speaks about the need for consistent fervent prayer. He concludes the parable of the unjust judge (the demanding widow) with an interesting statement: "When the son of man comes will he find faith on the earth?"(Luke 18:8).

Pastor Bill Langley of Severns Valley Baptist Church says the answer to Jesus' question is, "Yes, if He finds us faithful in fulfilling the Great Commission. My job as a pastor is to lead a people to be faithful followers of Jesus Christ who lead others to be faithful followers of Jesus Christ."

The pastor is key to the Great Commission church. Pastors who model, pray, promote, lead, and empower the Great Commission create churches that take on that personality. Further, people desire to be involved in those kinds of churches. People long to be where the Holy Spirit is moving and where people are getting saved. There is a spiritual momentum present that excites, energizes, and brings joy to a church. The faithfulness of a pastor who is modeling, empowering, promoting, providing resources, and recognizing evangelism creates an environment where people will become transformed, and they, in turn, will go out and transform their community and the world for Christ.

3

Issues in Every Member Evangelism

David Mills

THE POTENTIAL FOR EVANGELIZING the world staggers the imagina-
tion. At this time, more than seven hundred million evangelicals
around the globe trust Jesus Christ. Through evangelism, this mighty
force could make a large difference for the kingdom. If only 10 percent
of evangelicals witnessed every day, they could share the gospel with all
lost people in the world in less than four months. When Jesus said, "Make
disciples of all nations" (Matt 28:19), "preach the gospel to every creature"
(Mark 16:15), and witness "to the ends of the earth" (Acts 1:8), he was not
exaggerating. He really wants to be the Savior of all (1 Tim 2:4; 4:10), and
he has a plan to make this happen—every Christian a witness.

To make this happen, laypersons in local churches must view themselves as Christ does—as evangelistic witnesses. The New Testament reveals that laypersons involved themselves in evangelistic witnessing. Jesus
won a demoniac to salvation, and this man began to witness immediately
(Mark 5:1–20). Jesus won the Samaritan woman, and she began to witness at once (John 4:39–42). The 120 people assembled in the upper room
at Pentecost witnessed to the assembled pilgrims (Acts 2:11). Stephen and
Philip, both laymen, engaged in evangelistic witnessing (Acts 6–8). Many
more examples of laypersons evangelizing surface in the New Testament
besides these.

Despite great potential and New Testament precedence, survey
after survey reveals that laypeople do not observe Christ's imperative

commission of evangelism. Few laypersons know the joy of winning a person to Christ. With the magnanimous opportunities and the New Testament materials before them, why do so few laypersons share the gospel? This chapter will address these issues and seek to remedy them. Hope exists to remedy this disobedience and usher in a new day of evangelistic fruitfulness.

HYPER-SPIRITUALITY

God desires the Christians to develop in matters of the spirit. He wants to address his people as spiritual and not as carnal (1 Cor 3:1–3). This means that Christian people occupy themselves with spiritual matters. They view life in spiritual terms. They relate to people, spend their money, resolve their conflicts, and make their decisions in a spiritual manner. To live life this way requires biblical knowledge, prayer, instruction, contemplation, reflection, and spiritual counsel. Spiritual people wait on the Lord to direct them in these matters. God wants his people to observe this healthy approach to kingdom living. Like all good things from God, however, satanic forces have created counterfeits to spiritual living, and these counterfeits kill evangelism. Some label these counterfeit approaches to spiritual living "hyper-spiritual," and they injure evangelism.

Hyper-spirituality surfaces in a number of ways. To begin with, it may surface when a Christian attempts to dress disobedience in biblical or spiritual terms. For example, some Christians announce "I will witness when the Spirit leads me." This sounds spiritual, but it represents what has become the tradition of men that makes void the commands of God (Matt 15:3–9). Where does God instruct his people to obey him only when the Holy Spirit leads? Such an instruction does not appear in the Scripture. What if Christians applied this to giving, holiness, or moral purity? What if a church leader said, "I will give to my church when the Holy Spirit leads me"? What if a husband said, "I will remain faithful to my marriage vows when the Holy Spirit leads me"? Is there any doubt about the outcome?

Christians must distinguish between God's callings and God's commands. Christians do some things because God calls them to do them. Some pastor churches, but not all. Some serve as missionaries, but not all. Some participate in the music or student ministries of their churches, but not all. Not all Christians do all of these things, and they are not disobedient if they do not. Some things are unique callings from God. On the other hand, Christians do other things because God commands them. Among these are holiness, giving, church attendance, prayer, Bible study, and love. Evangelism falls into the latter category and not the former. Evangelism is not a calling but a command. Hyper-spirituality may surface in some Christians when they credit the Holy Spirit with disobedience to the Great Commission.

In addition, hyper-spirituality may surface when Christians comment, "We do not win them; the Holy Spirit wins them." Christians do well when they emphasize the Holy Spirit's role in evangelism. Christians and churches urgently need a daily touch from the Holy Spirit, but where does the Scripture say the Holy Spirit wins lost persons? The Scripture does not use the word *win* in reference to the Holy Spirit; it does use it reference to Christians winning the lost. Paul said, "Though I am free from all, I have made myself a servant to all, that I might *win* more of them. To the Jews I became as a Jew, or order to *win* Jews" (1 Cor 9:19 ESV; italics mine). In this passage (1 Cor 9:19–23), Paul used the word *win* five times. Besides Paul, Solomon wrote, "He that wins souls is wise." The Holy Spirit will do in evangelism what only he can do, but he will never compensate for the hyper-spirituality of disobedient witnesses. Christians are to win the lost to Christ and shun hyper-spiritual obstacles that hinder evangelism.

FEAR

Many Christians struggle with fear in witnessing. Many do not believe they can defeat fear, but feel paralyzed by it instead. They fear an angry response. They fear saying the wrong thing. They fear questions. They fear embarrassment. They fear losing friends and face. Despite these fears, the New Testament offers good news to those who struggle with fear in witnessing—they have good company in Paul. Paul experienced the Holy Spirit's power when evangelizing Corinth, but admitted he did so in "fear, weakness, and much trembling" (1 Cor 2:3–5). In Corinth, Paul did not feel well when empowered by the Spirit in evangelism. He felt fear, weakness, and much trembling. Fear did not exclude him, however, from the Spirit's assistance in evangelism, and it does not exclude today's witness either.

The Spirit's filling does not guarantee the absence of fear, nervousness, or awkwardness. In fact, fear of witnessing may not be fear at all. It may be sincerity. The witness believes the gospel and it has gripped the witness's heart. Fred Craddock said, "Nervousness is the way the body honors the seriousness of what you are doing."[1] At other times, the witness's fear may actually be a sense of the need to depend on God. Sometimes, the witness may have real fear. C. E. Autrey warned that fear of witnessing evidences "over concern" with oneself.[2] Fear, then, often comes from a self-centered spirit. To overcome this paralyzing fear, the witness should think more of Christ's glory and the lost person's need to know Christ.

Sometimes the witness experiences spiritual warfare and confuses it with fear. The enemy despises evangelism and creates turmoil in the witness's emotions. The enemy will use anything at his disposal to hinder witnessing, even spirituality. H. Clay Turnbull gave more than fifty years of his life to personal evangelism. He warned readers that Satan seeks to convince witnesses that they will harm the cause of Christ by witnessing; that sharing the gospel with unbelievers does more harm than good.

> From nearly half a century of such practice, I can say that I have spoken with thousands upon thousands. Yet, so far from my becoming accustomed to this matter, I find it as difficult to speak about it at the end of these years as at the beginning. Never to the present day can I speak to a single soul for Christ without being reminded by Satan that I am in danger of harming the cause by introducing it just now. If there is one thing that Satan is sensitive about, it is the danger of a Christian's harming the [evil] cause he loves by speaking of Christ to a needy soul. He has more than once kept me from speaking on the subject by his sensitive pious caution."[3]

Satan hates evangelism with such a white-hot intensity that he will use good things to hinder it. He even uses religion and piety with great skill to hinder evangelism (Matt 4:1–11). He convinces some witnesses that evangelism hinders Christ's cause, evangelism obstructs the gospel, and sharing the gospel embarrasses Christ. They should expect and anticipate such satanic resistance.

---

1. Tony Cartledge, "Fred Craddock, *Reflections on My Call to Preach: Connecting the Dots*," (St. Louis: Chalice, 2009), 111. March 21, 2009, http://www.tonycartledge.com, accessed March 23, 2009.

2. C. E. Autrey, *You Can Win Souls*, (Nashville: Broadman, 1961), 46.

3. H. Clay Trumbull, *Individual Work for Individuals: A Record of Personal Experiences and Convictions* (New York: Association, 1911), 168–69.

OPPORTUNITIES

Sometimes Christians fail to witness because they expect God to orchestrate perfect circumstances before they will share the gospel. Some will witness only if a lost person starts a conversation about the gospel. Some will witness only to children in Sunday school or Vacation Bible School. Some will witness only if they trust the lost person not to react angrily to the gospel and hurt the witness's feelings (when "earning the right to be heard" actually means "making lost people earn the right to hear"). Other unreasonable expectations abound. Some will witness if they feel no fear. If a Christian waits for perfect circumstances before witnessing, that Christian will probably witness only a few times in a lifetime. How does that reflect the love of God for the world?

Too often, some witnesses use one approach to personal evangelism and neglect other legitimate approaches. Without examining the New Testament or the research, they set one legitimate approach to personal evangelism against another legitimate approach. This happens especially in the relationship evangelism literature. Most effective personal witnesses pursue all legitimate approaches to personal evangelism. Among these are "scheduled and planned evangelism," "spontaneous and lifestyle evangelism," and "social and relationship evangelism." Each of these three approaches finds precedence in the New Testament, and witnesses should practice each of these three. First, witnesses can practice scheduled and planned evangelism. Jesus evangelized at scheduled times such as synagogue worship, which was his custom to attend (Luke 4:16–30). Paul maintained and practiced the custom of evangelizing in the synagogue as well (Acts 17:1–4). The early Christians did evangelism at a time that God placed on the Jewish calendar centuries before them—Pentecost (Acts 2:1–40). Scheduled and planned evangelism consists of witnessing at times when the church or witness schedules or plans opportunities. Some of these times may involve weekly processes such as during a weekly visitation, during the pulpit preaching and the invitation, or while teaching the gospel in Sunday school and explaining the invitation in each lesson. Some of these times involve events, and these may consist of block parties, fall festivals, wild game suppers, or revivals. The most effective evangelistic churches among Southern Baptists host seven to eight evangelistic events each year.[4]

4. "Evangelistic Event Research Report," (Alpharetta, GA: North American Mission Board, July 2009), 1.

Second, witnesses can practice spontaneous and lifestyle evangelism. Jesus told his disciples, "As you go, preach" (Matt 10:7). Jesus wanted his disciples to evangelize as they went through villages, towns, and homes. He expected them to witness spontaneously and in their daily life. Witnesses can evangelize spontaneously and in their daily life when they speak to the cashier at the gas station, the bag boy at the grocery store, and the pizza delivery person at the front door. They witness as they meet people. They start conversations with strangers and others, guide the conversation toward the gospel, and offer them Christ's gift: discipleship.

Third, witnesses can practice social and relationship evangelism. This approach involves witnessing to those within the witness's circle of relationships. These include family members, neighbors, and friends. In this approach, the witness has the opportunity to share the gospel, to cultivate the heart of the unbeliever, and demonstrate the resurrected life of Christ. Andrew witnessed to his brother Peter (John 1:40–42) and Jesus witnessed to residents of his hometown (Mark 6:1–6). Any layperson that has ever made a friend can make effective use of this approach to evangelism.

In social and friendship evangelism, however, witnessing can inadvertently be restricted to their circle of friends, and this is one of many reasons relationship evangelism has not produced the fruit it promised decades ago. As each year passes, witnesses tend to limit themselves to a shrinking group of friends and family members, thus excluding the rest of the world. Each day, then, the witness should take the initiative in making new friends (John 3, 4; Luke 19:10). Jesus initiated conversations with unbelievers. This means witnesses take opportunities that arise (John 3) and make opportunities where they do not exist (John 4).

MODELING

Many sincere Christian laypersons do not witness simply because they have never seen another Christian witness. These Christians are not lousy Christians. They do not hate the gospel. They do not desire that anyone perish. They would witness if someone showed them how to witness. Their problem is that churches do not have ministries that model personal evangelism. They canceled evangelistic modeling when they canceled weekly visitation. In most cases, the disappearance of weekly visitation has meant the disappearance of evangelistic modeling. Every local church should have a weekly visitation ministry in order to reach the lost and model evangelism for laypersons. If they do not do weekly visitation, they should do something better. Thus far, nothing has surfaced that models personal evangelism better than weekly visitation.

Sadly, weekly visitation has suffered from as many attacks as revivals and Sunday school evangelism. Authors and conference speakers have thrust undocumented blows at it for decades. Despite the smoke and fury, several justifications exist for weekly visitation. First, while Scripture does not command weekly visitation, Scripture does point to intentional evangelism and modeling. The Scripture models direct contact of unbelievers in face-to-face conversations about the gospel. Jesus' ministry involved face-to-face contacts with unbelievers. Jesus made frequent visits in people's homes.[5] Jesus came to "seek and to save that which was lost" (Luke 19:10).

Further, visitation has produced fruit in those churches that use it appropriately. When churches pray for, organize, and maintain visitation, visitation can produce fruit. Responding to criticism of this approach, Thom Rainer commented, "While a few churches can boast of dynamic growth with little follow up outreach, their examples are rare. And, unfortunately, many church leaders have followed those examples with disastrous results. . . . *Nearly all of the churches in our study had some well-planned, regular program for visitor follow-up.*"[6] Despite the critics, then, visitation provides evangelistic opportunities in 99 percent of churches that excel at evangelizing and keeping new converts.

Sometimes visitation can produce some surprises. In the author's last pastorate, witnesses visited people who had recently moved into the community. They began this ministry when the pastor arrived at the church. After a year, leaders complained that none of the new movers had visited the church. They did not want to give their time to an evangelism effort that produced no results, and who could blame them? The pastor's conscience, however would not allow any person in the community to suffer neglect. He knew that no other church worked to reach these people, and his mind would not rest knowing they had moved into the community without a gospel witness from the church. After a short time passed, the pastor noticed people attending the church that members

5. Matt 9:10, 28; 10:14; Mark 2:15; Luke 16:27–28; 19:5.
6. Thom Rainer, *High Expectations* (Nashville: Broadman, 1999), 92.

had not invited, and in that church's location, that was unusual. When he asked these guests how they learned of the church, they mentioned names no one recognized. Soon after that, the pastor reviewed the list of newcomers, and recognized those names. The newcomers did not visit the church, but they sent their friends. In essence, the church had lost people doing evangelism for them. Herschel Hobbs made this point, saying, "We didn't get all we went after, but we didn't go after some we got. If we had not gone after those we didn't get, we would not have gotten those we did not go after." God blesses churches that take the initiative in reaching the lost. God loves to see a "going spirit" in local churches.

Finally, visitation ensures the church will do at least some evangelism on a consistent basis. Long-term attention to worthy tasks provides the best opportunity for progress, and evangelism is no exception. When Christians believe in something, they practice it consistently. They attend church consistently. They tithe consistently. They pray consistently. They read and study the Bible consistently. Why should they evangelize sporadically or never at all? Could anything surpass winning a lost, hell bound sinner to free grace in Christ? Weekly visitation will ensure that evangelism receives at least weekly attention, which is far more attention than some churches give it today. Weekly attention to evangelism keeps evangelism consistent. It keeps evangelism before the people. It goads their conscience. It enlists their prayers. It reminds them of the lostness of unbelievers. Churches must conduct weekly visitation to reach unbelievers and model personal evangelism, or do something better.

NEGATIVISM

Negativism can hinder evangelism among laypersons. Negativism may expose a doubt in the promises and love of God for the lost world. It indicates a serious spiritual problem. Negativism can mean many things, but in evangelism, it means the Christian views the world so negatively that the Christian does not believe that people will receive the witness or the gospel. It involves the unproven assumption that no one will respond positively to a witness and that most everyone will respond negatively, angrily, dismissively, or derisively.

The problem with negativism is that it simply is not true. Jesus said, "The harvest truly is plenteous" (Matt 9:37–38). Jesus did not moan about the difficulties of reaching unbelievers. He viewed the evangelistic possibilities in optimistic terms. The number of people who would respond positively to the gospel ranked as "plenteous" to him. In fact, effective witnesses are incurable optimists. Effective witnesses report that unbelievers usually receive them in a warm and friendly manner. When a Christian says that lost people are more difficult to win to Christ today than ever before, that Christian reveals that he or she is not witnessing. The only people who are negative about evangelism are those who are not doing it. Those who do witness ignore the grumpy and negative, walk in faith, and witness.

Research shows that more than 80% of unbelievers are at least "somewhat likely" to accept an invitation to church, but only 21% of them have received an invitation to church from a Christian. In addition, 11% of lost people are "highly receptive" to the gospel, meaning they would turn to Christ now if someone would tell them. Another 27% are "receptive" to the gospel, meaning they would trust Christ soon if someone would patiently explain the gospel, pray for them, answer questions, and befriend them in this journey. This means that about sixty million lost people will accept Christ or are close to accepting Christ, but only 2% of them have had a Christian tell them the gospel. About 36% of lost people are "neutral" towards the gospel, and 21% are "resistant," but Christian witnesses can influence them to open themselves to it. Only about 5% are "highly resistant."[7] A negative view of evangelism implies that the Holy Spirit has failed at his work. Such a Christian is not likely to evangelize at all. Christians who trust scriptural promises and view the world biblically will grow in faith and go forth bearing precious gospel seed to sow in the world (Ps 126:5–6).

CONCLUSION

Christians of the twentieth and twenty-first centuries have benefited greatly from the personal evangelism of an almost anonymous nineteenth-century Sunday school teacher. This man won D. L. Moody to Christ. Moody had joined his Sunday school class a couple of weeks before, and the Sunday school teacher was upset about Moody's spiritual condition. Burdened for Moody's soul, he visited Moody at Holton's Shoe Store in Boston, his place of work. The Sunday school teacher was so nervous he almost did not visit Moody, but decided to go into the store, share quickly,

---

7. Thom Rainer, *The Unchurched Next Door* (Grand Rapids: Zondervan, 2004).

and get the whole matter over with as quickly as possible. Despite his reticence, Moody turned to Christ in the back part of the building.

Moody served Christ as the premier evangelist of the second half of the nineteenth century and he won F. B. Meyer to Christ. Meyer pastored a Baptist church in London, preached all over the English-speaking world, and wrote some of the best devotional works printed. Meyer won J. Wilbur Chapman. Chapman pastored churches and entered full time evangelism. He covered much of the globe with gospel, and in one service won William Sunday to Christ. Sunday had been a baseball player, and when he came to Christ, he turned to evangelism with the vigor of an athlete. In one of his crusades, Sunday won to Christ Mordecai Ham. Ham served as an evangelist until his death in 1961, winning at least three hundred thousand to Christ. The world knows one of those he won, a farm boy from North Carolina who came to Christ in the 1930s—Billy Graham. The lineage of evangelistic influence began with an ordinary Sunday school teacher from Boston named Edward Kimball.[8]

When laypeople win others to Christ, they may not realize how much good they will produce through the generations. Without laypeople evangelizing, the church will not win the world. If they evangelize every day, they could conceivably share the gospel with every person on the globe in a short time. Why in the world a layperson would refuse to witness is anyone's guess, but untold billions await a gospel word from a Christian witness. Will they hear it?

---

8. William R. Moody, *The Life of D .L. Moody by His Son* (New York: Revell, 1900), 41.

4

Considering Approaches to a
Great Commission Church

Will H. McRaney, Jr.

M Y COLLEGE PITCHING COACH used to tell us the only way to coast was downhill. He was very clear in telling us that if we did the natural, the normal, the easy and usual, we would not get better as players. A pitcher is either improving in some aspect of pitching or he was going downhill, getting worse as a pitcher. The same could be said of most any organization, including local churches. The coasting path of a church is downhill or at least inward toward organizational and personal concerns and preferences. It is the natural, the normal, the easy, and the usual way.

If the above is accurate, then the natural trajectory of most churches over time is inward toward itself and away from those who desperately need Christ. The default position is inward, toward the needs, wishes, concerns, stylistic preferences and desires of those who make up the membership, not toward the mission of the church or toward the expansion of God's Kingdom on earth. In other words, it is a position that benignly, not intentionally, neglects the Great Commission.

For churches to advance the mission of the church toward the Great Commission, the leadership will have to go uphill against gravity in a downhill world. The church will have to swim upstream, against the currents toward a different type of future.

As a person who grew up around the Gulf of Mexico and lots of lakes, I enjoy being around the water, whether on the beach, swimming, or some form of boating. Most of my life my family has had access to a small ski boat, so I learned to ski and to drive the boat at an early age. The one type of boating that I have not engaged in is sailboating. I am naturally inquisitive about how things work, and I watched with great interest the America's Cup sailing competition in the mid 1980s. In the finals it was the American boat, *Stars and Stripes* against the winner of the fleet of foreign boats. The competition was fierce and the TV coverage was widespread. I learned a great deal about the boats themselves, the crew, the strategies involved, and the impact of wind speeds on the various types of boats.

Part of the racing involved having wind speeds high enough to move the boats and crews through the waters. With the massive sails and boats, the winds were essential to racing. Without the winds, the boats would just drift in the ocean. I believe there is a parallel here to church life. Without an active engagement with the Great Commission, churches just drift through their existence and only end up where the currents of the times take them. The Great Commission puts wind in the sails of the boat and allows the boat to move in a positive direction toward the expansion of God's glory and purpose for the individual church. Part of what the leadership of a local church has to do is to make sure they put enough pressure (wind) into the sails of the church to keep the church on course and continue to move on course with the design of God.

In many regards, the Christian church, as a whole, in America is adrift. There are many reasons for this and, hence, many consequences and manifestations of this in our churches and in our country. The typical American church lacks both a course and wind for the sails to help them move toward their destination. This problem is becoming more evident but has been somewhat covered up with the increase in the life expectancy of Americans. While we owe a great debt of gratitude to the senior saints who have paved the way, there has been an increasing tendency for the church in America to coast along with a status quo that does not reproduce itself either in numbers of churches or in numbers of new followers of Christ.

However, with the increased pressures in the United States and around the world during difficult economic times, the church is having less and less financial and human resources to engage in the advancing ministries of his Kingdom. The pressures did not create the challenges the church is facing, they just exposed what has been there for some years. These problems could be seen more easily in the decline of mainline churches in the 1960s and 70s. However, those declines have now begun to impact the Southern Baptist Convention (SBC) churches. The vast majority of churches are experiencing challenges with attendance, with baptizing new first time converts, especially adults, with finances, and with growing people spiritually into the life and culture-changing character of Christ. The church in America, including the SBC, is in many ways adrift and people are beginning to ask questions. I trust they will be good questions, not just survival questions, but that is for another time.

No one modern book or no one chapter can provide easy answers to the complex challenges facing churches across the country. In this particular chapter, I will seek to write my perspective on various approaches to the Great Commission. At points I will simply be offering my perspective on what I see without much opinion. At other points I will be offering my perspective on what could or should be. At points I am sure I will blur the two. I trust you will find some nuggets along the way.

In 1992 I completed a year-long research and writing project for my dissertation for my PhD at New Orleans Baptist Theological Seminary. Having been both a student and a professor in doctoral studies, I have come to believe that a requirement for getting a doctorate is to have a dissertation title that is long and one that confuses most people who might read the title. My title was "The Purpose Driven Church: An Investigation into Developing and Implementing a Purpose Statement and Its Benefits to Church Growth."

Most dissertations are not the most exciting documents to read, so let me summarize the gist of the research. Church leaders and members unite to advance the health of their church when they operate according to their purpose statement. In other words, churches do better when they have a clear understanding of why they exist.

A professor colleague once noted that he believed that every organization should go out of business every ten years and then reexamine why they existed and then restart with a clear purpose and use the resources they had to accomplish their purpose. While this suggestion was and is not practical, it gets at the heart of the issue. Over time churches forget why they exist and lose focus on the essential: being a body of kingdom people who are sent by God to expand his glory by sharing what they have been entrusted to a world that God desperately loves. From my dissertation and personal observations through the years, churches that constantly strive to operate by the Great Commission actually tend to do better in fulfilling the Great Commission.

The tragedy of many individuals, churches, mission agencies, and denominations is that while they started with a worthy target and mission, with time they have largely forgotten why they exist and begin to, more naturally, serve their own needs. They forget they even have a God-given target. The reality is that if you aim at nothing, you will hit it every time.

CURRENT CONTEXT

With recent challenges, both morally and economically in the country as a whole and in Southern Baptist churches specifically, a growing number of the church's younger leaders are beginning to examine the church and the supporting parachurch organizations in the SBC with a more critical and concerned eye. They are asking questions such as what is our business and how is business. Church members and younger leaders are asking these questions in light of current declines in attendance, baptisms, and financial resources. It appears that while there is talk of fulfilling the Great Commission, true evangelism and effective discipleship are not taking place as they ought to be, neither on the local church level nor through the various supporting SBC organizations. Hence, some in the SBC are looking for a resurgence of the Great Commission as a priority.

WHAT IS THE GREAT COMMISSION?

While this chapter primarily focuses on approaches to the Great Commission, I must confess that I believe that unless a church or a denominational agency has a clear sense of purpose, and makes decisions consistent with that purpose in its daily tasks, the approach will not matter. Therefore, underlying everything is the need for a clear understanding of the biblical purpose of a local church, and in this particular book, a biblical understanding of the Great Commission.

My preaching professor said that words do not have meanings, they have usages. While there may be some commonly held characteristics of views and beliefs around the Great Commission, I do not operate under a false illusion that everyone uses the term in the same manner or approaches the Great Commission in the same manner.

In short, the imperative of the Great Commission is to make disciples of all the peoples of the world. This certainly would involve doing this with intentionality and doing this as we go through life. It involves both sharing the greatest news of Christ's plan of salvation and teaching to obey the commands of God as found in the Bible, including the teachings of Christ through his life and ministry. Ideally, sharing involves a verbal witness supported or validated by a life that actively follows the teachings and commands.

I believe that our understanding of the Great Commission will directly and dramatically impact our approaches to carry it out. So, if we do not have a biblical understanding, we will err in our approaches in spite of our good intentions. If we do not have a solid understanding, we will substitute mileposts or indicators as the final targets for the Great Commission.

MIXED UP APPROACHES BASED ON PARTIAL UNDERSTANDING OF THE GREAT COMMISSION

While making more disciples and teaching new converts to grow in Christ, the Great Commission can be carried out in some partial ways. These partial ways are not wrong, but they do not fully contain the calling and task of the Great Commission. Christian leaders can run into difficulty if they unknowingly communicate that the Great Commission, as the whole, is one of the following:

- Baptisms
- Evangelistic events
- Attendance
- Giving
- Teaching events
- Telling gospel

For some churches, effectiveness and success is measured by how many people they baptize. While this is important, it is not the whole of making disciples. The danger in this approach is the birthing of spiritual orphans in the worst case situation. Doing this makes it very difficult to carry out evangelism in the future as (1) it typically leaves the new convert without much practical and seen life-change, which does not endear them to share their new faith and (2) it leaves those without Christ, who are connected to them, a poor example of a new life in Christ. Research has also concluded that between two-thirds and three-quarters of all adult baptisms are for adults who are not professing Christ for the first time. So, we can believe we are doing better in reaching into the culture without Christ than we actually are. With these things said, baptism is very important and is a factor we should examine.

Making disciples involves more than just conducting evangelistic events, whether they are Vacation Bible School (VBS), revivals, seasonal musicals, seeker services, or even door-to-door visitation. While we are called to be faithful, we also want to examine the quantity and quality of fruit that is being produced. We do not need to buy into the belief that because we have acted in an evangelistic manner, we have completed the Great Commission or have been effective in even one aspect of the Great Commission.

With some level of kidding, but also some level of truth, Baptists accuse themselves with being concerned with three Bs: buildings, budgets, and baptisms. While attendance at our services and training is important, just because a person has come into our church building does not mean we have been fruitful or even helpful in the process of disciplemaking. Too many have come to falsely identify success as "getting as many people as possible to stop whatever they are doing, and come and do whatever it is we are doing." Churches in America have often bought into the Western education approach to disciplemaking, where there is a teacher who teaches and a student who learns by listening. This approach has its place in terms of providing information, but it is a limited and, might I say, lousy way to think about the process of making disciples. We tend to think about getting them there and what we are going to tell them, but not as much about how people actually grow spiritually. If we are trying only to give academic tests, this approach would be fine. However, if we are trying to help people grow in their relationship with Christ, we will have to ask some additional questions.

Budgets and giving reflect the priorities of the church and something of the level of commitment to the Great Commission, individually and cooperatively. For some people, they believe that because they give financially to their local church, they are fulfilling the Great Commission; that, somehow, someone will do Great Commission works on their behalf. Likewise, a church can falsely believe that because their church is participating financially in mission efforts either locally or through the Cooperative Program of the SBC, that they have fulfilled their responsibilities toward the Great Commission. While these are significant, they too are only part of the puzzle.

Southern Baptists have typically carried out mission efforts in a cooperative manner through the Cooperative Program (CP). Because individualism is on steroids in the United States, with the impact of postmodernism and the media, more churches are tempted to pull back their funds from the CP, thinking they can better use the resources in carrying out the Great Commission. This approach will have significant consequences, many of which might actually be detrimental to the overall task. Individual church members struggle with this as well, sometimes to the point of withholding their tithes and offerings. They believe that they know best how to use their giving toward the Great Commission.

We do live in an age where the world is smaller and more accessible to churches and individuals. But it is also true that the world is more complex in its nature and subcultures than ever before. However, there is work that can be done together, better than it can be done separately or individually. The Great Commission approach should include individual and cooperative efforts. No one person, church, or even denomination can complete the Great Commission by themselves. To believe otherwise would be a great act of arrogance toward God and the task before us.

GREAT COMMANDMENT AND
GREAT COMMISSION CONNECTION

Men are known in some circles as the gender that can more easily compartmentalize. At points, this serves them well, such as with their ability to focus on hunting for food (when men hunted for food). At other points, men's ability to compartmentalize does not serve them well. Many married men can give testimony to this fact. In order to protect the guilty, I will use a personal analogy. I have the great pleasure of having a wife of twenty-four years, and we share three daughters, so I am quite outnumbered. It could be possible that our house might burn down around me if I am totally engaged in a sports event on TV, or if I am engaged in some work activity on my computer. At these points, it is not good to be so singularly focused. Neither is it good to be so focused on these things if my wife, Sandy, is trying to talk with me.

Churches have the tendency to focus on whatever is important to the current pastor, if the pastor has established leadership by being trustworthy and exercising good judgment over a period of years. Some pastors do reach points in their ministry where they are giving actual leadership. Whereas in many older churches, because of a steady turnover in pastors, leadership resides within a few members of the local church body.

Pastors who are leading their congregation tend to quite naturally lead out of their strengths and their passions. Wise pastors will also evaluate the ministry context around the local church and the ministry context within the local church. At different points in the life of a congregation, they may in fact need a strong emphasis in a particular area, even though they realize there are other parts or functions to a local church.

Few churches across America are truly focused on the Great Commission. Most are focused primarily on the internal needs of their church. Still others are focused on the needs of others, out concern for the Great Commandment. My observation through the years has led me to believe that most churches are focused neither on the Great Commission nor on the Great Commandment. These churches are typically lukewarm and seem to be slowly dying across the church landscape of America.

I am supportive of a call for renewed emphasis on the Great Commission. I am also supportive of a call toward the Great Commandment. I would be neglectful not to state what may be obvious to some; that is, the Great Commission is a priority expression of the Great Commandment. It all begins with a vital love relationship with God. Without this, we lack the power and credibility to be effective in the Great Commission. In addition, the Great Commission needs to flow out of the Great Commandment as its primary motivating factor, so that we see people as God sees them and act toward them in a way that honors Christ. People need to see and experience our love toward them, which certainly includes helping them know Christ and grow in Christ. The application, or living out of, the Great Commandment will be more effective and fruitful as followers of Christ in our churches give serious personal attention to loving God with all their hearts, minds, and souls, and love their neighbor as themselves.

Please allow me a few words to overstate a case, or to use hyperbole. Much of the evangelism in America today focuses on getting Christians who may not be experiencing it to express the love of God. We, as evange-lism leaders and pastors, may be trying to motivate lackadaisical Christians to share Jesus with a lost, hostile, and spiritually confused world. I would say that the American form of Christianity is focused more on what God can do for us, and less on how can live in a vital relationship with him and for him and for his glory and benefit. We have American Christians who live in a pluralistic world and who are confused spiritually about who God really is, and then we as church and denominational leaders are asking them to face the attack of the world and to attack the gates of hell with the gospel that they do not experience on a daily basis.

No amount of additional "how to's" will overcome the significant "don't want to" among some Christians. Christians have to first believe that God is the power unto salvation; there is no other name by which people can and must be saved, that in addition to prayer to attack the spir-itual battles taking place, the next greatest weapon we have is a changed life that is the daily experience of the love of God and living toward others out of that love and obedience to Christ.

Telling the story of Christ and teaching the commands of Christ are essential, but they are not the whole by themselves. Telling and teaching need each other. In fact, the church suffers as we neglect one or the other. Our goal is faithfulness and fruitfulness. We are to act faithfully and trust the Lord as he gives the increase in fruit. We do want to make sure that we are acting in such a way as to honor the Lord with our efforts and to not be of hindrance to his message we are sharing, so we continually need to examine our approaches to look for God's hands in our work.

Some may want to look to the seminaries as a problem. Some will want to look to our national and state agencies as a problem. Some will look to the cultural mess and mixed up religious views as the problem. While I agree, changes can and should be made when necessary, the larg-er challenge from my perspective is the LOVE problem. As Christians fall more in love with God and live their lives out of this love toward others, we have a greater opportunity to have impact with a refocusing on the Great Commission.

ASPIRED VERSUS ACTUAL VALUE

My mentor, Pastor Harold Bullock, taught me that every person and every church operates out of their perspectives and their values. Their behaviors, actions, will flow through the filters of what they see (perceive) and what really matters to them (value).Churches are famous for having statements of faith and statements of purpose, including ones around the Great Commission, but often those are neglected over time.

Individuals and churches tend to do what they truly value, not just what they say or write that they value. Aubrey Malphurs, in his book *Values Driven Leadership*, uses a term that I have found quite helpful through the years: "aspired" values.[1] These are the values the church or organization says are important but may not in fact be "actual" values of the church or organization.

APPROACHES TOWARD THE GREAT COMMISSION

God is creative in his creative activity. He chose to make thousands of different kinds of animals and plants. Each one is unique even if they share similar qualities. With people, God was and is also creative. He made man and then he made women, each similar and each unique at the same time.

Humans are similar in so many ways, but each one carries their own DNA descriptors and each one has a unique fingerprint that is shared with no other person. In the same way, all churches are different. They are unique, and they take unique approaches to church. And, of those churches across America that are committed to ministry toward the Great Commission, they too take different approaches to advancing the command of Jesus to make disciples of all the nations.

VIEWS OF THE GREAT COMMISSION

Everyone physically sees through their eyes. If the eyes are poor, the whole body has difficulty in functioning. We need good sight. Having passed forty years of age, my eyes have changed. Instead of single vision contacts and glasses, I now primarily wear progressive lenses to help me see more clearly both up close and at a distance. These years are also causing me to examine the past, the current situation, and the future of the church, particularly the church in America.

Some see the Great Commission through the eyes or perspective of the imperative verb and command to *make* disciples, particularly through academic or intellectual lenses. Their focus is on seeing people mature

---

1. Aubrey Malphurs, *Values Driven Leadership* (Grand Rapids: Baker, 2004).

in their faith, often maturing through Biblical knowledge and individual spiritual growth.

Still others see the Great Commission through the lenses of evangelism. For them, the Great Commandment and evangelism are synonyms. The measure of effectiveness in the Great Commission is the number of baptisms or evangelistic activity.

It seems that while there is a measure of truth in the two perspectives, the Great Commission is better fulfilled if the focus includes the best of each of these narrowly focused perspectives. The Great Commission involves helping more people come to know Christ both initially (evangelism) and for a lifetime (disciplemaking). Some would like to draw very strong lines between the two and proclaim their application of the Great Commission the one that is worthy of attention and giving only a token glance at the other side of the exact same coin. I think that proclamation is not only unwise and ineffective but not true to the biblical calling.

Along with a host of others, I raise my hand in support of a view of the Great Commission that unmistakably and quite intentionally links the better parts of making disciples, as we are commanded to do in the Great Commission. We cannot simply birth spiritual babies and walk off and leave them to fend for themselves in the midst of Satan and demonic beings—who seek to destroy them before they can grow into Christlikeness. So, too, we cannot help saved people to grow intellectually in their faith and grow in their personal relationships without engaging them in the harvest field for those who have yet to be saved.

If you will allow me, let me borrow a business or sales analogy that might be helpful to us. While this is extreme, I trust it will help us see more clearly. If Christianity were a business, we could not continue as a business unless we sold more products. In the same way, the church cannot continue to exist in a vibrant manner without evangelism. The obvious—every person who knows Christ is a product or fruit of various evangelistic efforts in partnership with the drawing of the Holy Spirit.

Likewise, if Christianity were a business, we could not continue as a business unless we did more quality control of our output, our desired product. In the same way, the church cannot continue to have an impact on the world for Christ without effectively helping people continue to live out their faith effectively at home, in the workplace, and in their social gatherings. The obvious—the credibility of the gospel in evangelism is significantly connected to the credibility of the witness.

If churches produce poor products (followers of Christ), evangelism will be increasingly difficult. To make a point, it appears that the divorce rate in Southern Baptist regions of the United States was higher than the national average in the year 2000.[2] If this research is accurate, and we as Christians are about the ministry of reconciliation (2 Cor 5), how much harder is evangelism to the lost relatives and friends of those Christians who have experienced the pain of divorce? I come from a home where the marriage was not healthy and it ultimately dissolved into divorce; so my intentions are not to cast stones or to make this the number one sin, but to illustrate why evangelism and disciplemaking processes are connected.

Paul said come follow me as I follow Christ. If our lives are not reflecting more of Christ, we are relegated to telling people to follow Christ in spite of ourselves, which does have a kernel of truth, but not completely. We can no longer simply tell people to believe the truth regardless of how the church is living or how I am living. I know the gospel is still true, but in terms of how people determine what is real, they are watching our lives. Jesus said that they would know us by our fruit and by our love for others and that they should see the hope and inquire as to the hope within us.

This has and will continue to impact our methods of evangelism, our approaches to the Great Commission. Without a credible, not perfect, messenger, evangelism can become limited to evangelism with strangers we do not know. While God has drawn complete strangers to me to himself, this approach to evangelism not only limits the number of people who might engage in evangelism, it makes follow-through very challenging; not impossible, but challenging.

It seems to me, Christians need to be ready to share the hope that is within them at all times, as the Scripture teaches—whether with neighbors or with strangers. Our greater opportunity to make disciples is to credibly live in word and deed the gospel in front of those who know us best and those with whom we engage on a regular basis.

Evangelism is inevitably linked with post salvation working out of the salvation. We cannot effectively have one without out the other.

2. "On the Scandal of Southern Baptist Divorce," SBC Resolution (Orlando, Florida: June 2010).

DIFFERENT APPROACHES OR DELIVERY SYSTEMS

One way to approach or consider the Great Commission is to consider the various delivery systems that are used. There was a period in time, as the use of radio expanded, that not only did various mission and ministry organizations begin to use the radio to broadcast the gospel into various parts of the world, they came to believe that radio would be the way the Great Commission was accomplished. While a helpful tool in some way, with a few decades of perspective and experience, we can see this has not happened.

The following are other delivery systems that have and are being used in different parts of the world to communicate the gospel: short-wave radio, radio, TV, Internet, media, print tracts and Bibles, and large public gatherings, such as crusades and other mass evangelism efforts. In the United States some churches have begun to use their primary public weekly gathering to evangelize their area. This has carried several names and nuances, but it is often referred to as seeker-target or seeker-focused services.

POSSIBLE APPROACHES TO GREAT COMMISSION

- Radio
- Shortwave radio
- TV
- Internet
- Media
- Print tracts and Bibles
- Personal evangelism
- Public worship—seeker sensitive
- Mass evangelism

Regardless of the delivery system used, eventually it takes disciples to make more disciples. Disciples tend to reproduce their own kind.

INDIVIDUAL CHURCH GROWTH AND/OR CHURCH PLANTING

For several decades in the latter part of the twentieth century, much of what was written and discussed in American church circles was around the topic of how to numerically grow an individual church. As with any movement or emphasis, there are both strengths to this approach and there are limitations. God is concerned about numbers, but not just one church's numbers. We in America tend to think about what we can see, what we can count, and what the more immediate result is.

With the opportunities afforded to large churches because of their size, let me say we need large churches that exercise significant strength and voice into a given region, or even nationally. Most churches need to grow larger, but it is also true that many churches need to expand their view of church growth to include planting churches across North America and the world, as a part of their calling to the Great Commission. Many church leaders have been trained to believe this is a foreign concept, when in fact it is quite biblical and essential to our overall work.

As one who has led and taught in church planting, I am always surprised at the looks I receive when I say to a group that "every church that exists was started." It is so very obvious but often overlooked. While church planting does not solve all the problems, and in fact it may create some new ones, it too is an essential part of carrying the gospel to all the peoples of the world.

DO VERSUS BE

Some approaches to the Great Commission impact what and where the church does what it does. Churches can compartmentalize what it means to carry out the Great Commission to refer only to projects that they put on their calendars. The Great Commission can also be relegated to taking up offerings to support missionaries either locally or nationally or internationally. Yet, it is true that carrying out the Great Commission is reflected in budgets, calendared events, and planned trips and activities.

Another approach, or misconception, to carrying out the Great Commission is seen in churches that believe that everything they do is somehow connected in an unintentional manner to the Great Commission. Churches can come to a false belief that because they exist, hold worship gatherings, have a pastor, and do various meetings and projects that they are carrying out the Great Commission. By looking at the lives of those in their fellowship and the results of their gatherings, one from the outside would not see a church that was focused on the Great Commission.

However, it is possible for churches to get focused on their primary task of the Great Commandment and live it out through the Great Commission. It seems the goal is not to assume everything a church does is advancing the Great Commission. It also seems the goal is not to just carry out Great Commission activities, although intentional activities are significant. The church is wise, as it approaches the Great Commission, by making it the filter by which it lives, both who it is and what it does.

FOCUS

One way to examine the ways church approach the Great Commission is to examine the location of their focus. Some churches are focused on the nations to the ends of the earth through international missions. They are known for their engagement with their time and financial resources to one or more places of the world. Indeed, the world is becoming smaller. Churches and people can get to most places of the world both physically and electronically as well.

Other churches are more focused on reaching and discipling those who are close to the physical location of their primary worship site, their Jerusalem. On a local level, their members are personally involved in reaching people in their community—their neighbors and co-workers— as a matter of focus. But they do not look beyond their local community. For those connected to the Southern Baptist Convention, however, they can be involved in their region of the state through the work and ministry of their local association. These associations are made up of churches in the region that voluntarily partner together, to carry out ministry that can be done better through a cooperative effort of the churches.

Southern Baptist churches are also involved through their Cooperative Program giving. These funds are sent to their state conventions, which in turn divide those funds between missions' needs in the state and the national missional causes. The funds that reach the national offices of the SBC are then divided among national mission causes in North America (through the North American Mission Board), and international mission causes (through the International Mission Board), and vocational ministers (through the six Southern Baptist Seminaries).

In addition to local and international focuses, some churches are focused on reaching North America through the planting of churches and participating in evangelistic efforts throughout the United States and

Canada. The majority of Southern Baptist churches are small churches that are located in small and mid-sized cities in the southern part of the United States. These churches are involved in Great Commission endeavors in the West or in the Northeast, where major population centers exist but are not heavily populated with churches affiliated with the SBC.

In conclusion, we find that some churches focus on evangelism, others on disciplemaking. Some churches emphasize church planting and still other churches growth. Some emphasize "doing" and others "being." The healthy church will understand that all these are vitally important in the life of the Great Commission church. For this reason pastors and deacons need to understand and evaluate their congregation, constantly seeking to improve its ministry. Just like pitching in baseball, coasting is not an option. The church must press on to remain vital and truly be a Great Commission church.

5

How to Develop a Great Commission Church

William D. Henard III

IT WAS NEARING THE end of 1991 when I received a phone call from a friend and mentor. He had just returned from a trip to the former Soviet Union and was planning a return junket. The purpose of his phone call was to invite me to go with him in 1992. I told him that I would pray about it, gave it a cursory thought, and declined. God had called me to pastor a local church, and my mission field involved my city and my state. Though I had a great respect for those on the mission field, the world was their oyster, not mine . . . end of story . . . or so I thought.

He called later, in early 1992, to ask me again to go with him. I once more declined gracefully, citing some spiritual reason. A third call came not two weeks before the departure date. It seems that one of the travelers was unable to go due to health reasons but wanted to pay for someone to take his place. My friend determined that I was that someone. All I had to pay for was a plane ticket to New York's Kennedy Airport and my visa. The benefactor had covered the rest of the costs. My most erudite spiritual thoughts surfaced. Why not? What have I got to lose?

I went to my church on Sunday, throwing out a proverbial "fleece," figuring that the church members would not want me to go. Instead, the church not only embraced the trip, but I had several people approach me with promises of financial help with the plane ticket and extras. One gentleman eventually used his preferred airlines' SkyMiles to buy me a first class ticket to New York. Another individual volunteered to drive me to New Orleans to "walk through" my passport application. Passport in hand, I overnighted it and my visa application to the New York travel agency, receiving it back a few days before departure.

The trip was a disaster. First, I was sick the entire time I was gone. I ended up with an ear infection (which bothers me to this day), bronchitis, laryngitis . . . just to whine for a while. I also got all of my camera equipment stolen (video and still).The beds were hard. The food was terrible, and I got lost in a city of five million people, not knowing a word of Russian.

Yet if you were to ask me what I thought about the trip, my answer would be simple. It was the most life-changing event in my ministry. We handed out Bibles under the arch in Victory Square in Kiev, Ukraine, and were mobbed by literally hundreds of people wanting a copy of the Scriptures. On my lost adventure, I handed out what tracts I had on my person, met a Ukrainian Air Force pilot, who did his best to help me find my way back to my hotel, and ended up with an entourage of people who sought to help me reconnect with my group. I even was able to lead a young couple, who were part of the entourage, to Christ, as the Air Force pilot prayed silently nearby.

The most interesting part of the whole escapade was meeting up with those two college students who offered their assistance in relocating my lodging. We finally arrived after several hours. I treated the young couple and the pilot to a late night snack, spending time to carefully share the gospel as best I could. It is amazing what one can do through God's help in communication, even when an incredible language barrier exists. I had already figured out through hand signals that the pilot was a believer. The two college students were not, but one of them spoke broken English. Standing in the foyer of the hotel, I slowly shared how one could know God through Christ. The pilot stood nearby praying and listening. The young man translated to his girlfriend the words I shared. In the end, both of them prayed to receive Christ, and I was able to refer them to a local pastor for follow-up. These circumstances served as the catalysts for me to become a Great Commission pastor committed to building a Great Commission church.

How to communicate this newfound passion with my church now became the biggest concern from the entire event. Most Christians have heard boring missionary stories or have listened to testimonies that seemed to be more about brow-beating and self-exaltation than a challenge for believers to fulfill the Great Commission. It is also true that, while churches talk a good talk about missions, many of them become defensive and resistant to actual hands-on, sacrificial missions giving and involvement. So the question remains, "How do you develop a Great Commission church with Great Commission Christians?" This chapter proposes to answer that question.

THE ROLE OF THE PASTOR

The most critical element in developing a Great Commission church comes from the role of the lead pastor of the church. Another chapter in this book handles the specifics of this proposition, but it remains important to reiterate the need for the individual who leads the church and brings vision to the church to be totally committed to the idea of building a Great Commission church. Without good leadership, the church, in most situations, will never develop that particular commitment on its own.

STEPS FOR DEVELOPING VISION

I want to be careful in introducing this section because I do not want to convey that, if one will follow these steps exactly, it will result in an immediate global focus. Most of these steps involve concurrent, not consecutive processes. One must do these things together, repeating the steps often. In other words, these principles must be applied and re-applied throughout the process of Great Commission development.

1. Preach the Word

In my opinion, no greater need exists in the church today than for a consistent proclamation of God's Word. While stories move people emotionally, God's Word speaks to the spirit. A Great Commission church must be born through conviction, and the most formidable way comes from proclamation.

Larry Reesor reminds us that the Bible is "about God and His purpose, not about us."[1] It is important, through the preaching of the Word,[2]

---

1. Larry Reesor, *Growing a Great Commission Church* (Woodstock, GA: Global Focus, 1999), 7.

2. It is my personal conviction that the use of expository messages provides the most functional means for accomplishing this goal. See H. C. Brown Jr., H. Gordon Clinard, Jesse J. Northcutt, and Al Fasol, *Steps to the Sermon: An Eight-Step Plan for Preaching*

that the pastor instills a passion in his people for the Great Commission and for those who are lost. Take the church through the passages of Scripture that remind them of the Great Commission.[3] Allow them to respond, in some way, to the message. In Simon Peter's sermon on the day of Pentecost, Luke records, "And with many other words he testified and strongly urged them, saying, 'Be saved from this corrupt generation.'"[4] The words "strongly urged" (*parakaleo* in the Greek text) are found approximately 108 times in the New Testament. Of these occurrences, the context suggests pleading or begging in at least sixty-one of the usages. Five times,[5] the words are used in direct connection with evangelism.[6]

My point is not so much about the benefits, or lack thereof, of the public invitation but the need for the pastor to challenge people to respond to the preaching of the Word. Do not underestimate the power that God's Word has to quickly change the heart of the congregation. Show them in the text the call to evangelism and mission for every Christian, and it will impact many lives and change many hearts.

Another important task in preaching is to remind believers about the lostness of the world. Estimates are that 6.9 billion people lived on this earth in 2010. Within these billions, approximately 5,850 Last Frontier people groups exist. A Last Frontier people group is defined as "a people group which is unreached and has not had a new evangelical church started within the last two years."[7] At present, this group encompasses around 1.6 billion people.[8]

The definition for an unreached people group is "a people group in which less than 2% of the population is Christian."[9] This population involves 630 different people groups, with numbers exceeding 2.4 bil-

---

with Confidence, rev.ed. (Nashville: B&H, 1996), John MacArthur Jr., ed., *Rediscovering Expository Preaching: Balancing the Science and Art of Biblical Exposition* (Dallas: Word, 1992), Jim Shaddix, *The Passion-Driven Sermon* (Nashville: B&H, 2003).

3. See Matt 28:16–20; Mark 16:16; Luke 24:44–48; John 20:19–23; and Acts 1:8.

4. All Scripture references are quoted from the HCSB, unless otherwise noted.

5. Acts 2:40; Acts 11:22; 2 Cor 5:20; 2 Tim 4:5; and Titus 1:9.

6. R. Allen Streett, *The Effective Invitation: A Practical Guide for the Pastor* (Grand Rapids: Kregel, 2004), 62–65.

7. "Global Status of Evangelical Christianity," accessed June 27, 2009, http://www.imb.org/globalresearch/sge.asp.

8. Ibid.

9. Ibid.

lion people.[10] Still another 977 people groups, encompassing 1.85 billion people, only have an evangelical population of greater than 2% but less than 5% of the population.[11] These numbers represent the vast lostness of our world.

Even in North America, the last bastion of evangelicalism, it appears that only 25% of the population is Christian.[12] This statistic indicates that 255 million people are not believers in the United States and Canada. Global Focus, a ministry that empowers local churches for global impact, estimated that only 11% of the world's population is Christian.[13] If this statistic is true, it means that at least 6 billion people do not know Christ today in our world, and the numbers continue to grow.[14]

While statistics alone may not motivate anyone to missions and evangelism, they give insight and depth to the need for every Christian to get out on the mission field. The preaching of the Word and the call to decision will facilitate a passion among church members. This process must consistently be presented to the congregation. It cannot be a one-time event, with the expectation that the church will develop and keep a passion for the world. Preach the Word and keep preaching the Word to them!

2. Develop an "Acts 1:8" Strategy

In Acts 1:8, Jesus says, "But you will receive power when the Holy Spirit has come upon you, and you will be My witnesses in Jerusalem, in all Judea and Samaria, and to the ends of the earth." This verse references the call placed upon the disciples' lives as they prepared to embark on the task of fulfilling the Great Commission. John MacArthur states about this commissioning, "Beginning in *Jerusalem*, the apostles carried out the Lord's mandate. . . . Today, believers continue to have the responsibility for

10. "Global Status of Evangelical Christianity," accessed June 27, 2009, http://www.peoplegroups.org/Downloads/2009-04%20GSEC%20Overview.pdf, 1–2.

11. Ibid.

12. From "North American Mission Board Report" by Geoff Hammond, president, Southern Baptist Convention, June 24, 2009.

13. Larry Reesor, *Growing a Great Commission Church* (Woodstock, GA: Global Focus, 1999) 20.

14. At the Southern Baptist Convention 2009, the statistic was given during the International Mission Board Report that the number of people who have no access to the gospel grows by 81,499 each day.

being Christ's witnesses throughout this world. The sphere for witnessing is as extensive as the kingdom–all the world. That was and is the mission for the church until Jesus comes."[15] John Phillips concurs, explaining: "How quickly our world could be evangelized, even at this late date in the church's history, if every church would take this plan seriously and begin with its own immediate community, reach out to its own country, and become involved in missionary activity to the farthest reaches of its own continent, and then send out its ambassadors to all nations. The world would be invaded by armies of believers from all nations reaching out to all peoples in all parts of the world."[16]

The command to go was not just one given to the apostles or the first-century church; it is a command for all believers.

The details for this strategy are simple. Jerusalem represents one's local community, town, or city. Judea can be interpreted as the state. Samaria symbolizes the country. And the ends of the earth signify the world. Sometimes people are resistant to developing a global focus because they cannot understand why someone would go halfway around the world to tell people about Jesus when nonbelievers live in their own city. This concern may arise out of a genuine passion for those outside of Christ. Oftentimes, it is more of an excuse, because many of those who share this perspective are rarely themselves involved in any kind of personal evangelism or local missions.

Many times a hesitance regarding global missions comes from a lack of biblical understanding. People are not against going around the world; they just do not understand the biblical mandate placed upon all Christians and churches. Therefore, teach what the Bible commands about the Great Commission and then show how it can be fulfilled through your local church. Where is your Jerusalem, Judea, Samaria, and world? An Acts 1:8 Strategy will help church members avoid compartmentalizing each aspect of missions, as though one part is more important than another. Additionally, it will aid the church in removing jealousy among mission volunteers and mission projects.

Finally, putting together a global mission team or committee will provide a helpful way to get many people involved in this strategy. Divide them into groups of four, each with the assignment of dreaming, research-

---

15. John MacArthur, *Acts 1–12*, in *The MacArthur New Testament Commentary* (Chicago: Moody, 1994), 22, emphasis original.

16. John Phillips, *Acts 1–12*, vol. 1 of *Exploring Acts* (Chicago: Moody, 1986), 21–22.

ing, strategizing, and implementing a specific part of Acts 1:8. Thus, each part of the Great Commission is equal in emphasis and importance. It also allows for a large number of people to catch the vision of reaching the world, to communicate that perspective to the rest of the church, and to provide immediate volunteers who have developed a passion for that part of the world, whether local or international.

3. Take People on a Mission Trip

One of the best ways to get someone to develop a heart for missions is to simply get them on the mission field. Getting them there is not as easy as it sounds, though. If the pastor, however, is capitalizing on the preaching of the Word and is ready for when people respond and commit, then the chance for success becomes excellent. Keep in mind several things.

First, not everyone will go, but that reluctance does not necessarily mean that they are opposed to missions. Second, not everyone will go on an international mission trip, but that fact does not diminish their passion for reaching the lost. Third, going on a mission trip does not necessarily indicate that the person going is more spiritual than those who stay. One of the greatest detriments to developing a Great Commission church is the people who go on the trips. Unfortunately, becoming a mission volunteer can create an attitude of self-righteousness and false spirituality.

Providing a variety of venues for fulfilling the Great Commission offers some solution to a part of the problem. Acts 1:8 challenges the church to be witnesses "in Jerusalem, in all Judea and Samaria, and to the ends of the earth." Therefore, develop trips or opportunities that will allow the church to fulfill at least two or more of these calls.

Many possibilities exist for fulfilling this task, which is good news. For those who are Southern Baptists, your state convention will have various opportunities for the local church to get connected in hands-on mission projects. The North American Mission Board can link your church with mission activities around North America. The International Mission Board can do the same for trips outside of the United States. My encouragement would be to contact your state convention and talk with the person who handles mission trips. Various levels of involvement are available, so start out small and build to greater participation. Do not think that your church has to be on the cutting edge from the start. Work toward the goals that you set for your church.

4. Provide the Proper Training

As already mentioned, one of the problems that surfaces within churches that will spell the end of missions is the people who go on trips. To be quite honest, mission trips, especially international ones, sometimes draw people who are not spiritually, emotionally, or personally ready. They are attracted because of the adventure or the attention they receive. The dilemma presents a delicate balance because we do not want to discourage anyone from growing in his or her faith, but we also need to protect the integrity of the mission endeavor and ministry.

In order to help control this problem, I would suggest that every church require that everyone who signs up for a trip or demonstrates an interest in going attend a training event. The length of the training may vary based upon the significance, difficulty, or purpose of the mission; but provide training nonetheless. A training manual that can be distributed to the mission volunteers is quite helpful. In it, include the following:

1. The "Deciding to Go" Checklist. This list includes helping the volunteer decide what God is saying in leading them in missions, knowing how to discern the reaction of family and friends, discerning the right time for going, seeking God for his provision financially and otherwise, and knowing how to decide if it is not time for a short-term mission trip. A person is not ready to go if he or she: a) has trouble giving up personal rights to comfort and control of the agenda, b) finds it difficult to follow the assigned leadership, c) has difficulty working as part of a team, d) has trouble being punctual at all times, and e) has fears that outweigh faith and are distracting from the task at hand.

2. Protocol. In this section, include the requirements for the mission team. These standards are probably generalized for every trip, but the leader can give specifics as needed. Protocol items include that all team members will: a) meet at the specified time at the location specified by the team leader, b) dress appropriately while traveling, representing the church and Christ well, c) assist other team members with regard to baggage, passport checks, security, and in managing/safekeeping of their personal property while traveling, d) be aware of where the other team members are at all times; no one travels alone, and e) keep passports and visas protected on their person at all times.

3.   Medical Guidelines. This section should include specific needs or requirements for each trip, including medications and/or shots required. Give specific details of how to acquire or fulfill the necessary medical specifications. It is important that each volunteer sign a medical release form that includes important personal information and a consent-for-treatment release statement. Unfortunately, medical emergencies do arise during trips, and it is important to protect both the volunteer and the church.

4.   Building Team Unity. Team unity proves to be one of the most essential elements of a successful mission trip. The best advertising for missions and for building a Great Commission church and spirit is the people who go on trips and have life-changing experiences. Take the team through some of the biblical mandates and models for unity, including 1 Cor 3:6–9; Col 3:12–17; Gal 6:2; and Eph 6:18–19.Spend time praying with and for one another and include in the manual a "Release of Rights" form that every volunteer signs.

5.   Fund-Raising. If your church allows fund-raising, it is important to include a section that sets the guidelines for how team members can approach church members and others outside of the church for assistance in raising needed funds. Raising funds can be a delicate issue, so make sure that specific standards are given.

6.   Financial Guidelines. Provide information on each person's responsibilities financially, along with dates and timetables for payments. While money is not the most important issue for the trip, if individuals do not pay their share of the costs, it can cause some resentment and resistance to missions, especially if your church is conducting several trips during the year. One sure way to kill a Great Commission passion is to place an unnecessary financial burden on the church due to the negligence of a few mission volunteers.

Have the group meet several times, if possible, before they embark on the trip. Praying together, getting to know one another, sharing hopes and fears, and dreaming together all have an important part in preparing the team for missions.

5. Adopt a People Group

One of the drawbacks of how churches have done missions in the past is that people do not know who they are trying to reach. The lostness of the world is nothing more than an ambiguous idea; it is difficult to grasp and impossible to understand. While preaching the Great Commission stirs the spirit, seeing the Great Commission impassions the heart.

The priority of engaging and reaching people groups represents a major philosophical change that has occurred recently at the International Mission Board of the Southern Baptist Convention. Previously, missionaries focused on regions of the world. The world, however, has changed and come to us. People groups are rarely found in single regions or locations. They are often scattered around the globe. Therefore, a church can focus on reaching a people group that, not only is found in a particular country in another part of the world, but may also be living right in one's own city in the United States.

Adopting a people group allows the church to see real people and to understand real lostness. A person's spiritual condition now becomes a substantial issue, having flesh and blood. The church no longer speaks of just "lost people," but it envisions those people as individuals in need of a Savior. The International Missions Board (IMB) can provide assistance in adopting a people group for your church.[17] The process is simple, but it allows your church to take huge steps toward becoming a Great Commission church.

6. Have a Global Mission Celebration

Another downfall of the local church in developing a Great Commission passion originates from the church's inability to connect with missionaries. Unfortunately, many churches involve themselves in praying for missionaries, naming missionaries, talking about missionaries, but no one in the church has ever met a missionary. Occasionally, the church has a missionary come and speak, but this opportunity rarely results in a real passion for missions. Sometimes it does more harm than good. The only real recollection people have about missions is the boring mission sermon and the disconnected slide show. Thus, this sad fact results in many misconceptions about those on the mission field and a genu-

17. Go to this website: http://www.imb.org/main/lead/page.asp?StoryID=8718& LanguageID=1709; or navigate through imb.org.

ine lack of passion for missions. The solution is simple: have a Global Mission Celebration.

In order to develop a Great Commission church, one must celebrate the Great Commission. It must become a priority and a special event in the church. Several suggestions are apropos:

1. With the aim of preparing the church for the celebration, decorate the church year-round with mission paraphernalia. Surround the church worship center with flags representing various countries and states (flags can be purchased for a relatively low cost from a variety of merchants). Develop a Missions Wall of Honor where highlights can be given for the various mission trips or missionaries the church supports. Display a map that highlights the lostness of the world. Highlight passages of Scripture in bold letters that point to the Great Commission. These activities represent a way to involve a significant number of people in missions' education and promotion.

2. Set aside a specific weekend for the event. Some churches will go two weekends and some an entire week. Make this event as important as anything else that the church does. Promote the celebration as an opportunity that no one wants to miss.

3. Invite a reasonable number of missionaries. Mission boards, state conventions, and local associations can help in this process. Invite them early. Waiting until the last minute will only hinder the celebration.

4. Ask Sunday school classes or Bible study small groups to sponsor or host a missionary. Set up opportunities for these classes/groups to fellowship specifically with individual missionaries. Let them hear the missionary's stories. That event alone will change people's hearts towards missions.

5. Put on a mission fair. Decorate thematically areas of the church for the missionaries. Set up tables or booths for people to come by and meet the missionaries personally. *Provide food.* If you feed them, they will come! Have food from the various countries. If you have a large area where people can congregate, invite the choirs of the church to sing. Use gifts from various countries, especially from countries, cities, and states where the church has served, as giveaways. Without trying to sound irreverent, the

mission fair should have a carnival atmosphere. It should be exciting and engaging.

6.   Conclude with a commitment-celebration service. On Sunday morning, develop the worship service around celebration missions. Find a theme song that the choir/praise team/praise band can lead. Have a mass choir, including adults, students, and children. During the singing of the theme song, have a parade of flags, ensuring a sense of elegance and grandeur. This activity can be perceived as irrelevant and as a distraction if not done with a sense of importance. Introduce the missionaries who are present and celebrate their attendance and work. Missionaries serve as the heroes of the church. They may be embarrassed by the attention, but the church should realize that these missionaries are the real warriors. Thank them for their service to Christ and the church. Be careful with allowing one to share in the service, as it might unintentionally hurt another's feelings. The best suggestion is to invite someone to be the special speaker for the morning and use the service as a time for personal commitment and consecration. This service also provides a good opportunity for members to make financial commitments toward missions and mission trips.

CONCLUSION

When it comes to evaluating our own nation, think about these statistics. Currently, 162 million people (58%) live in the fifty largest metropolitan areas of the United States. An estimated 100 million lost persons live in these large metros. New York (21 million) and Los Angeles (16 million) continued to lead the population in 2000. One of every 7.5 Americans lives in these two metropolitan areas. Metros experiencing the largest net and percentage growth are in the Southern and Western regions. The fifty largest metros account for 63% of the nation's net population growth between 1990 and 2000 (net gain was 20.5 million in these areas). Las Vegas (83%), Austin (48%), and Phoenix (45%) were the fastest growing metros.[18]

18.   "Population Change and Distribution: 1990-2000," accessed April 11, 2011, http://www.census.gov/population/www/cen2000/briefs.

Those statistics reveal that the world in which we live, even our own nation, is in need of a Savior. The church cannot continue to just talk about missions and evangelism as subjects for Bible study. Christians must be about the business of fulfilling the Great Commission. The task seems impossible and daunting, but the world can be reached if churches can grasp this one thought: do what it takes to develop the church into a Great Commission church.

6

Building a Great Commission Denomination

Charles E. Lawless Jr.

THE FUTURE OF DENOMINATIONALISM has been in question for years. Some argue that denominations will not be in existence within the next few decades. Others argue that young generations of leaders have no allegiance to denominations, even if those denominational systems have made it possible for these men and women to become leaders. Still others argue that economic struggles will slowly drain denominational coffers to the point that they can no longer be effective. While there is an element of truth in each of these thoughts, one truth about denominations is clear: few, if any, denominations are effectively doing the work of the Great Commission (Matt 28:18–20).

More than one person has noted the failure of our own denomination, the Southern Baptist Convention, in the Great Commission task.[1] We are reaching no more people today than we did in the 1950s. The rate of population increase continues to outdistance the rate of our denomination's growth. Our international missions' endeavors are more effective in reaching nonbelievers, though some question whether the churches planted are as solid as they should be. If a strongly evangelical denomination such as ours struggles to focus on the Great Commission, how much

---

1. E.g., "Study: SBC's Conservative Resurgence Failed in Evangelism," accessed April 11, 2011 at http://www.floridabaptistwitness.com/sb/4258.article.

more must that be the case for denominations whose commitment to the Word is less clear?

The goal of this chapter is to address the issue of building a Great Commission denomination. The very nature of this book demands emphasis on the Southern Baptist Convention, but the principles herein are broadly applicable to other denominations.

THE TITLE: A MISNOMER?

By definition, a denomination is "a religious organization whose congregations are united in their adherence to its beliefs and practices."[2] It is the fifth word of this definition—"congregations"—that should most capture our attention. Though denominational structures and polities differ, no denomination would exist without local church congregations. In that sense, a Great Commission denomination is not possible without Great Commission congregations. Furthermore, Great Commission congregations seldom exist apart from pastoral leaders who are themselves Great Commission pastors.

In some ways, a summary of this chapter is as simple as these bullet points:

- God calls all believers to be Great Commission minded.
- A Great Commission pastor leads a Great Commission congregation.
- When many Great Commission pastors lead many Great Commission congregations . . .
- The result is a Great Commission denomination.

Other writers in this text are addressing in depth the topics of leaders and congregations. Should the principles and concepts in those chapters *not* be followed, there will likely be no Great Commission denomination. This chapter will address these topics as needed, while also speaking more broadly to the topic of denominations.

2. "Denomination," in *Merriam-Webster Online Dictionary*, accessed at http://www
.merriam-webster.com/dictionary/denomination.

A GREAT COMMISSION DENOMINATION MUST TAKE THE
WORD OF GOD SERIOUSLY

The church is the body of Christ (1 Cor 12:12–27), the people of God living out their faith in a local context. We are God's chosen vessel to proclaim and teach the gospel of Jesus Christ to an unbelieving world. Only through reading and applying God's Word can we truly understand who we are to be and how we are to live; thus, the church must be built on a solidly biblical foundation. If that foundation does not exist, doctrines related to the Great Commission are often the first to be jettisoned.

Consider, for example, what often happens to evangelism if a church's teachings are not based on the Bible. The exclusivity of Christ (John 14:6; Rom 10:9) is denied in the face of political correctness; after all, how can there be only one way to God? The doctrine of hell is viewed as an outdated teaching that cannot possibly reflect a loving God. More specifically, the lostness of humanity (Rom 3:23) is itself questioned if the Bible's teachings are ignored. The church may still grow in numbers, but the growth will not be conversion growth that makes an eternal difference. Evangelism, a central piece of the Great Commission puzzle, no longer matters.

That is not to suggest, though, that a stated belief in the Scriptures automatically leads to a Great Commission focus. Southern Baptists have loudly and consistently proclaimed for thirty years that we believe in the authority of the inerrant Word—a Word that at least four times mandates the Great Commission (Matt 28:18–20; Luke 24:46–47; John 20:21; Acts 1:8). As I have written elsewhere, however, we have stood faithfully for a message that we have chosen to keep to ourselves.[3] When a denomination's stated belief in the Word is not matched with practical obedience to that Word, the denomination will not be a Great Commission denomination.

A GREAT COMMISSION DENOMINATION
MUST FACE BRUTAL FACTS

If obedience to the Great Commission is the scriptural standard, denominational leaders must be willing to admit when denominational churches miss the mark. Doing so is not easy, especially when energy,

3. Chuck Lawless, "The Great Commission and the Local Church," in *Toward a Great Commission Resurgence* (Nashville: Lifeway, 2008).

dollars, and people have been devoted to achieving the denomination's goals. Accountability often hurts, but no needed change will take place without honest reflection.

Recognizing again that denominations do not exist apart from local congregations, I encourage denominational and church leaders to ask at least the following accountability questions about their individual churches:

1. *Is the church's teaching based on the Bible?* Where that particular gospel is not taught, something less than the New Testament church exists.

2. *Is the church a praying church?* Legitimate Great Commission church growth is a gift of God, who empowers his followers and draws others unto himself.

3. *Is the church reaching nonbelievers?* Here, the possibility of overemphasizing numbers becomes apparent, but the question must be asked: are nonbelievers coming to know the Lord through the church's ministry? If growth is primarily transfer growth, something must change.

4. *Is the church keeping the new believers who join?* Reaching nonbelievers, while losing them soon thereafter, fails to fulfill the Great Commission order to make disciples.

5. *Is the church both locally and globally minded?* At the risk of understatement, the world is *always* bigger than any local church. As many as 1.6 billion people in the world have little access to the gospel. Great Commission churches minister from their Jerusalem to the ends of the earth.

6. *Are the leaders committed to the Great Commission?* By far, the most common problem we see in unhealthy churches is poor or unfocused leadership. Leaders who are not committed to the Great Commission do not often lead a church to lasting Great Commission growth.

7. *Are young leaders on board?* Churches (and by extension, denominations) cannot survive if future generations "jump ship." Without compromising the church's commitment to the Word, leaders must disciple and lead the next generation.

These questions are just a beginning, but every analysis must start somewhere. Honest diagnosis is the first step toward prescription and better health. The seriousness of the Great Commission task demands that churches and denominations continually ask the hard questions.

A GREAT COMMISSION DENOMINATION
MUST BE A PRAYING DENOMINATION

Accompanying each of the aforementioned New Testament references to the Great Commission is a promise of the power of God to accomplish the task. Jesus promised that his presence would be with his followers to the end of the age (Matt 28:20). He told his disciples to wait in Jerusalem until they were empowered from on high (Luke 24:49). As he prepared the disciples, he breathed the Spirit upon them in a foreshadowing of the day of Pentecost (John 20:22). Likewise, he assured them of the power of the Spirit who would lead them to be witnesses to the ends of the earth (Acts 1:8). What was the point of these multiple references to power? Simply stated, the early church could not do what God called them to do apart from his authority and power.

Almost by definition, denominations risk missing this point. One small congregation longing to make a dent in spiritual darkness seeks God's presence and power, knowing that they can do little on their own. Unite their efforts with the larger church down the street, though, and their own weakness may not be as apparent. Multiply that factor exponentially as thousands of churches form a denomination, and it becomes increasingly easier to trust denominational structures and programs more than God. The result is a denomination—perhaps even a growing one—that lacks life-changing power.

Indeed, denominations are by nature "fixers." We come by this practice honestly, as our structures give us the "know-how" and the experience to tackle the problems that we face. Local associations or districts, state organizations, national mission boards, Bible colleges, seminaries, funding agencies, research institutes—some denominations have all the resources to address the issues they face. Though unstated, our practical prayer philosophy becomes:

- Try hard, give it our best, and turn to God only if our best is not good enough.
- Turn to God as a last resort rather than a first and only hope ("all we can do now is pray").
- Work to correct the problem, and then pray only when we realize that we can't fix it.

That is what concerns me about the Southern Baptist Convention. My fear is that we will respond to our call for a Great Commission resurgence by meeting, organizing, planning, strategizing, and suggesting correctives—but genuinely praying *only when we have to.* No Great Commission denomination will develop from that kind of praying.

A GREAT COMMISSION DENOMINATION'S TRAINING INSTITUTIONS MUST EMPHASIZE THE GREAT COMMISSION

As the dean of the Billy Graham School of Missions and Evangelism, I admit my bias here. God gave me a passion for the Great Commission many years ago, and I have the privilege now of focusing on this task. My point, however, is larger than my personal interests.

Most denominations recognize the importance of trained leaders for their churches. From the Bible training center on the mission field to the seminary that offers doctoral degrees, denominations provide opportunities for needed ministry training. Too often, however, that education sacrifices practical training on the altar of other theological disciplines.

Allow me to be elaborate in order to be clear. I believe strongly in the classical theological disciplines. Knowing the Scriptures is critical to effective ministry. The church leader who does not know Christian theology is not best prepared for ministry. Knowing how church history and Christian ethics inform the Church today can be invaluable to church leadership. All of these disciplines are indeed foundational to theological education and ministry.

In addition, I also believe that practical training is best accomplished through the local church. The local church pastor who teaches others to do evangelism and missions is often the most effective educator as he pours his life into young believers. Many of us can speak of pastors or other church leaders who had just such an influence in our own lives.

At the same time, though, I do not believe that practical training should be limited to the local church. Most church leaders do not train well (hence, the training must at least start elsewhere for now). In addition, the best teaching of theological disciplines also provides occasion to make direct application to life. For example, teaching a theology of the Bible affords opportunity to show how the Scriptures differ from the holy books of the world's false religions—thus providing missiological training as well. Every discipline should be taught in such a way that students not only understand what Christians believe but also know how to proclaim and live those truths before nonbelievers.

More specifically, teachers and professors can have tremendous influence on students as they model their faith before them. Students will remember the New Testament professor who leads a mission trip or the Christian philosophy professor who speaks of his latest evangelism attempts. Great Commission passion is memorable, regardless of the discipline taught.

A GREAT COMMISSION DENOMINATION MUST EMPHASIZE GREAT COMMISSION TRAINING AND EDUCATION FOR CHILDREN

Ask our children who their heroes are, and I fear they would speak of a cartoon figure, a movie character, or a television superhero. I hope they would name their parents, but I am not persuaded that would always happen. I am fairly certain the children would not name their pastor, and I am convinced most children would not identify a missionary as their hero. I doubt most could even name a missionary. William Carey and Lottie Moon are often unknowns, and present-day missionaries are equally unfamiliar.

That reality is tragic. Who of the next generation will take the gospel to the ends of the earth if they do not know the stories of missionaries? How many of our boys will be open to a call to ministry because their pastor has been a hero? How many will long to be like their pastor who preaches the Word, lives a holy life, models personal evangelism, and loves God's church? One of my pastoral heroes, Jack Tichenor, preached God's Word for over sixty years. Never did I hear him say a negative word about another person, and nor did I ever see him miss an opportunity to speak a good word about Jesus. He was a pastoral evangelist until the day he died. If God were to allow me to be even somewhat like "Brother Jack," I would be honored.

My point is not to rob God of his glory by being anthropocentric. Rather, it is to call denominations to emphasize again Great Commission training and education of children. Produce the best material that is both exciting and challenging for children. Strongly encourage church leaders to invite furloughing missionaries to speak to their congregations. Provide resources that teach children about the world and show them how to tell their friends about Jesus. Make certain that all children's programs include a clear Great Commission component.

Children can evangelize, and they can do missions. In fact, their enthusiasm for doing both sometimes puts to shame the unenthusiastic response of adults. The denomination whose churches prioritize giving their children an evangelistic, globally focused worldview will reap Great Commission dividends for years to come.

A GREAT COMMISSION DENOMINATION MUST PRIORITIZE THE GREAT COMMISSION

This principle is perhaps the most obvious and yet most difficult one, as it demands an assessment of programs, personnel, and dollars. While not everyone agrees with Rick Warren's concept of the "purpose-driven church," his philosophy has influenced thousands of churches to plan according to purpose—and to delete activities that do not contribute to the purpose.[4] Denominations that seek to be Great Commission-minded will need to do the same.

The needs of the lost world are so great that denominations cannot afford to dilute their Great Commission focus. Dollars spent on sacred cows that drag energy from the Great Commission must be redirected. Programs that point believers more inwardly than outwardly must be redesigned or discarded. Structures that drain dollars and personnel, while the denomination wanes in Great Commission results, must be changed.

Here, the real task of the denomination—not to do the Great Commission but to assist *churches* in fulfilling the Great Commission— is most significant. The Great Commission task is a bottom-up task rather than a top-down one. Church members do the hard work of investing in relationships with nonbelievers, evangelizing their friends, and discipling new believers. Congregations raise up missionaries, send them out, and support them with additional short-term mission teams. Pastors are on the front lines of leading believers to be Great Commission-oriented. Denominational funding originates in the pocketbooks of church members. For at least these reasons, it is imperative that denominational leaders listen when church leaders seek change to re-focus on the Great Commission.

---

4. See Rick Warren, *The Purpose Driven Church* (Grand Rapids: Zondervan, 1995).

Moreover, denominational leaders must lead the way in making changes needed to prioritize the Great Commission. Frankly, this final principle hits home for me as a denominational employee. If I genuinely believe this principle, it is possible that my own denomination would suggest change that affects my own position. If so, I pray that I would graciously follow, believing and modeling that the Great Commission is not about me.

CONCLUSION

I have the privilege of serving as a consultant with the Southern Baptist Convention's International Mission Board. In that role, I have traveled in multiple countries in the last year. I have visited with tribal people who worship idols as well as wealthy entrepreneurs who still offer fruit sacrifices to their gods. I have spoken with atheistic Westerners and animistic Africans. The world desperately needs a denomination that will focus again on the Great Commission.

More recently, I have intentionally invested in nonbelievers in my city and state. I have not only realized how separated I had become from the lost world, but I have also seen again just how much the people around me need Jesus. North America, too, cries out for a denomination committed to the Great Commission.

May that denomination be mine—and yours.

7

Understanding the Gift of the Evangelist in the Local Church

Darrell W. Robinson

THE EVANGELIST IS CENTRAL in the plan of God: for his church to get the gospel of the good news of Jesus Christ to every person in his world. God took initiative when he came into our sinful world in and through the person of Jesus Christ to provide forgiveness and eternal salvation for every person who will believe in him. John 3:16 is the greatest evangelistic line ever written: "For God loved the world in this way: He gave His One and Only Son, so that everyone who believes in Him will not perish but have eternal life." Without passionate evangelistic ministries that led people to Christ and started churches, the gospel would not have survived the first century.

JESUS—OUR MODEL EVANGELIST

Throughout his earthly ministry, Jesus did the work of the evangelist. He refused to be dominated by the religious system of the Pharisees and Sadducees and went "to all the towns and villages, teaching in their synagogues, preaching the good news of the kingdom, and healing every disease and every sickness. When He saw the crowds, He felt compassion for them, because they were weary and worn out, like sheep without a shepherd. Then He said to His disciples, 'The harvest is abundant, but the workers are few. Therefore, pray to the Lord of the harvest to send out workers into His harvest'" (Matt 9:35–38, HCSB).[1]

The first Southern Baptist Director of Evangelism Dr. C. E. Matthews stated in his book, *The Southern Baptist Program of Evangelism* on page 1, "There are only two methods of evangelism taught in the Bible; namely, mass and personal. Any soul that was ever won to Christ by another—regardless of time, place, or condition—was reached through either mass evangelism or personal evangelism."[2]

Jesus is our model, our mentor, and our Master! He did both mass evangelism and personal evangelism. He engaged the multitudes through mass evangelism. The Sermon on the Mount is a classic example of mass evangelism. "When He saw the crowds, He went up on the mountain, and after He sat down, His disciples came to Him. Then He began to teach them, saying, 'Blessed are the poor in spirit, because the kingdom of heaven is theirs'" (Matt 5:1–3). He continued and told them what they needed to do, "But seek first the kingdom of God and His righteousness, and all these things will be provided for you" (Matt 6:33).

Personal evangelism was done with mighty power by our Master, Jesus. He personally dealt with every spectrum of the society in which he lived. Jesus gave the good news of the new birth in a late night setting when he spoke with the wealthy religious leader, Nicodemus. This Pharisee, who occupied a seat in the Sanhedrin, became a follower of our Lord (John 3:1–18). Jesus engaged the adulterous "woman at the well" in conversation. He gently drew out of her a confession of her sins and offered her "the water of Life" which would quench her thirst forever. He taught her the nature of true worship and revealed to her that he is indeed the Messiah. She went back into the town of Samaria and told the men, "Come, see a man who told me everything I ever did! Could this be the Messiah?" (John 4:29).

Jesus called to Levi (Matthew), a hated tax collector, "Follow Me! So leaving everything behind, he got up and began to follow Him" (Luke 5:27b–28). Levi hosted a grand banquet for him. But the Pharisees and scribes complained and tried to discredit him. "Jesus replied to them, 'The healthy don't need a doctor, but the sick do. I have not come to call the righteous, but sinners to repentance'" (Luke 5:31–32).

1. All biblical quotations in this chapter are from the HCSB.

2. C. E. Matthews, *The Southern Baptist Program of Evangelism* (Atlanta: Home Mission Board, SBC, 1949) 1.

Jesus saved a noted cheat and crook, Zacchaeus, in Jericho. Zacchaeus prepared a meal for him. Again, the religious critics attacked Jesus and accused him of consorting with a sinful man. Jesus answered them, "For the Son of Man has come to seek and to save the lost" (Luke 19:10).

THE EVANGELIST TODAY FOLLOWS
THE MODEL OF THE MASTER!

Among the many evangelists whose ministries are recorded in the New Testament are Philip and Paul. Philip went to Samaria when the disciples scattered at the stoning of Stephen and went everywhere evangelizing. In Acts 8, Philip, "the evangelist" (Acts 21:8), did both mass and personal evangelism. There, a great revival movement of the Holy Spirit resulted in many coming to Christ. Then, the Holy Spirit led Philip into the desert of Gaza to meet one man, the treasurer of the queen of Ethiopia. The dynamic conversion of the Ethiopian happened through Philip's obedient witness for Christ in personal evangelism.

Paul went from place to place leading people to Christ and starting churches. Through Paul's ministry of personal and mass evangelism in Ephesus for two years, God did a mighty work. Paul led people to Christ and equipped them to lead others to Christ. "And this went on for two years, so that all the inhabitants of the province of Asia, both Jews and Greeks, heard the word of the Lord" (Acts 19:10). Paul led the Philippian jailer to Christ. He led Lydia and her household to Christ and multitudes of others throughout his ministry.

Paul wrote: "For Christ did not send me to baptize, but to preach the gospel (evangelize)—not with clever words, so that the cross of Christ will not be emptied of its effect" (1 Cor 1:17). "And woe to me if I do not preach the gospel (evangelize)" (1 Cor 9:16b).

THE EVANGELIST TODAY FOLLOWS THE GREAT HERITAGE OF
EVANGELISTS IN THE BIBLE!

The Evangelist Is a Gift from God!

> And He personally gave some to be apostles, some prophets, some evangelists, some pastors and teachers, for the training of the saints in the work of ministry to build up the body of Christ. (Eph 4:11–12)

According to Ephesians 4, the gift of the evangelist is one of the five leadership gifts given to the church. The evangelist is God's provision to enable the church to carry out the Great Commission of Christ. To ignore or minimize the use of the evangelist will cause the church to fail in the evangelistic mission of Christ.

The Evangelist Is a Gift of God to the Church!

Along with apostles, prophets, pastors, and teachers, the evangelist is a leadership gift to the church. When a church neglects to utilize any of God's gifts to the church, it minimizes its effectiveness in building up the body of Christ by maturing the members and by reaching the lost and incorporating them into the church. Evangelists are essential to the effective work of local churches.

In my own experience as a pastor, I led the church to use a vocational evangelist each year. Our people loved the evangelists and generously supported them. The result was that many lost people came to Christ through their preaching of the gospel. The evangelists were used of God to ignite the fires of revival in the church. They taught our people their particular techniques in soul-winning. They helped to create passion for the lost in the hearts of members of the church. They assisted us in training and using invitation counselors. The churches where I was pastor were mightily blessed through the ministries of godly evangelists.

The Evangelist Is a Gift to Equip the Saints!

Those who have the gift of the evangelist have the anointing of God to "draw the net" and lead people through the conversion experience to receive Christ. Some evangelists are called to the work of the vocational ministry in evangelism. They move from place to place and church to church assisting churches in mass evangelism such as revivals, crusades, harvest days, and so forth. They are of great value to the churches and to the growth of the Kingdom of God. However, some members of a church, also, have the gift of the evangelist.

Some have estimated that between 5 percent and 10 percent of church members have the gift of evangelism.[3] These people suggest that only those with the "gift of evangelism" ought to do evangelism for the

---

3. For example, C. Peter Wagner, *Your Spiritual Gifts Can Help Your Church Grow* (Ventura, CA: Regal, 1979, 1994), 160.

church. Meanwhile, they say, other members are to operate in the area of their giftedness.

The problem with this concept is that there is no such thing as a gift of evangelism. The gift given by Christ in Ephesians 4 is that of "The Evangelist." Every member has the assignment of evangelism. Witnessing is every Christian's job. What every Christian is to do is to use every gift God has given to witness and lead others to Christ.

In my book, *Incredibly Gifted*, I analyze the nineteen gifts listed in the Scriptures and how they can be used in evangelism.[4] The thesis of the book is "Every gift has been given by our Sovereign God through individual members to the body of Christ for carrying out the Great Commission. Every gift is a Great Commission Gift! Therefore, every gift is for evangelism and can be used to lead the lost to Christ!" I believe that every Christian desires to witness and if they are equipped, they can share the gospel and lead people to Christ through the power of the Holy Spirit.

Those who have the gift of the evangelist, whether a vocational evangelist or a church member, are equippers "of the saints for the work of ministry to build up the body of Christ" (Eph 4:12). Their equipping will be in the area of enlisting, training, and engaging all the members in witnessing and reaching the lost. Again, in my pastoral experience, I asked each vocational evangelist to teach our people how to lead a person to Christ. Each evangelist's technique of personally leading the lost to Christ would "ring the bell" for some of our people. They would use his approach to lead people to Christ. The personalities and gifts of all the people are different. One technique of sharing the gospel will fit some and another will fit others. By using different evangelists to equip our people, we continued to increase the army of witnesses in our churches and led many more of the lost to Christ.

Laypeople with the gift of the evangelist can be utilized by a church to help enlist, equip, and engage other members in evangelism. They are equippers along with the pastor. But, the pastor must train them, organize for equipping them, and develop the evangelistic systems to enable them. One such member was George, age sixty-five, who chose to retire from his position of professor of music at the University of Houston. I was his new pastor. George spoke to me, "Pastor, God has told me to retire early and be available to Him twenty-four hours a day, seven days a week, to go

4. Darrell Robinson, *Incredibly Gifted* (Garland, TX: Hannibal Press, 2002).

wherever He sends me to share Jesus with anyone anywhere. I am going to do it."

But, George had a problem. He said that he did not know how to witness effectively. He asked me to train and equip him. He said he had asked three pastors to train him and none ever would. Of course, I was thrilled and said, "George, you are talking my language! Be in my office every Monday morning at 8:00 a.m." Each Monday I gave him a list of ten lost people to see that week. I took him with me to witness. He participated in our witness training seminar.

George became a prolific soul-winner. Then, he began to train and equip others in our church. Soon he was called on by other churches to help equip their members to witness. Ultimately, his equipping ministry led him to be a minister in evangelism nationally and internationally. This continued until his death when he was eighty-nine years of age. I preached his funeral on a Christmas Eve. His son told me, "Pastor, you did not know my Dad before, but his life began at sixty-five." George, a lay person, had the gift of the evangelist.

The Gift of the Evangelist Is to Build Up the Body of Christ!

Jesus, himself, builds the church. "[A]nd on this rock I will build My church, and the forces of Hades will not overpower it" (Matt 16:18b).

While Jesus has built his church, he uses evangelists to "build up the church," his body. The question is, "How does this happen?" It can happen when God-anointed evangelists motivate churches, help them disciple their members, help them equip the members to witness, and join them in reaching the lost for Christ and incorporating the new converts into the churches.

THE EFFECT OF THE GOD-ANOINTED EVANGELIST

The Evangelist Sows the Gospel Seed!

Whether from preaching revivals, crusades, harvest meetings, or personal soul-winning, the evangelist sows the gospel seed. Like Philip, the evangelist sows the seed of the gospel through sharing Jesus with contacts in everyday life. Every evangelist is a personal soul-winner who becomes a model for Christians in the churches. This model is critically important in a day when many have come to the conclusion that "you cannot do that anymore." They do not do it and they do not know anyone in the church who does. They need the role model of the evangelist. They respond positively when they have exposure to the influence of an evangelist.

The Evangelist Harvests Souls for Christ!

Through mass evangelism revivals, crusades, and harvest events led by evangelists, God has an impact on churches and areas for Christ. In this way, people who would never be reached through the ongoing ministry of the church come to Christ. The evangelist is gifted by God to preach the convicting message of the sinfulness of humanity, the drastic consequences of sin in the present life and in hell separated from God throughout eternity. He has the gift to clearly proclaim the death of Jesus on the cross as our substitute to pay the wages of our sin and extend the offer of God's forgiveness. He has the gift of calling the lost to repentance and to commit their lives to Christ. The evangelist has the gift of extending a public invitation for people to publicly confess Christ as Savior and Lord.

Evangelists are anointed to preach and draw the net like Peter in Acts 2. Peter proclaimed the death, burial, and resurrection of our Lord. He confronted the people with their sin:

> When they heard this, they were pierced to the heart and said to Peter and the rest of the apostles: 'Brothers, what must we do?' Repent, Peter said to them, and be baptized, each of you, in the name of Jesus the Messiah for the forgiveness of your sins, and you will receive the gift of the Holy Spirit. For the promise is for you and for your children, and for all who are far off, as many as the Lord our God will call. And with many other words he testified and strongly urged them, saying, 'Be saved from this corrupt generation!' So those who accepted his message were baptized, and that day about 3,000 people were added to them. And they devoted themselves to the apostles' teaching, to fellowship, to the breaking of bread, and to prayers. (Acts 2:37–41)

A great example of the gift of the evangelist calling people to Christ, drawing the net, is something that happened in my pastorate at Dauphin Way Baptist Church in Mobile, Alabama. My friend, Evangelist Freddie Gage, was to begin a citywide crusade that Sunday night. He was present at our Sunday morning service. In fairness to all the other churches, he did not preach for us that morning. We had numbers of professions of faith that morning. At the end of service, I introduced Freddie and invited everyone to the crusade that night. Freddie came forward to give the greeting that I had asked him to give. Instead of a greeting, Freddie said, "I believe there are still people here who need Christ. Turn from your sins and receive Christ right now! Step into the aisle and come to Christ!" Would you believe, fifteen more people came forward and received Christ. What a gift and calling! As a true evangelist, he was gifted by God to draw the net.

The Evangelist Inspires God's People!

Revival in the church comes through God-inspired evangelism. When I was at the Home Mission Board, our staff did a survey. At that time the survey showed that no more than 5 percent of our church members ever witness to anyone for Christ. If that is true, 95 percent of members of the average church are living in perpetual disobedience to the command and commission of our Lord. How can God bless such disobedience with revival? We may pray, "Oh God, give us revival and an outpouring of the Holy Spirit."

I think God must shake his head and say, "Why should I give you revival? What would you do with it if I did? You already have all of the Holy Spirit that there is within you, but you are disobeying Him. You ask for power, but you are not using the power I have already given you!"

The God-anointed evangelist preaches the truth to the church and confronts it with its sin. He calls the people of God to repentance. Peter said, "For the time has come for judgment to begin with God's household" (1 Peter 4:17). The evangelist will be God's instrument to call God's household to repentance and obedience to him and his mission. God will give revival and the result will be many lost people coming to Christ.

The evangelist fans the flame of revival and soul-winning. God uses him to ignite the fire of Holy Spirit passion for souls in the hearts of believers in the church.

The Evangelist Challenges the Church to
Saturate Its Jerusalem with the Gospel!

But you will receive power when the Holy Spirit has come upon you, and you will be My witnesses in Jerusalem, in all Judea and Samaria, and to the ends of the earth. (Acts 1:8)

Acts 1:8 is the Jesus' strategy to reach the world with the gospel. He was speaking to a small group of 120 followers. He charged them to saturate their world with the gospel beginning with Jerusalem. Why begin with Jerusalem? That was where they were. His commission was to saturate Jerusalem with the gospel; let it overflow throughout Judea, Samaria, and to the ends of the earth. Though they were so few and had such an overwhelming task, they did it. They saturated Jerusalem by going to every person with the gospel. How do I know they did it? The Bible says they did! "When they had brought them in, they had them stand before the Sanhedrin and the high priest asked, 'Didn't we strictly order you not to teach in this name? And look, you have filled Jerusalem with your teaching and are determined to bring this man's blood on us!'" Acts 5:27–28.

Jesus' strategy would have every church identify its Jerusalem (primary ministry area) and saturate it with the gospel, not overlooking any person. The church must go where the people are and share Jesus with them. They need a one-on-one personal witness. *This is a new paradigm two thousand years old.* It is new because so few are doing it. It is two thousand years old because it is what Jesus told us to do two thousand years ago.

In my books, *Synergistic Evangelism* and *Total Church Life*, I show a simple Biblical plan for a church to implement Jesus' strategy.[5]

POPULAR MYTHS ABOUT EVANGELISM!

The evangelist preaches and, through the power of the Holy Spirit, helps the pastor convince the people to unite as God's army to saturate its Jerusalem with the Good News of Jesus. The evangelist dispels the present myths about evangelism in the church. There are several evangelism myths that are popular.

1. *The myth that "it is not my job, but that of the pastor, the evangelist, and maybe a few leaders in the church."* The evangelist proclaims that witnessing is every Christian's job! He shows them how to lead people to Christ and leads them to be a part of what God is doing in bringing the lost to him. The evangelist inspires the believer to believe that "witnessing is my job and I will do it!"

5. Darrell Robinson, *Synergistic Evangelism* (Nashville: CrossBooks, 2009); *Total Church Life* (Nashville: Broadman, 1997).

2. *The myth that "you cannot do that anymore."* The evangelist helps the people of the church get started by contacting every person and seeking to share Jesus with them in preparation for the evangelistic meeting. He helps them get started. He helps train them to do it.

3. *The myth that people do not want Christians to come to their homes or businesses to share Christ with them.* The evangelist proves that this myth is false. People are interested in Jesus and spiritual things. If we will go in obedience to Christ and even go door-to-door, it has been proven that most people will respond positively. We have done door-to-door witnessing all over the world including the great cities of America and many rural areas. Each time we presented the gospel six times, one person prayed and received Christ. Further, we do not go because they want us to come. *We go because he sent us!*

What happens as we saturate our Jerusalem? First, some are saved immediately because the Holy Spirit has prepared their hearts. Second, we discover people who are possibilities for us to reach. We record their names and addresses and follow up. Third, our people are involved in the joyful ministry of sharing Jesus. Fourth, we create a God-consciousness and a climate of evangelism in the community. Fifth, we obey Jesus in his strategy to saturate our community with the gospel.

Recently, I assisted a church that had relocated in an affluent community. They had no idea of how to reach the community. I suggested the above-quoted plan of Jesus to saturate the community. They responded that they could not do it. "These people do not want us to come to their homes. These are large and nice homes." I continued to urge them to just try what Jesus said. We set up Operation Saturation and one hundred people went out door-to-door on a Sunday afternoon. When we came back from the saturation effort, every person was excited. They said, "We were welcomed. They thanked us for coming." Only one or two had anyone be rude to them. The church began to reach its community.

THE EVANGELIST CREATES A CLIMATE FOR EVANGELISM IN THE CHURCH AND A GOD-CONSCIOUSNESS IN THE COMMUNITY!

During my pastoral experience, I have led my churches to participate in many area-wide evangelistic crusades. Some area pastors refused to participate, saying that they would not receive any new members and it would be too much effort and expense. I told my church that we need to participate even if we do not receive one new member. Periodically our community needs to have the churches make a "big splash" for Jesus that will call people's attention toward God. Evangelists lift up Jesus and lead the churches to call the attention of a community to God and his purpose for them.

As a result, we did reach new members as we followed up with those who had come to the crusade. Even more than that, for years to come we reached people who had come to the crusade. As we counseled with them, they would indicate that they had made a decision at the crusade and now, though time had passed, they wanted to follow Christ in the church.

THE EVANGELIST TODAY!

The office of the evangelist has been minimized today by both denominations and churches. Therefore, support for evangelists and the number of evangelists have declined. As a result, the numbers of people being saved and baptized also continues to decline. Denominations and churches try to resolve the situation by pouring mass amounts of money and programmatic effort into "creative" approaches to increase baptisms and church memberships, while continuing to ignore the office of the evangelist. These approaches will never succeed in reaching our world for Christ. As the office of the evangelist and evangelism continue to be ignored and minimized, the trend will not change. We are out-of-step with God!

WHAT CAN BE DONE?

Denominations and churches must repent! Change—get with God in his plan to reach the lost for Christ!

- Honor the office of the evangelist!
- Utilize and give support to evangelists!

- Get back to New Testament evangelism!
- Evangelists must continue to be faithful to the gift and calling of God! Depend on him and obey him in taking the gospel to every person! "God's gracious gifts and calling are irrevocable" (Rom 11:29). God is the source and resource of the evangelist.

8

Keys to Benefiting from a Revival Meeting

Jake Roudkovski

W HILE THE USE OF revival meetings in the Southern Baptist Convention (SBC) is in decline, these meetings continue to yield the best evangelistic results. The key to benefiting from a revival meeting is in understanding what it is and what it is not. Positive results are also dependent upon the preparation of the pastor and the evangelist. This chapter will focus on the how and why of revival meetings.

A significant number of SBC churches continue to use revival meetings for evangelism and revitalization. According to one study in 1984, about 75 percent of evangelistic churches scheduled one or more revival meetings annually.[1] In another study published in 1996, nearly one-half of the evangelistic churches in the sample group used local church revivals as an effective evangelistic tool.[2] According to the study conducted by the Georgia Baptist Convention in 2001, 58 percent of the churches in the state conducted a local church revival.[3] In a 2009 survey by LifeWay Research, revival meetings were among five of the most often used evangelistic events in Southern Baptist churches.[4]

---

1. Bill Cathey, *A New Day in Church Revivals* (Nashville: Broadman, 1984), 5.

2. Thom Rainer, *Effective Evangelistic Churches* (Nashville: Broadman, 1996), 32.

3. *Revival Preparation Manual* (Atlanta: North American Mission Board, 2009), 10.

4. Mark Kelly, "LifeWay Research Reveals Top Evangelistic Activities," accessed April 11, 2011, http://news.wooeb.com/NewsStory.aspx?id=127997&cat=13.

When church leadership chooses to schedule a revival meeting, how can they prepare for such an event? This chapter attempts to assist church leaders develop an appreciation for the SBC heritage of revivalism; examine causes of perceived ineffectiveness; and suggest practical ways for churches to benefit from a revival meeting. In this chapter, the term *revival* is defined as the sovereign movement of God, through the work of the Holy Spirit, to revitalize believers in Jesus Christ to pursue a more vital spiritual life, work, and witness. *Revival meetings* refer to a period of time set aside by a church for the purpose of spiritual revitalization and/ or evangelism.

HERITAGE OF REVIVALISM IN SBC

Southern Baptist churches have inherited a rich heritage of revivalism. In a classic resource on the history of revival meetings in Southern Baptist life, Chuck Kelley asserts that revivalism was one of the major factors which contributed to the enormous growth of the denomination in the past.[5] According to Kelley, three major factors have shaped the development of revival meetings: the Great Awakening, the frontier camp meetings, and the methodological developments of Charles G. Finney.[6] One can delineate four phases of the development of revival meetings in Southern Baptist evangelism history: the institutionalization, the popularization, the maximization, and the diversification.

At the very first Southern Baptist Convention in 1845, the assembled believed the unifying passion for Baptists had been and should continue to be evangelism. The first expression of that passion was the creation of a Board for Foreign Missions and a Board for Domestic Missions (or Foreign Mission Board and Home Mission Board). The first missionaries appointed by the Home Mission Board were pastors for mission churches or church planters who were expected to start churches in the areas without Baptist churches. Evangelists were appointed as well, but they concentrated generally on establishing new churches rather than leading evangelistic campaigns.[7] In 1866, the Convention instructed the Home Mission Board to make evangelism its major work and to promote a comprehensive system of evangelism, including the appointment of evan-

5. Chuck Kelley, *How Did They Do It?* (New Orleans: Insight, 1993), 115.

6. Ibid., 100–105.

7. Ibid., 106.

gelists.[8] The change took place in 1906 when the Convention instructed the Home Mission Board to create the Department of Evangelism. The Department of Evangelism was designed for one purpose, which was to plan, promote, and lead revival meetings.[9] The leader of the department was identified as a general evangelist. His staff consisted of other evangelists and singers who traveled from place to place leading revivals. This approach was adopted because other denominations and churches were employing revival meetings to effectively reach the lost people.[10] After the formation of the department, revival meetings were institutionalized as a method of evangelism within Southern Baptist life.

W. W. Hamilton was the first secretary of evangelism for Southern Baptists. The evangelism strategy (simultaneous revival meetings) adapted by Hamilton to meet the needs of Southern Baptist churches called for crusades to be organized to involve Baptist churches in the community. Every Baptist church was used for night services, and one central church hosted united day services. The campaigns concluded with the praise service held in the largest meeting place in the city on the last Sunday afternoon. To implement the plan on a denominational scale, Hamilton recruited a staff of evangelists and singers to plan and lead crusades. He chose competent staff, paid them a salary, and made them available to churches based on need rather than ability to pay. During his tenure, the staff grew to include more than forty evangelists and singers. The purpose of the department was to do the work of evangelism.[11] Hamilton's contribution to revival methodology was that revivals were popularized among Southern Baptist churches.

In 1936, C. E. Matthews was the pastor of Travis Avenue Baptist Church in Texas. One day during that year, Matthews and evangelist Hyman Appleman were discussing evangelism. Matthews suggested that mass evangelism, using the simultaneous associational crusade, was the method of evangelism closest to the New Testament approach. Not long after that conversation, Matthews had what he felt was a divine revelation. He felt that God gave him a strategy for the Baptist General Convention

---

8. Arthur Rutledge, *Missions to America: A Century and a Quarter of Southern Baptist Home Missions* (Nashville: Broadman, 1969), 212.

9. J. B. Lawrence, *History of Home Mission Board* (Nashville: Broadman, 1958), 100.

10. Chuck Kelley, *How Did They Do It?* (New Orleans: Insight, 1993), 15.

11. Ibid., 17–20.

of Texas.[12] According to the plan, the state convention should implement organizational and promotional innovations. He suggested the creation of the office of secretary of evangelism in the state and the employment of an annual simultaneous crusade in every association for the purpose of evangelism.[13]

After Matthews was asked to become the evangelism leader of the convention, he implemented his Texas plan for the entire convention. The chosen methodology for his plan was revival meetings. Matthews believed that there were only two forms of evangelism: personal and mass. His research and experience convinced him that mass evangelism was the most productive form for his day. The evangelism secretary wanted every church to have two revival meetings each year. He suggested that one be the meeting for the church alone. The other was to be some form of a simultaneous crusade.[14] By simultaneous crusade, Matthews meant a two-week period when all the churches of a given area conduct revival meetings at the same time. The meetings were to start and to end at the same time. During the first week, attention was given to church members and the status of their relationship with God. The prayer was that revival would break among the Christians by the end of the week. The second week focused on evangelism, with messages on salvation and strong evangelistic appeal. Most churches would see the largest number of conversions during the second week.[15]

Matthews' plan, when implemented in the convention, ushered in the golden era of Southern Baptist evangelism. Annual baptisms topped four hundred thousand a year by the end of the Matthews' tenure and remained near that level for the next six years. John Havlik calculated that the convention grew five times faster than the population of the United States at a time when the nation's population was exploding.[16] During this period, the revival meeting methodology reached its maximum effectiveness.

12. C. E. Wilbanks, *What God Hath Wrought Through C. E. Matthews* (Atlanta: Home Mission Board of the Southern Baptist Convention, 1957), 110–15.

13. Ibid., 115.

14. Donald Wilton, "A Critical Investigation of Charles Everett Matthews' Concepts of Evangelism and an Assessment of his Impact upon the Southern Baptist Program of Evangelism" (ThD diss., New Orleans Baptist Theological Seminary, 1986), 123–24.

15. Ibid., 124.

16. John Havlik, "Back to the Bible?" *Missions USA*, March-April 1982, 53.

Leonard Sanderson succeeded Matthews as evangelism leader in 1956. Sanderson gave a greater emphasis than Matthews to personal evangelism. He encouraged churches to think in terms of reaching the lost each week, rather than once or twice a year during a revival meeting.[17] When C. E. Autrey followed Sanderson, he fully intended to use revival meetings as a part of his strategy. He soon discovered, however, that many pastors were ready for a change. Although Autrey was an advocate for the two week meetings, an eight day meeting became the norm, with some churches going to four days or weekend revivals. Youth-led and layperson-led revivals were especially encouraged. These were organized in much the same way as typical revival meetings, but youth or laypersons were given the leadership positions.[18] A study of SBC churches conducted during this period indicated that about 60 percent of churches had two-week revival meetings and about 83 percent of churches had one-week revival meetings.[19]

As revival meetings continued to diversify in length, format, and emphasis, evangelism leaders who followed Sanderson recognized the proliferation of other methodologies for doing evangelism in a local church. For example, when Darrell Robinson came to the Home Mission Board in 1990, his emphasis was on total church evangelism. He wrote, "Revival meetings, harvest crusades, music events, age and interest group events, Lay Renewal Weekends, Lay Discipleship Weekends, Prayer for Spiritual Awakening Conferences, Interfaith Witness training seminars and classes, ministry evangelism activities, and other such events should be scheduled to grow the spiritual life of a church and to reach the lost for Christ."[20] Church revival meetings became one of many methodologies for evangelism.

Revival meetings have undergone the four stages of development in Southern Baptist history. With the formation of the department of evangelism, the convention institutionalized the methodology of revival meetings. Hamilton and his successors popularized revival meetings among local churches. Under Matthew's leadership, the revival meetings

17. Rutledge, Mission to America: A century and a quarter of Southern Baptist home missions (Nashville: Broadman, 1976), 216.

18. Ibid., 43.

19. Robert Proctor, "70 Onward Integrative Studies" (Nashville: Report to the Inter-Agency Council of the Southern Baptist Convention, 1964), 32.

20. Darrell Robinson, *Total Church Life* (Nashville: Broadman, 1993), 212.

were maximized in their effectiveness for evangelism. Beginning with the leadership of Sanderson, the revival meetings have diversified in length, format, and emphasis, becoming one of many tools available for churches to reach their communities for Christ.

In preparation for a revival meeting, church leadership can benefit from the study of the use of the revival meeting in SBC history. By developing an appreciation for the heritage of revivalism and its contribution to the growth of the SBC, church leadership acquires a proper historical framework for the use of revivals in their ministry. The study of SBC revivalism has helped me personally to be more informed and more motivated in the usage of revival meetings.

CAUSES FOR PERCEIVED INEFFECTIVENESS

After a brief historical analysis of revival meetings, one must examine reasons that have led some to abandon the usage of revival meetings altogether or pronounce them ineffective for reaching people for Christ. Several years ago, a prominent pastor made the following statement, "Local church revivals are dead, I am sorry to say. I am doing five a year but the average church has about a Sunday night crowd average. We have them because old habits do not easily die." What have caused some Christian leaders to assert that revival meetings are "dead"?

The first reason for the perceived ineffectiveness is the spiritual condition of many churches. At times, Christian leaders tend to blame methodology but fail to understand that Western Christianity is in need of spiritual awakening. The church must pray for an awakening and cleanse herself from sin and live the life of holiness. Then we could reach others for Christ. Effective revival meetings should begin with the theology of spiritual awakening taught to the local church.

The second reason for the perceived ineffectiveness of local church revival meetings is the lack of purpose for those meetings. Many churches schedule a revival meeting because of tradition. I have preached in several churches that scheduled revival meetings the second week of August out of tradition without considering the purpose for those meetings.

The third reason for the perceived ineffectiveness of local church revivals is the lack of preparation. Many churches do not prepare or plan for revival meetings. Church leaders want evangelistic results in local revivals without prior cultivation. In the previously mentioned study by the Georgia Baptist Convention, the baptism-to-member ratio of churches that did not use revival meetings was one baptism per thirty-six members. The ratio of churches that did use revival meetings was one to twenty-four. The ratio for churches even with minimal preparation was one to nineteen. Revival preparation provided ways of cultivation for evangelistic harvest.

The fourth reason for perceived ineffectiveness of revival meetings is cultural trends. Pastors cannot overlook the fact that during the golden era of revivalism the entire community gathered around revival meetings. In the past, local schools were shut down for revival meetings, like in the case of Pine Grove Community in Mississippi. Those meetings might have been the only major local event going on in the community, and the lost people came to it. Now, improved roads provide access for people in rural areas to travel to an urban area in a relatively short period of time. Movie theaters, video rentals, computer programs, sports activities, and the Internet have provided competing alternatives to local church revivals.

The fifth reason for the perceived ineffectiveness of revival meetings is the proliferation of other evangelistic methodologies. When revival meetings in SBC experienced their golden era, the revival meeting was the prevalent methodology for evangelism. Today, churches enjoy a variety of methodologies for evangelism. Evangelistic crusades, Christmas and Easter productions, lay renewals, business lunches, and judgment houses are just a few examples of available methodologies.

PRACTICAL WAYS FOR REVIVAL PREPARATION

Although some have pronounced local church revival meetings "dead," they are much alive in many churches. It is my conviction that the effectiveness of revival meetings will depend on the stewardship of that methodology by the local church. The more churches are willing to prepare, the more they place themselves in the position to reach people for Christ. Let me suggest several practical ways that may help churches benefit from a revival meeting.

Purpose

When church leadership begins to sense that God is leading them to schedule a revival meeting, they need to ask what the purpose of such an event should be. Will it be primarily for evangelism or revitalization of a local congregation? The purpose will dictate a strategy for preparation. If the primary purpose is evangelism, the strategy may differ from one whose primary purpose is revitalization. Even though a church selects the primary purpose as evangelism, it may experience a spiritual renewal among the membership. In turn, a church that chooses the primary purpose as revitalization may reach people for Christ along the way. A clear purpose will enable church leadership to be more proactive in matching the purpose with a strategy for preparation and resources.

Personalities

Once the primary purpose is established, the church leadership should select prayerfully a revival team. I have to confess that for the first ten years as a pastor, I invited my pastor friends to preach revival meetings. However, I came to the conclusion that if I really believed that an evangelist was a God's gift to the church, I should be willing to employ vocational evangelists in the churches God allowed me to serve. The Conference of Southern Baptist Evangelists is a group of full-time evangelists who serve as an excellent resource for selecting leaders to preach and lead music in revival meetings. I have used Ron Herrod, former president of COSBE (Conference of Southern Baptist Evangelists), among others, in four churches that I served as pastor or interim pastor. The churches benefited greatly from the giftedness of vocational evangelists, and the meetings were blessed with people coming to Christ and believers renewed in their faith.

Several considerations should be given in regard to the revival team. It is my opinion that the church leadership should secure the revival team at least one year before the event. When the church leadership begins to communicate with the revival team, they should be notified of the primary purpose of the meeting. Then the church leadership should consider, together with the revival team, what theme and format may be used in accomplishing the primary purpose. Many evangelists have developed proven themes and formats, and they have used them effectively in many churches. The church leadership should be open to what the revival teams may bring to the table concerning theme and format. One year, I was sharing with an evangelist that the main purpose of the meeting would be evangelism. I found out that one of the themes he used frequently was an emphasis on the family. Further, a format that this evangelist employed was a Saturday through Monday meeting. Previously, the more common formats for me were Sunday through Wednesday or Thursday through Sunday meetings. After prayerful consideration, we agreed to conduct a revival meeting with a theme *Focusing on the Family* while employing a Saturday through Monday format. God blessed that event with over forty people giving their lives to Christ!

Another consideration in relation to the revival teams should be clarity about finances. It has been my practice as a pastor to initiate the conversation about finances with an evangelist. Typically, we would budget the money for expenses (travel, food, lodging, and incidentals) and use a love offering to provide an honorarium for the revival team. If you choose this method, make sure that the love offering will be given to the team in its entirety. Some churches would budget an entire amount for expenses and honorariums. Regardless of the approach used, the church leadership and the revival team must be clear about finances at the onset of the process. If the church decides to use the love offering method to reimburse the revival team, the pastor needs to plan a thoughtful and prayerful love offering. For full-time evangelists, this money is the way God provides for their families. In addition, church leaders should be gracious hosts to the revival team. Church members observe how pastors and staff treat the revival team and in many instances, that is how church members learn how to treat their leaders!

Preparation

After the church leadership establishes the purpose and secures a spiritually gifted revival team, they are ready to develop a strategy for preparation. Many state conventions publish manuals on revival preparation. The North American Mission Board has an excellent, recently published resource, *Revival Preparation Manual: Practical Suggestions for Planning a Revival in Your Church.* The church must begin preparations three to six months in advance. Church leadership should share enthusiastically with the church council, deacons, teachers, and other key leaders about the upcoming revival. The more that church members are involved in preparation of the revival meeting, the more they will be willing to attend and invite their friends to come. Revival manuals provide concrete ways of how to involve church membership in preparation and participation in revival meetings. The attempt should be made to involve as many church members as possible in various tasks associated with revival preparation and the revival meeting itself.

Publicity

One critical aspect of revival preparation is publicity. The most effective way to publicize is with a personal invitation to attend. A business card with information about the event could be printed and distributed to church members to use in inviting their family, friends, co-workers, and neighbors. We have found that distributing such a card one to two months in advance creates excitement, provides focus in prayer, and gives church members a tangible way to invite others. Church literature such as newsletters, worship guides, and websites should provide pertinent information about the event. Depending on the budget allocated to publicity, the church could publicize the event via a local newspaper, television, yard signs, and billboards. Publicity via Facebook, Twitter, blogs, and other viral marketing strategies by the church and church members can generate a buzz about the event in the community and beyond.

Personal Evangelism

From my experience and observation, personal evangelism is the most productive way of preparation for revival meetings. Even though throughout the year as a pastor I cultivated relationships with the lost, revival meetings provided an impetus for greater prayer and contacts with those without Christ. For three months preceding the revival, I typically scheduled meetings with the prospects who were on the verge of making a commitment for Christ. If they were ready to trust Christ, they would become the most faithful in inviting their friends and family to the revival meeting. If they were not ready, I would extend an invitation for them to attend revival services with a prayer and a hope, and an evangelist may be able to harvest the seeds of the gospel planted in their lives.

Revival preparation provides a unique opportunity to train church members in personal evangelism. One of the most productive revival meetings took place in my ministerial tenure when we intentionally equipped church members in personal evangelism a week before the revival meeting. Then we went out as a church to share Christ and give out a package containing a brochure about the upcoming revival and a gift. During the Sunday morning service of the revival, we registered the highest worship attendance and the greatest number of people receiving Christ in one service in the history of that church. The Sunday of the revival was the watershed moment in my ministry and the ministry of that church.

Program for Children

One oftentimes neglected aspect of revival preparation is what to do with children. In one church that I served as pastor, I became concerned about an apparent lack of participation by young couples. When asked, they responded by pointing out that the church did not have anything for children during the revival week. From that day forward, in addition to the typical childcare, we provided a specialized program for children during revival services. When young couples knew that their children were taken care of spiritually, they were more inclined to participate and invite their lost friends and family members to attend.

Possible Meals

Another response the young couples gave me for their lack of participation was that they did not have time to prepare a meal and get to the worship service after work. As a result, we began to provide catered meals during week nights. We offered tickets for a nominal price with a major portion of the meal subsidized by our church budget. Church members were more predisposed to invite people to their church during a busy week when their invitation was accompanied by an invitation to a nice meal before the service.

Post-Event Follow-Up

In preparation for revival meetings, post-event follow-up should not be overlooked. Billy Graham once commented that the most difficult part of his crusades was not what happened before the crusade but what happened after it was conducted. The same is true for local church revival meetings. Training on post-event follow-up may be incorporated into the training for commitment counselors. As commitment counselors are taught how to lead people to Christ, how to provide assurance of salvation, and how to explore issues of church membership, an emphasis can placed on taking accurate records of those making spiritual commitments. As soon as the revival meeting concludes, names of those who made spiritual commitments can be distributed among deacons and/or Bible Study group members for further follow-up. In the churches that I served as pastor or interim pastor, we continued to baptize people who were identified as potential prospects during the event months after the conclusion of the revival meetings.

Prayer

The most significant aspect of revival meetings must be prayer. The genuine revival can be brought only by God. Only God can save individuals through his Holy Spirit. As the church leadership and membership engages in prayer, they acknowledge their dependence on God. From establishing the primary purpose of the revival meeting to seeking the right individuals for the revival team; from producing publicity to carrying out personal evangelism; from taking care of the spiritual needs of children to following up on the post-event, the church leadership and membership must prioritize prayer. Church leaders should set aside personal time to pray for genuine revival in their church as well as provide opportunities for church members to pray for God's movement in their church. Among various avenues for engaging membership in prayer for revival, some churches employ cottage prayer meetings in the home of church members, while other churches open up their prayer rooms for continual prayer for revival, and some others assemble prayer chains for praying for revival.

By developing an appreciation for the heritage of revivalism in the SBC, churches become more informed about the tool that God has used to reach many for Christ. In identifying causes of perceived ineffectiveness of revival meetings, church leaders become more equipped to address challenges. By employing simple ways such as prayer, purpose, publicity, preparation, and so forth, churches place themselves in the position for God to bring a harvest of souls.

9

The Call to Preach:
Revitalizing Pulpit Evangelism

Paul H. Chitwood

SOME SAY THEY HAVE been "called" to preach. I contend preaching is not a special calling from God. Everybody I know, when they set their mind to it, can preach. My three year old daughter can preach—she learned how from her mother, one of the best preachers I know! Anyone can preach. But those men truly called of God who mount the pulpit are charged to preach the gospel of the Lord Jesus Christ.

I am not suggesting that every sermon should *just* tell people how to be saved; but my conviction is that every sermon should *at least* tell people how to be saved. There is nothing wrong with preaching about God-honoring relationships, however, a gospel preacher must not leave out the fact that the only way to have a relationship with God is through the shed blood of Christ. When preaching about the sanctity of life, why would the gospel preacher neglect to mention the one who so valued life that he laid down his life so all who trust him could receive life abundant and eternal? When preaching on the Christian home, is the door not open to exalt the one who left his home in heaven and "for the joy set before him endured the cross" (Heb 12:2, NIV)?

The subjects addressed by a preacher of the gospel are as diverse as the subjects addressed by the holy book from which we preach. And just as the grand subject of the Bible (God's plan of redemption) undergirds

97

every page, so should that grand subject undergird every sermon. To the extent that it does, the pulpit will be home to evangelism.

How can we ensure our pulpits accomplish the high and holy task of evangelism? Preachers are leaders. To be an evangelist in your pulpit, be a LEADER. Here is how.

L = LET EVERY SERMON MAKE A JOURNEY TO THE CROSS

In keeping with the tradition of country churches, while holding revival services in a rural farming area of central Kentucky, I was invited daily to the homes of church members to dine. On one particular evening, I was the guest of Mr. and Mrs. Hugh Ray in their humble little farmhouse. Nothing, however, was humble about the meal Mrs. Ray put on the table. She robbed the garden, the smokehouse, and the henhouse! During our dinner conversation, I noticed several old photographs of soldiers hanging on the wall. When I asked about the photographs, I learned that Mr. Ray's great-grandfather fought during the Civil War. His father was a veteran of WWI. His uncle was a casualty. Ray and his brother both served in WWII. His brother was killed in combat. Ray's middle son, representing a fourth generation of soldiers, was killed while on patrol in Vietnam. The Ray family is one of those families whose personal sacrifice is directly responsible for the freedoms enjoyed by every American.

After identifying each photograph, Ray then recounted the story of the day he met the owner of the Cincinnati ship building company where he worked for many years after WWII. The owner was none other than George Steinbrenner. Just after the body of Ray's son had been flown back from Vietnam, Ray made a plan to erect a flagpole over his son's grave. He asked his supervisor if he could take home a section of a steel pole from the salvage pile to fashion into a flagpole. The supervisor told him no. As Ray turned to walk away, the supervisor said, "No, you can't have a pole from the salvage pile, but you can have one of the new ones from the ship." They were in the process of taking that new pole off the ship when they ran into Steinbrenner, who immediately inquired about their plans for the company's pole. The supervisor spoke up first, took the blame, and explained the need. Steinbrenner glared at them for a few moments, and then said to the supervisor, "You'd better put in an order to replace that pole. And while you're at it, order two flags to fly over the grave of Hugh's son."

When the story was over, I didn't ask the old veteran why it was so important for him to fly the flag over his son's grave. I didn't have to. That flag symbolized all the reasons three generations of his family had been lowered into the grave.

As followers of the Lord Jesus, we have a symbol of his death and our salvation—the cross.

All who are his are his because of the cross. If more will become his, it will be through the cross! Paul reminds us that the message of the cross is the power of God for those who are being saved (1Cor 1:18). The preaching of the cross is the way that message, carrying God's saving power, is communicated. If the cross is not preached, the mystery and power of the gospel remain hidden. When the cross is preached, that mystery and power are revealed.

Making a journey to the cross is not a stretch for most sermon texts or topics. The stories, themes, and lessons of Scripture all serve to undergird the overarching theme of God's glory displayed through the love, mercy, and grace of the cross. The task of the Bible preacher is to craft the sermon so as to showcase that display.

The importance of unveiling the message of the cross cannot be overstated. People in the pews will not be quick to see the cross unless it is shown to them. The poor lost sinner will never hear of the cross unless a convicted preacher proclaims it to him. The journey to the cross isn't far. Use the pulpit to lead saints and sinners to it.

E = EVANGELIZE ON PURPOSE

The old Methodist catechism said it well—"You have nothing to do but save souls. Therefore spend and be spent in that work." The preacher's job is to caution sinners, sinners like you and me, but unlike you and me in that they have not yet trusted in Jesus Christ. We are to caution them that Jesus is coming and hell awaits all who do not belong to him. That is our role in the kingdom. People in heaven don't share the gospel. They stand around the throne of God celebrating the Author of the gospel. Angels don't share the gospel. They long to look upon the gospel. The sun, moon, and stars don't share the gospel, even though they serve as a witness to the majesty of the gospel's architect. Lost people don't share the gospel. They stand in need of the gospel. Sharing the gospel is the job of those who have been saved, ours alone. If we fail to do it, then it does not get done. If the preacher does not stand in the pulpit for the chief purpose of sharing the gospel then his high calling has been forsaken.

I recall attending a funeral service for a middle-aged man whose parents occasionally attended the church I was serving as pastor. The minister who conducted the funeral did a marvelous job of eulogizing the man, although he admitted he only knew the man's children. He presented the man as sensitive, well-liked, and a consummate family man. The large crowd of mourners gave evidence to the truth of his words. The minister also spoke of the death and resurrection of Christ as the key to having hope in the face of death. Yet, for all the truth he spoke, the pastor failed to describe to the overwhelmingly unchurched crowd in front of him *how* hope is found in the death and resurrection of Christ. He failed to tell them *how* to be saved. I don't think he purposely left out the part about how to be saved. Nor did he purposely include it.

The Bible does more than announce the crucifixion and resurrection of Jesus. The Bible calls sinners to repent of sin, believe in the Savior, and confess Jesus is Lord, promising that anyone who does so will be saved. To tell a lost man the facts of the gospel but fail to answer his questions about how to act on the gospel is to leave the job half done. The pulpit that heralds the glory of Christ's cross and empty tomb but does not purposely tell the listener how to benefit from the same is like the trumpet that does not sound a clear call. "Who will get ready for battle" (1Cor 14:8)? Or, in the case of the pulpit, who will rush to the Savior? Who will repent of sin? Who will confess Jesus as Lord? Evangelizing on purpose means we share the facts of the gospel *and* how to act on the gospel.

A = ASK FOR A RESPONSE

Public invitations have been critiqued, debated, and, by some, abandoned. One of the primary concerns is the emotional wrangling and manipulation that often accompany a public invitation. Another concern is the danger of a false assurance of salvation assumed by many who have "walked the aisle and prayed the prayer" but have exhibited no evidence of conversion or genuine life change. Rather than offer a public invitation, some churches opt for response cards, directions to a counseling room at the end of worship, or a host of other techniques designed to assist those who have questions about the gospel or feel ready to make a profession of faith in Christ.

The debate over invitation methods helps us sharpen our own methods and guard the integrity of our evangelism, but the appropriateness of an appeal for sinners to repent of their sins and trust in Christ alone for their salvation is not debatable. Again, the gospel itself is more than facts about who Jesus is or what he has done. The gospel includes an appeal to "confess with your mouth 'Jesus as Lord' and believe in your heart God raised him from the dead" (Romans 10:9). To challenge people to that end is not only acceptable, it is essential.

No preacher who has clearly presented the facts and demands of the gospel should fear calling on everyone within his hearing to respond immediately to the gospel. Jesus asked the rich young ruler to respond. Peter called on the crowd in Solomon's colonnade to respond. Paul persuaded the Jews and Greeks at the synagogue in Corinth to respond and challenged King Agrippa to respond. The gospel demands a response. Ask for one.

D = DON'T FORGET THE URGENCY OF THE GOSPEL

On an episode of *Dateline* a couple of years ago, video footage showed a man dangling from the side of a bridge threatening to jump. A local reporter had happened by, turned on his video camera, and filmed the man in such desperation that he was considering ending his life. Dozens of onlookers soon gathered, as did a host of fire trucks, police cars, and emergency workers. A real-life tragedy was unfolding on film. After a significant period of negotiations with police and firefighters, the man suddenly let go of the railing and plummeted through the air. He disappeared beneath the surface of the water with a splash. Just as quickly, the man reappeared, frantically struggling to keep his head above water. His cries for help were a faint sound captured by the camera's external microphone. An officer threw a life ring but the man could not reach it. After that, the officials seemed to do nothing at all. No boat. No helicopter. No one dove in. They just stood and watched. After a few painstaking moments, the focal point of the camera shifted to the shoreline where an onlooker could be seen jumping into the water and swimming out to the man. The *Dateline* program host explained that the onlooker had once been a lifeguard. The river was so wide that, by the time the Good Samaritan made it out to the struggling man, he had disappeared again beneath the water. The lifeguard began diving and when he came to the surface with the unconscious victim, the crowd of onlookers began to cheer. By this time another man had swum to them. The host identified him as a nurse who had seen the emergency vehicles and stopped to help. He was so exhausted from the swim that he could not assist the lifeguard. With heroic effort, the lifeguard managed to make it back to the shore with the victim all on his own. Sadly, the effort was in vain. The man could not be resuscitated. He was dead.

The Bible teaches us that every human being is in the same condition as the drowning man. We have willingly plunged ourselves into lostness by our sin. We do not have the ability to save ourselves and, upon death, will complete our journey to the depths of hell. However, God, who is rich in mercy, has called and equipped a mighty army of rescue workers. Some have been trained to lead the effort. Yet, most of them seem to be standing safely on the bridge tossing in an occasional life ring. Few are willing to dive into the rushing waters. And many are the corpses who bear testimony to our complacency. The stakes could be no higher, nor the tragedy more real. With every tick of the clock, souls are swallowed into eternity. Who will be concerned for their destiny?

The final chapter of the final book of the Bible records a thrice repeated promise from our Lord: "I am coming soon!" He is not coming for the world. He is coming for his adopted sons and daughters. When the sky breaks on that great day, the destiny of every person who has sat under our preaching, as well as every other living person, will be sealed. That is why the advice to "preach every sermon as if it were your last" carries with it the urgent need of the gospel in every sermon where a lost soul might be present to hear.

E = EXPECT RESULTS

The player convinced of having no hope for victory rarely plays his best game. The student whose grade point average ensures failure seldom gives her all in preparation for the final exam. Likewise, the preacher who prepares and delivers his sermon with no expectation that God will use it to rescue the perishing will usually lack the passion and conviction of one who speaks as a dying man to dying men. No surprise that the gospel might be overlooked or intentionally left out by the preacher who anticipates no replies to an appeal made on Christ's behalf.

Jonah denied his calling because he feared a response. He was right. When he finally did preach, the response was overwhelming. Jeremiah, on the other hand, continued to preach with passion even though no one responded. Stephen declared the gospel even when the response was his stoning. Throughout the Bible, we see examples of men preaching the word of God with the expectation that God will bring the results he had willed.

A pulpit will be filled with evangelistic fervor when the one filling the pulpit prays for souls to be saved, calls on souls to be saved, and expects souls to be saved. God has given many promises to fortify this expectation. He has pledged his word will not return void. He has pointed to fields white unto harvest. He has provided the Holy Spirit to convict of sin, convince of truth, and convert the lost. He has prophesied of "a great multitude that no one could count, from every nation, tribe, people and language, standing before the throne and in front of the Lamb" (Rev 7:9). God will accomplish his stated purpose of saving lost souls. He will do it by the means he has determined. He will do it through the preaching of the gospel. Paul expresses this fact when he writes, "For since in the wisdom of God the world through its wisdom did not know him, God was pleased through the foolishness of what was preached to save those who believe" (1 Cor 1:21). Expectation should accompany the preaching of the gospel.

R = RELY ON THE HOLY SPIRIT

I recall a visit with a missionary couple serving in a small, impoverished Muslim village on the edge of the Sahara desert. They were in their twentieth year of working in the midst of disease, starvation, suffocating sandstorms, and smothering heat. In those twenty years, they had seen only ten people profess their faith in Christ. Just three of those converts had managed to endure the isolation, intimidation, and persecution and so remain true to their confession. I wondered then, and now, how that couple continues to remain faithful to their task of evangelizing the Muslim people in the midst of such physical hardship and spiritual drought.

Expecting results admittedly is hard when no results are visible. How does the pulpit evangelist guard against disappointment and discouragement during seasons of decision drought? Understanding the role of the Holy Spirit and learning to rely on him is the key.

The Bible is very clear on the multifaceted role of the Holy Spirit in evangelism. The Holy Spirit appoints and commissions those who preach the gospel, directs them where to preach and where not to preach, and what to preach. He convicts sinners of their sin and convinces them of the truth of the gospel. He is the author of the new birth, the down payment and seal of salvation, who also guides the process of sanctification.

To know all that is to know that the Holy Spirit is ultimately responsible for any harvest of souls wrought from our ministry. If we have been faithful preachers of God's word and faithful in the other areas of our ministry, we have done what we are charged to do. Rather than allowing our hearts to be broken for want of visible results, let our hearts always be trusting in "him who works out everything in conformity with the purpose of his will" (Eph 1:11).

Not only does relying on the Holy Spirit guard the pulpit evangelist from disappointment and discouragement during seasons of decision drought, that reliance also opens up the possibility for a truly miraculous harvest. The Apostle Paul communicated to the Corinthians the importance of relying on God to bring forth the harvest: "What, after all, is Apollos? And what is Paul? Only servants through whom you came to believe—as the Lord has assigned to each his task. I planted the seed, Apollos watered it, but God made it grow" (1 Cor 3:5–6, NIV). God saves. We do not. Relying on God, rather than relying on our own gifts and methods, keeps us focused on our tasks of planting and watering and leaves to our great God the task of making the harvest grow.

Finally, relying on the Holy Spirit helps us maintain our humility as servants of our Lord. Knowing that results in evangelism are impossible to achieve apart from the regenerating work of the Holy Spirit should guard the evangelist against taking pride in any response to the gospel call. We must preach with boldness and to the full extent of our gifts but never allow our boldness and skill to manufacture pride. The Lord's own words set the tone for our ministry: "So you also, when you have done everything you were told to do, should say, 'We are unworthy servants; we have only done our duty'" (Luke 17:10). For a preacher of the gospel, that duty is evangelism! When every sermon makes a journey to the cross, when we are evangelizing on purpose, asking for a response with a sense of urgency and expectation, and relying on the Holy Spirit, our pulpits will be home to leaders accomplishing the high and holy task of evangelism.

10

Invitations with Integrity

Mark Tolbert

I AM CONCERNED ABOUT a dear friend. God has greatly used this proven friend not only in my life but also in the lives of countless others. This seasoned ally has been an incredible blessing and vehicle for multitudes to experience comfort, freedom, forgiveness, and untold joy. Although once a very familiar mainstay in evangelical circles, over time this friend has become the victim of misunderstanding, abuse, neglect, ridicule, scorn, slander and now near abandonment. This familiar friend is at risk of being portrayed, at the least, as a marginalized relic or, at the worst, a dangerous charlatan. I am concerned about that friend: the current state of the public invitation.

One's integrity is crucial and it works hand-in-hand with delivering meaningful public invitations. To have your integrity questioned is far more serious than having one question your competency or skills. There is a serious challenge today concerning the very integrity of the public invitation. I would have to agree with those who would charge that the public invitation sometimes has been abused or mishandled, sometimes by the use of coercion and manipulation. Perhaps a more common abuse is the extension of invitations that are unclear, superficial, or perfunctory. I would heartily support a move to ensure that invitations are better prepared and extended with more clarity and integrity. This article addresses a more serious issue, however—the very integrity of the public invitation as well as the integrity of those who extend it, no matter in what form.

There is a rising tide of criticism that questions the very legitimacy of extending a public invitation, evangelistic or otherwise, as an appropriate means of response to biblical proclamation. The public invitation is this issue which must be examined.

I came to know Jesus Christ as Savior and Lord in response to a public evangelistic invitation. At the age of sixteen, I attended a Billy Graham movie at a local theater while on a date with my girlfriend. For me it was just another Friday night at the movies. I did not realize we were attending a religious film or I probably would not have attended. That movie made me aware that, although I was a church member, I did not have a relationship with Christ. I was deeply moved and convicted of my sin and need for forgiveness. I understood that I needed Christ's forgiveness and salvation. Sitting in my seat, watching the final scenes of the film, I purposed that I would commit my life to Christ someday.

At the conclusion of that movie, a man gave an appeal for those who wished to make a commitment to Christ to come to the front of the theater and speak with a counselor. Prior to that night, I was unaware of a need to make such a commitment. I had not gone to the movie that night with any intention of coming to Christ. No Christians had been talking with me about my need for Christ. I had never been exposed to the message of the gospel. I had never heard a public evangelistic invitation. He quoted a scriptural invitation that night as he paraphrased an Old Testament reference that asked, "How long will you hesitate between two opinions? If God be God follow Him!" As the challenge was given, I realized my need to respond to the invitation and to make a commitment to Christ. I went to the front of the theater and a trained counselor assisted me in making my commitment to Christ. The gospel was made clear; I freely acknowledged my need for Christ, and God wondrously saved me. From personal experience, I bear witness to the legitimate place of extending public evangelistic invitations.

Tragically, the public invitation is in trouble. No longer is the invitation a near-universal part of evangelical worship. What once was a tool that was implemented for the evangelization of the masses is now a mere shadow of the past. Even churches that continue the practice of extending public invitations, often do so with little precision or purpose. How could the once mighty and respected practice have drifted so far?

Criticisms of the public invitation move along four levels. First, some charge that the public invitation is without scriptural warrant. Second, it is alleged that the public invitation is a modern invention. Third, some contend that the call for a public response adds the work of man to salvation, rather than it coming solely by the grace of God. Still others have eliminated the public invitation following the public proclamation of the gospel, in favor of exclusively supporting relational evangelism. Let us respond to these various criticisms.

BIBLICAL PUBLIC INVITATIONS WITH INTEGRITY

The spirit and principle of the public evangelistic invitation is evident in the Bible. There are Old Testament examples. When Moses came down from Mount Sinai, he discovered the people giving themselves over to idolatry and worshipping the golden calf, and he confronted the people by asking, "Who is on the Lord's side? Let him come unto me!" (Exod 32:26). That was a clear call to his people to make a public declaration and to take a public stand for the Lord. After Moses' death, Joshua was commanded to lead the nation of Israel; the people lapsed into idolatry. Toward the end of Joshua's life he called all the tribes together and said, "[C]hoose you this day whom ye will serve; whether the gods which your fathers served that [were] on the other side of the flood, or the gods of the Amorites, in whose land ye dwell: but as for me and my house, we will serve the Lord" (Josh 24:15). That, too, was a call for a public commitment of loyalty to God.

Centuries later, idolatry again was the issue. This time Elijah was God's chosen instrument. Standing on Mount Carmel it is recorded: "And Elijah came unto all the people, and said, 'How long halt ye between two opinions? If the Lord [be] God, follow him: but if Baal, [then] follow him'" (1 Kgs 18:21). This was a clear and powerful call to public commitment and identification as a follower of God. In Ezra 10:5, this great scribe called upon his contemporaries to swear publicly that they would carry out the principles of his reform. Nehemiah's book also indicates that the Jewish leaders were required to commit themselves to a covenant of loyalty to the Lord after their revival (Neh 9:39). Hosea urged the people to return to the Lord and receive his forgiveness (Hos 14:2). Throughout the Old Testament, one sees a clear picture of the man of God publicly calling people to make a public commitment to the Lord.

The New Testament records the urging appeal to people to decide publicly for Christ. The apostle Paul announced to the church at Corinth that Christians have been given the ministry of reconciliation (2 Cor 5:18–20). This ministry charges the believer to seek to join together sinful man and holy God. Further, this ministry compels the Christian to urge the hearer to decide for Christ. The gospel is not to be presented in a casual, perfunctory manner, but with a sense of urgency, appeal, and persuasion (2 Cor 5:11), as Paul did when he reasoned with and persuaded the people of Ephesus (Acts 19:8) and as Jesus did when he charged his disciples to do the same (Luke 14:23). This urging is to be done while relying on the Spirit of God. The evangelist must do his best to urge men to come to Christ, but there also must be a dependence upon the Holy Spirit to convict and draw men (John 16:8).

Jesus made numerous appeals for people to decide publicly for him. The launching of his ministry included a public proclamation of the gospel and a public call to repentance (Matt 4:17). When he called Andrew and John, his first disciples, he extended a public appeal to follow him (Matt 4:19), as he did with the woman of Sychar (John 4:4–42), Philip (John 1:43), Matthew (Luke 5:27), the rich, young ruler (Luke 18:18–34), and Zacchaeus (Luke 19:1–10). There are also general appeals that Jesus gave in group settings (Matt 11:28, 29; John 7:37, 38). The Lord Jesus Christ gave us a personal example of his public invitations to people to follow him as Lord and Savior.

There are other New Testament examples of preachers who called for a public decision. Aside from Jesus, the most outstanding example is John the Baptist. John came preaching a message of repentance (Luke 3:23), but the chief characteristic of his ministry was baptizing the people who responded to his message (John 1:28). His ministry, preaching, and appeal were public, and those who responded to his appeal did so publicly.

The followers of Jesus also extended public invitations. Andrew sought out his brother, Peter, and brought him to Jesus (John 1:42). After he went on to become a powerful spokesman for our Lord, Peter called for an immediate public commitment to Christ, as evidenced in his sermon on the day of Pentecost (Acts 2:39–40), and in his preaching to the household of Cornelius (Acts 10:28–48). Philip preached to the Ethiopian eunuch and those in his caravan as they traveled along a desert road (Acts 8:26–38). The public proclamation of the gospel was basic to the ministry of the apostle Paul (1 Cor 15:1–11; 1 Thess 1:5–11). His preaching and appeals for Christ were often in a public arena, usually in the setting of the Jewish synagogues. This was his practice in Pisidian Antioch (Acts

13:14–48), in Iconium (Acts 14:1-7), in Thessalonica (Acts 17:1–4), in Berea (Acts 17:10–12), in Corinth (Acts 18:1–4), and in Ephesus (Acts 19:1–10). Paul and Silas challenged the jailer at Philippi to place his faith in Christ amid the public spectacle of a crowded jail cell (Acts 16:25–31). The Bible concludes with an invitation to come to Christ (Rev 22:17). Throughout the New Testament, we discover ample evidence for the practice of public proclamation of the gospel, with an appeal for a public declaration of faith in Christ.

From an examination of Scripture, one discovers the clear basis for public evangelistic invitations. When the preacher of the gospel makes an appeal for people to decide openly for Christ, he is on solid biblical ground. As the minister of the gospel applies biblical principles of public evangelistic invitations, he can do so with the blessing of heaven.

CRITICISM OF AND USE OF PUBLIC INVITATIONS WITH INTEGRITY

Critics of the public invitation make the claim that the practice started with Charles G. Finney (1792–1875). Although it is true that Finney's "new measures" popularized the practice, public evangelistic invitations can be traced back centuries before Finney. The preachers of the first century called upon people to offer themselves as candidates for repentance, faith, and baptism. These invitations continued until AD 324 when Emperor Constantine declared Christianity the state religion of the Roman Empire. In one sudden move, all citizens of Rome, whether believers or not, were swept into the church and were proclaimed to be Christians. Adults and infants alike were baptized as they became members of the church. As these infants grew, the need for adult baptism diminished, and the practice of the public invitation declined.

Among Christians who continued to issue a public invitation were the Anabaptists. They opposed the Roman Catholic Church on several issues, including infant baptism. They were faithful in calling for the repentance of sins, faith in Christ, and the outward sign of rebaptism.

The Anabaptists were opposed by both Catholics and Protestants. This opposition came because the Protestant reformers proclaimed the message of salvation by grace through faith, and believed in the final authority of scripture, but they opposed the public invitation, believing it to be an addition to faith and, therefore, unbiblical.

The Separatists, founded by Thomas Helwys, were other proponents of public invitations; they broke away from the Church of England in 1609. They believed that people must repent and believe on Christ in order to be saved. They invited people to confess Christ publicly through believer's baptism. Famous Separatists included John Bunyan, author of *Pilgrim's Progress*.[1] He advocated a call for a public profession of faith in Christ. One Separatist congregation was the Pilgrims who were on board the Mayflower to America in 1620, seeking religious and political liberty.

The eighteenth century saw unusually gifted and anointed preachers who employed a variety of public invitations to come to Christ. Jonathan Edwards and George Whitefield would conclude their sermons with an appeal for seekers to meet with them following the service to seek private spiritual guidance. This was the standard invitational model of the eighteenth century. Another of their contemporaries, John Wesley, would also invite seekers to come forward and sit at the "Anxious Seat" where they would receive spiritual counsel. This occurred some fifty years before Finney, who is often cited as the inventor of the modern altar call for the invitation. According to noted historian Leon McBeth, Separate Baptists in the southern United States are known to have extended invitations for people to come to the front of the service with the singing of a hymn to make immediate commitments to Christ as early as 1758.[2] In 1799, at a Methodist camp meeting in Red River, Kentucky, an altar was erected in front of the pulpit where seekers might come for prayer and instruction. So popular was it that an altar became a permanent fixture in many Methodist churches.

The nineteenth century saw the ministry of Charles G. Finney popularize the modern pattern of coming to the front of the service at the time of invitation to commit to Christ. Charles Haddon Spurgeon employed a type of invitation similar to the eighteenth-century model, due in part to the physical limitations of his house of worship, the Metropolitan Tabernacle. Although Finney certainly is credited with the paradigm with which we are now familiar, the spirit and practice of public invitations is well documented in church history.

What about the charge that calling for a response in a public invitation is adding human means to the grace of God? In extending a public

1. John Bunyan, *Pilgrim's Progress* (London: Robert Ponder, 1693).

2. H. Leon McBeth, *The Baptist Heritage: Four Centuries of Baptist Witness* (Nashville: Broadman, 1987).

invitation, the preacher should make every effort to separate the need for an inner decision to the call for an external expression. A person is justified solely by the grace of God and apart from human effort (Rom 4:1–5). The Apostle Paul argued to the Romans that we are right with God based on the inward condition of our heart (Rom 4:29). Yet, the one who has a genuine inner relationship of the heart will validate it in an external expression. After Peter's sermon at Pentecost, the people asked, "What shall we do? And Peter said to them, 'Repent, and let each of you be baptized in the name of Jesus Christ, for the forgiveness of sins.'" (Acts 2:38–39). In the tenth chapter of his letter to the Romans, Paul describes the relationship between inward decision and outward expression: "That if you confess with your mouth, 'Jesus is Lord.' And believe in your heart that God raised him from the dead, you will be saved. For it is with your heart that you believe and are justified, and it is with your mouth that you confess and are saved" (Rom 10:9–10).

Outward expression is to be evidence of inner grace. To claim inner grace without external expression is to cheapen the gospel of grace. The charge of cheap grace or "easy believism" is often made by those who are of the Reformed persuasion. Our Reformed brothers are right in expecting evidence of professed faith. It is true that one is saved not by walking an aisle, raising a hand, or praying a prayer. One is saved by committing oneself to him as Savior and Lord. However, to question the integrity of the public invitation is to eliminate a legitimate and biblical means of external expression, as well as diminishing the necessary and legitimate place of works following genuine faith in Christ (Eph 2:8–10).

Others have abandoned the practice of extending a public invitation in favor of relational evangelism. The preference for relational witness has become an exclusive preference: relational evangelism as the only means of proper witness. Adherents of this position do not merely prefer relational evangelism; they see it as the only legitimate way to evangelize. They do more than merely minimize the legitimacy of the public invitation; they question its very integrity. This view would disparage those who would extend the public invitation as well as those who would practice direct conversational evangelism with a casual acquaintance or a stranger. Although personal relationships can be a valid, perhaps even the preferred means of presenting the gospel, should it be the exclusive approach? It was not the exclusive approach of Jesus Christ, who witnessed to individuals after a brief introduction (John 3:1–21; 4:1–26), as well as to the masses (John 7:37-38). The early church employed relational evangelism as recorded in the book of Acts. Philip witnessed to the Ethiopian eunuch (Acts 8:25–40), Peter to Cornelius (Acts 10), Paul and Silas to a jailer (Acts 16:25–34), and Paul before Festus (Acts 25:13–22) and before Agrippa (Acts 26:1–23). However, Philip also preached to crowds in Samaria (Acts 8:4–8), Peter to the thousands at Pentecost (Acts 2:1–40), and Paul to entire cities (Acts 13:44) in the synagogues (Acts 17:1–2), as was his custom, and to other large gatherings (Acts 17:22). Clearly, evangelism is to be done to individuals as well as corporate assemblies. Invitations should accompany both approaches when the gospel is presented.

I am passionate about the public invitation. God used it the night I came to faith in Christ. I am also passionate in my desire to see it implemented with clarity and integrity. To extend the invitation to manipulate or coerce is shameful. I resent coercion and manipulation in any context; I detest it in the setting of a public invitation. At the other extreme is the practice of extending the invitation in a passionless and perfunctory manner. To extend an invitation in a casual, unprepared, and careless manner is another type of abusing the invitation. An invitation to Christ should be done with urgency, passion, and even persuasion. Paul told the Corinthians:

"Therefore, knowing the fear of the Lord, we persuade men, but we are made manifest to God; and I hope that we are made manifest also in your consciences. . . . Therefore, we are ambassadors for Christ, as though God were entreating through us; we beg you on behalf of Christ, be reconciled to God" (2 Cor 11:5, 20).

The church needs a revitalized view and practice of the public evangelistic invitation. We do not need to implement a practice or methodology that is dishonoring to God. It is my contention that we need to recognize that the public evangelistic invitation is a tool, to be used with great integrity. Further, when it is implemented properly, its integrity is maintained through the character and methodology of the minister to ensure that it is consistent in both biblical and historical contexts.

May God use even the critics to refine our methods and our motives. May God revitalize our passion and our practice. May we stand to proclaim the gospel as God's gracious gift of redemption and salvation, and may God entreat people through us, as we beg the individual and the multitudes to be reconciled to God.

11

Splashing Your Way to Evangelistic Effectiveness

Kenneth S. Hemphill

WE ARE WELL AWARE of the research that indicates that the evangelical community is losing ground numerically. Baptisms in most major denominations have been in a fifty year decline, while the general population increases and spiritual hunger remains unabated. The proliferation of religious options might be blamed as the culprit. However, the obvious shallowness of most of those claims to religious enlightenment indicates another cause.

Theological liberalism and naïveté are issues that must be addressed. Recent studies indicate that many of the people sitting in the pews and classrooms of evangelical churches do not believe in the proposition that "there is no other name under heaven whereby men might be saved" (Acts 4:12). The exclusivity of Jesus has certainly been challenged by the religiously pluralistic climate of our day. At a recent pastor's conference, I was commenting on the finding that many evangelicals no longer believe that Jesus is the only means of access to the father. One pastor at the conference confessed that a youth had asked his Sunday school teacher where Muslims went when they died. To his utter chagrin, the teacher responded, "To Muslim heaven I suppose." So, to the teacher, there is not only another "way," there is another "destination."

Yet, I suspect that the biggest culprit to evangelistic effectiveness is the same today as it was in the first century. Just before Jesus commissioned the twelve and sent them to the lost sheep of the house of Israel, he declared, "The harvest is plentiful, but the workers are few. Therefore beseech the Lord of the harvest to send out workers into His harvest" (Matt 9:37–38). The twin problems are still the number of laborers and the lack of prayer. The two are inextricably bound together.

Thus, while we can and must discuss methodology and seek new effective ways to share the good news, we must also build on the twin foundations of prayer and the empowering of the Spirit. We must regain an unshakeable confidence that we have news that is both *good* and *effective*. It appears that in some quarters we have lost our conviction that God's word itself is powerful—that it is like a hammer breaking stone and a sword lying bare the thoughts and intents of the heart. We do not have to convince men that Jesus is the way, we must simply point men to the Way and he will draw them to himself.

IF IT IS THAT SIMPLE, WHAT'S THE PROBLEM?

When we look at the simplicity of the gospel and the means of its dissemination—person to person—we have to again ask ourselves, "what's the problem?" I have had the privilege of traveling broadly across America during my forty years of active ministry. I have conducted a not-so-scientific survey to determine why less than 5 percent of evangelical Christians have ever told anyone about their personal relationship to Christ.

My survey methodology is profoundly simple. I ask people why they find it difficult to share their faith. Many of the reasons given were not unexpected. The respondents listed, in no particular order, issues such as fear, lack of the gift of evangelism, not a confrontational person, inability to memorize a gospel presentation, hesitancy to talk about religion, inability to answer objections, no awareness of opportunities to share the gospel, and uncertainty as to how to begin a conversation about Christ.

We could probably add others to the list, but the truth is they are all simply *excuses* that must be overcome for the sake of the King and the kingdom. The truth is that witnessing and praying will always be challenging because both engage the Christian in the realm of spiritual warfare and most of us are reluctant to go into battle. If we glance again at Matthew 10, which recounts the sending of the twelve, we will notice that Jesus indicated that he was sending them out "as sheep in the midst of wolves" (v. 16). This is certainly not the normal recruiting speech for enrolling people in an evangelism training workshop.

As I have conducted my simple survey, I have come to believe that one of the greatest hurdles for most believers is that of bridging the gap from talking about daily affairs to talking about spiritual truth. It is the age-old question, "How do I engage people in a conversation about spiritual matters?" Any of us who have attempted to witness while on the go have struggled with this issue ourselves. Thus, those who want to improve evangelistic effectiveness in their church must address this issue while at the same time lead people to pray for the lost and witness in the power of the Spirit.

THE CONFUSING SIGNALS SENT BY THE CHURCH

I have come to believe that the church has further complicated the mobilization of the laity for the sharing of their faith by sending out several confusing signals that provided people the excuse for which they were looking.

1. The church has made evangelism a program. That, in turn, led to the conclusion that evangelism is the work of the pastor/staff. I believe that some members think, "They are our church employees and we pay them to run the programs, one of which is the evangelism program." I will never forget my first foray into training laity how to share their faith. I was pastor of a small seminary church. I began a discipleship program on how to share your faith not long after I was called as pastor. I grew the program from twenty people down to about five in a few weeks time. One evening before the total dissolution of the program, a deacon plucked up the courage to ask me why I was teaching the church members how to witness. When he saw the confusion written on my face, he quickly added. "Pastor, that's what we hired you to do."

2. Church leaders have connected evangelism too closely with church growth. Some might merely think, "We need to reach our community that we might grow the church." Once again, many laity thinks that church growth is the concern of the pastor and staff. For many laity, church growth is often seen as so much talk about nickels and noses. Many are actually unconcerned about church growth because they like the church the way it is.

3. Denominational leaders have inadvertently made evangelism too difficult. Evangelism programs grew in complexity and length. Then we followed the initial program with the second

level which began to address apologetic issues. Many laypersons felt they had neither the time nor the brain power to complete the complicated programs that required the memorization of a lengthy presentation.

4. The interest in spiritual gifts led some church leaders to talk about the gift of evangelism. I actually heard one leading pastor declare that only about 10 percent of the congregation had the gift of evangelism and thus we should not attempt to equip the other 90 percent. This was the theological confirmation for which many reluctant witnesses were waiting.

5. Church leaders made evangelism the sharing of a presentation and not the sharing of a person. This may have been our most strategic error. Many people today immediately turn the speaker off if they sense they are hearing a canned presentation. We have all received that phone call with the canned sales pitch just as we sat down for dinner with the family. It began with a feigned but futile attempt to call us by our name and then proceeded to share the good news that we have been chosen to receive a free all expense paid vacation to some exotic destination. Most of us are wary of such calls and quickly respond that we are not interested. In the same way, people today do not want to hear what they refer to as "a religious presentation."

I don't think anyone in the church intended to send confusing messages, but we did and we have reaped the results.

We must return evangelism to the home and the marketplace. Evangelism is not about growing the church; it is about expanding the kingdom, and it is every believer's responsibility and privilege. I still like the classic definition that evangelism is nothing more than one beggar telling another beggar where he found bread. Simplicity is the key to effectiveness. Evangelism is the telling of your story linked to the power of God's word undergirded by the work of the Spirit. While some persons may be more gifted in evangelism, every believer is called to be a witness. A witness is who we are before it is what we do. It is helpful to give people a structure or outline to guide them in sharing the gospel, but the day of the canned presentation is quickly fading from effectiveness. We must teach people to share Christ by telling their story in a dialogically.

I make these points with profound humility because I know that God can, and does, use anything we offer to him. I am quick to tell anyone, "If you have a strategy that you have used with effectiveness, I like it." However, all of us would agree that we must explore avenues to help the 95 percent who have yet to share the gospel with their neighbor, co-worker, or friend.

A SERENDIPITOUS DISCOVERY!

I was in Memphis to visit my youngest daughter and her husband. The reason behind the visit was the arrival of my oldest daughter, who is engaged in taking the gospel to the "ends of the earth." My oldest daughter, who was coming home for a few weeks, along with her husband, was able to manage a brief stopover in Memphis. And so my wife, Paula, and I quickly headed for Memphis to visit two of our girls, their husbands, and our first granddaughter. Lois was now six months old and we had only seen her when she was a newborn. She was the main attraction.

After a brief time of recovery from jet lag, Lois quickly began to entertain all of us with her antics. The smiles and the attempts at crawling were applauded by everyone. As evening approached, my daughter began preparations to bathe Lois. My youngest daughter, who was a newlywed, had none of the appropriate baby apparatus and thus the kitchen sink became a makeshift baby bath. It was soon apparent that Lois loved the warm water. She began to flail her arms like she was leading an unseen symphony. She laughed and splashed and water covered the counter top, the kitchen floor, and all the participants and onlookers.

As I stepped away from Lois's frolic in the sink, the Holy Spirit spoke to me. "That's what evangelism should look like. When you get around a believer in love with me, you can't help getting splashed with Living Water." At least, that is my translation of what the Spirit impressed upon me that night.

I began telling that story as I spoke on witnessing in churches across America. To my surprise, people not only responded to the story, but they wanted to know how to splash the love of God all around them. They indicated that what I was describing sounded like something they could do and they wanted more information.

That request caused me to think more seriously about what I had experienced at the kitchen sink and how it could be translated into a practical process for helping people to tell people about their love affair with Jesus. I am not usually good at acrostics, but I was soon pondering the word SPLASH. The idea jumped from the page—Show People Love And Share Him.

The concept and the acrostic were catchy, but I wanted something more substantial that would help those people who thought they could never effectively share their faith. I wanted something that was thoroughly biblical as well as practical and simple.

A STUDY OF THE EVANGELISM STRATEGY OF THE MASTER

I often tell people that the longer I am involved in ministry, the simpler my approach to ministry has become. I then quote one of my fundamental principles—"Nothing changes anyone's heart and mind except the word of God applied by the spirit of God." A second principle flows from it—"You must first change the heart before you can change the thinking and you must change the thinking before you can change the behavior." We have often attempted to enroll people in evangelism training through the not-so-subtle manipulation of guilt-laden appeals. Such an approach might temporarily help us meet our quota for an outreach program, but it will not change a person's passion or thinking and thus not lead to a lifetime of sharing.

Thus, my first priority was to look at the life of the Master Evangelist. I began once again to read through the gospels with special attention to the evangelistic encounters of our Lord. I began to see a clear pattern emerge that was similar to the Splash strategy. Jesus always demonstrated the gospel before he articulated it. Nonetheless, he consistently added explanation to demonstration.

For example, one could look at the classic encounter of Jesus with the woman at the well (John 4). He demonstrated the gospel by asking this "social outcast" for a personal favor. She is startled that a Jewish man would speak to a Samaritan woman. His loving action provided the forum for explaining that he was the great I Am, the awaited Messiah.

The story of Zaccheus is similar in that Jesus asked Zaccheus for a favor, inviting himself to dinner (Luke 19). Zaccheus was not only looked down upon for his diminutive size, he was despised for his profession, tax collector. Jesus knew that Zaccheus was desperately lonely, and thus Jesus met Zacchaeus's physical need for friendship so that his deep need for redemption might also be met.

Jesus showed love to the woman taken in adultery by stooping to write in the sand, thus drawing all eyes away from the unclothed woman (John 8). He met her immediate need by helping her escape the lustful glances of those who would stone her. This loving action provided the platform to talk with her about the bigger issue of sin.

The pattern of loving action accompanied with clear explanation was present in many of the ministry encounters of our Lord and seems to me to provide a workable pattern for our witness today.

A PRACTICAL PLAN EMERGES

Following principle one—"nothing changes anyone's mind but the word of God applied by the spirit of God"—I decided to write a Bible study guide focused on the ministry of Jesus. I invited my wife to join me in this task since I wanted it to have a woman's perspective. I wanted the material to communicate with young and old, men and women.

I generally suggest that it be studied through the Sunday school or cell groups to obtain the largest possible audience, and I suggest that it not be advertized as an evangelism program. Many people, who could profit from the study and discover practical ways to share their faith, will stay away if it is presented as another evangelism program. It is best simply to indicate that it is a study about how Jesus accomplished effective ministry and touched the lives of those around him. We who participate in this study learn how to apply the insights learned from Jesus to our own lives and to our church.

The goal of the study is to mobilize the 95 percent who will not attend a regular evangelism training program. I believe that when people are exposed to God's word and are given this biblical pattern, they will begin to embody these principles in their own lives. This is a simple strategy to mobilize laity to look for daily opportunities to Splash their family, friends, neighbors, colleagues, and enemies with the Living Water.

I borrowed from the classic *Concentric Circles of Concern* by Oscar Thompson and created Splash Zones.[1] By week two, participants are filling out Splash Zones cards that lead them to pray for people they identify as having spiritual needs. The next step is to find a Splash Effectiveness

---

1. W. Oscar Thompson Jr., *Concentric Circles of Concern* (Nashville: Broadman, 1981).

Partner who joins them as they pray together for the persons in their Splash Zones. This not only provides the necessary prayer support, it also creates essential accountability.

The natural progression of the Splash study leads persons to commit to loving actions that they can take to show Christ's love as preparation for sharing him. A key chapter in the study is the chapter entitled "And." It focuses on Jesus' commitment of attaching verbal witness to loving action. Without this focus the study would be little more than the "old social gospel" which often failed to actually present the gospel. The premise is rather simple—if Jesus, who fully embodied the character of the Father, found it necessary to accompany action with verbal presentation, we can do no less.

While Splash trainers suggest various means of presenting the gospel, from marking a New Testament with the Roman road presentation to the use of tracts and small evangelistic books, the key is *your story plus Scripture told in the power of the Spirit.* "Your story" is defined in broader terms than one's testimony about their salvation. We do encourage writing out one's testimony, but we encourage them to learn how to talk about their "current story." What has God done for you or said to you recently. The key to the approach is learning to "brag on Jesus" in your daily context with persons who are not Christians. We sing "my best friend is Jesus" but we fail to tell anyone about our best friend when we leave church.

When one talks conversationally about their story, they are actually "showing" what it means to have a personal relationship with God through his Son, Jesus Christ. Thus the very act of "bragging on Jesus" illustrates that one can have an intimate and personal relationship with God.

Splash trainers teach participants to attach their story to Scripture and then to continue to pray for the person they splashed. For example, suppose someone has commented to you that the current recession is causing them undue stress and they want to know how you are coping with it. Your commitment to Splash makes you aware that this is a kingdom moment. You might respond, "Sometimes I let the downturn make me anxious as well. But recently when I was talking to my heavenly Father, he reminded me of a verse I learned when I was a young person. It is found in Philippians 4:6 and 7. You then quote the verse. If you wonder what you do next, the answer is wait, and see how your friend responds. We have sometimes been guilty of running into the stream attempting to beat a fish into submission with a huge pulpit Bible rather than casting the bait before them and allow them to respond. Trust me, the word of God will have an impact and they will come back for another Splash of living water.

As noted earlier, we recommend avoiding a canned presentation. We want people to talk about a *person* not a *presentation.* To avoid misunderstanding, I do think it is helpful to give people an outline such as those from Faith, Evangelism Explosion, or Got Life, but it should serve as an outline for dialogue not as a monologue for presentation.

Splash creates a mindset that causes one to think about discovering and capitalizing on everyday events for sharing one's personal faith. It enables you to make the best of each situation, even when there is not adequate time to fully explain the gospel. It takes seriously the promise that the word of God is itself powerful unto salvation.

THE EARLY RETURNS ARE IN

Even though the material is relatively new, the early returns have been encouraging. The Bible study has been used in all size churches in both rural and urban centers. People have not simply enjoyed the study, they are beginning to discover the joy of demonstrating and explaining what it means to have a personal relationship with God through his one and only Son.

Feedback from early participants has led us to add helpful tools to the Splashinfo.com website. All of the tools to promote and teach the Splash study are provided free online. Most of these tools, including power point presentations for teachers and sermons to accompany the study, have been provided by pastors and educators who simply want to help others to discover evangelistic effectiveness. It has been wonderful to see churches helping other churches to advance the kingdom.

There are currently Splash envelopes available which will provide a fifty-two week reminder of the need to continually Splash those around us. They will also help churches to track Splash activity. A Splash discipling guide that will assist those who lead someone to Christ is available to begin the process of mentoring a new believer. A number of Splash materials are now available for those who are interested.[2]

---

2. For further information on these and other Splash materials, please go to www .auxanopress.com and click on products and resources.

Therefore, while the evangelical church may be losing ground in the United States, it doesn't need to continue in that direction. Pastors can find ways to mobilize the 95 percent of Christians in their churches who are not sharing their faith. Splash Evangelism can make that difference!

12

Preparing for Spiritual Warfare in Evangelism

Preston L. Nix

WHETHER YOU ARE PARTICIPATING in an athletic contest or playing a video game, you know that in order to win the game you must beat your opponent. In order to win the battle in a war you must defeat your enemy. You and I as believers are commanded to win the world to Christ. The Lord himself commissioned the church to "go and make disciples of all nations" (Matt 28:19).[1] As a result, followers of Christ for the past two millennia have been proclaiming publically and sharing personally the gospel in order to fulfill the mandate of the Great Commission.

With the power of the Holy Spirit and the Holy Scripture, as well as the authority of Christ which he gave to the church, you would think that by now the world would be won to Christ! Since it is not, then what is the problem? Why is the task of evangelizing the world not easy? One of the main problems is that there is great opposition to the advance of the gospel, which impedes its progress in this world. The reason that evangelism and missions are not easy is because there is an adversary, the devil, along with his demons who come against individual believers and the corporate body of Christ as they attempt to communicate their faith to a lost and dying world in need of a Savior. When people respond to the message of the gospel in repentance and faith, trusting Christ alone for

---

1. Unless otherwise noted, all Scripture citations will be from the New American Standard Bible.

salvation, they are transferred from the devil's "domain of darkness" to God's "marvelous kingdom of light."[2]

Since the devil does not like losing those who he has held in the bondage of sin to do his will, he comes against the church to try to stop any transfer of souls from his kingdom to God's kingdom. This battle for the souls of men and women, boys and girls has been raging since the beginning of creation and the church must be willing to engage the enemy in spiritual warfare in order to fulfill the Great Commission and win the world to faith in Jesus Christ. The church and the individual believer must come to know, as well as put into practice, solid biblical principles in order to prepare for spiritual warfare in evangelism.

BE AWARE OF THE REALITY OF SPIRITUAL WARFARE IN EVANGELISM

Being prepared for waging spiritual warfare begins with an awareness of the reality of the spiritual battle between good and evil that continually rages around us. Very simply defined, spiritual warfare is *the conflict of two opposing wills*—namely that of God and his followers versus Satan and his followers."[3] The Bible clearly affirms the reality of spiritual warfare and our Christian experience certainly bears witness to that fact. The word of God reveals, "For our struggle is not against flesh and blood, but against the rulers, against the powers, against the world forces of this darkness, against the spiritual forces of wickedness in the heavenly places" (Eph 6:12). The Scripture further asserts that "though we walk in the flesh, we do not war according to the flesh for the weapons of our warfare are not of the flesh but divinely powerful" (2 Cor 10:3–4). As Lawless plainly stated, "We cannot ignore the reality of spiritual warfare."[4] To do so is to invite frustration and failure, especially as it relates to evangelism and to the fulfillment of the Great Commission.

In one of the first books written by a Southern Baptist author on the subject of spiritual warfare entitled *Victory Over the Devil*, Jack Taylor proposed that believers must discern that there is a spiritual war to be

2. See Acts 26:18; Col 1:13; and 1 Pet 2:9.

3. John Franklin and Chuck Lawless, *Spiritual Warfare: Biblical Truth for Victory* (Nashville: LifeWay, 2001), 7. Italics from original.

4. Chuck Lawless, *Discipled Warriors: Growing Healthy Churches That Are Equipped for Spiritual Warfare* (Grand Rapids: Kregel, 2002), 16.

fought in order for spiritual victory to be achieved.[5] This sentiment was echoed in the recently published book *Spiritual Warfare* by Jerry Rankin, president of the International Mission Board of the Southern Baptist Convention, who stated, "A major part of victory in spiritual warfare is *awareness*—recognizing and understanding the *reality* of the battle on a day-to-day basis."[6] These assertions are particularly relevant to the discussion of spiritual warfare and evangelism. The church and individual believers who make up the body of Christ must recognize that evangelism involves spiritual warfare. The battle for souls is real. As Chuck Lawless clearly articulated in his book *Discipled Warriors*:

> Evangelism is about reaching out to people who are caught in the Devil's snare. *Evangelism is itself a spiritual battle, as we take the gospel of light into the kingdom of darkness.* The healthy church that is ready to expand its efforts of evangelism had better be prepared to face spiritual warfare.[7]

As Lawless pointedly declared, "To evangelize is to march into a spiritual battle."[8] The assertion that evangelism is spiritual warfare was also reflected in The Lausanne Covenant adopted at the International Congress for World Evangelization held in Lausanne, Switzerland, during the summer of 1974. Under Article 12 of the Covenant, entitled "Spiritual Conflict," evangelists from over 150 nations affirmed the spiritual battle that ensues wherever the gospel is proclaimed. "We believe that we are engaged in constant spiritual warfare with the principalities and powers of evil, who are seeking to overthrow the church and frustrate its task of world evangelization. We know our need to equip ourselves with God's armor and to fight this battle with the spiritual weapons of truth and prayer."[9]

I personally came to understand the reality of spiritual warfare in evangelism in the first church I pastored. I was informed sometime after I came that the church had, prior to my arrival, voted at a business meeting

5. Jack Taylor, *Victory Over the Devil* (Nashville: Broadman, 1973), 5.

6. Jerry Rankin, *Spiritual Warfare: The Battle for God's Glory* (Nashville: Broadman, 2009), 23. Italics mine.

7. Lawless, *Discipled Warriors*, 83.

8. Chuck Lawless, "Spiritual Warfare and Evangelism," *SBJT* Vol.5, No.1 (Spring 2001): 30.

9. "The Lausanne Covenant," Article 12, in *Let the Earth Hear His Voice*, ed. J. D. Douglas (Minneapolis: World Wide, 1975), 7.

to be a more evangelistic church. It is almost humorous to think about a church officially voting to be evangelistic, but when you consider the results that followed maybe more of our Southern Baptist congregations need to consider such a motion at their next business meeting! I was young, zealous, and very evangelistic, and my personality and giftedness matched the desire of the church to reach out to the community. The church was in an urban setting with plenty of lost people surrounding us to reach. Immediately we began to see many precious souls come to faith in Christ, resulting in the church baptizing more people in one year (and for four years in a row) than in the entire fifty-year history of the church.

It was exciting to be a part of such a movement of the spirit of God and see so many people come into the kingdom of God. What began to unfold, though, shocked me and thrust me into a new dimension of ministry I had never known before this time. Personal attacks on my character began to be made. Criticism of the direction I was taking the church was voiced. Varied demonic manifestations began to occur in our midst. These were mainly in the form of unusual individuals showing up who were unquestionably influenced by Satan. As we attempted to deal with them, we found out that they were demonized to different degrees from strong oppression to outright possession. I began to realize that they were sent to consume our time, distract us from the work of soul winning, and intimidate us so that we would quit being so evangelistically aggressive in our community.

These experiences gave rise to a statement which I made that I believe captures an observable phenomenon that occurs when a church gets serious about the work of evangelism. It is this: *Spiritual activity breeds spiritual activity.* When God's spirit begins to move through a church and the church starts reaching many souls with the gospel, then Satan begins to come against that church to try to stop the work of evangelism. He will begin to attack the congregation both from the inside as well as from the outside. Not only have I observed this in my own ministry but also have had numerous pastor friends relate to me similar experiences. You would think that all of the church members would be happy that, as a pastor, you are leading the church to reach many people with the gospel, but this is simply not the case. You make some people unhappy with the kinds of changes that occur when there is an influx of new people into the life of the church; but you especially upset the devil if you become an evangelistic church! He will not stand idly by and allow a church to "cut in on his territory." He will come against that church in any and every way that he can to try to stop souls from being transferred from his kingdom of darkness to God's kingdom of light.

Churches that begin to take seriously the Great Commission, and begin to reach out to the lost in their communities with the gospel, need to realize that in so doing they enter the spiritual battleground of evangelism. When the church and individual Christians begin to share their faith consistently, they must be aware that they will experience "push back" from Satan in the form of spiritual warfare. Satan hates those who win souls to Christ and will oppose them every step of the way.

Particularly, and consistently, have I observed the reality of spiritual warfare in evangelism when attempting to lead someone to personal faith in Jesus Christ. Experienced soul winners call this moment in the evangelistic encounter "drawing the net," when the witness as a "fisher of men" specifically calls for a response to be saved from the individual with whom he is sharing. Over and over again, at the very point in time when someone is about to make this life changing decision, I have seen all manner of interruptions occur in order to distract the person from praying to receive Christ. I have watched children suddenly cry out or run into the room wanting their mom or dad. I have seen pets, for seemingly no reason, begin to make noise or start moving around seeking their owner's attention. Sometimes other people have shown up, causing distraction. The most frequent interruption I have experienced when "drawing the net" is the ringing of the telephone, which has become even more common now that everyone has cell phones. On at least one occasion, bees began to swarm around me and a person with whom I was sharing the gospel while we were seated on an outside patio. Someone might say that these were simply coincidences, but I will need that person to explain to me the amazing timing and alarming consistency of these interruptions: always at the very point of a decision for Christ in the evangelistic encounter. What I believe I have observed over the years is simply the physical manifestation of the usually unseen spiritual battle for the souls of humanity. In a moment of desperation to keep from losing another soul, which he has held captive, Satan makes a last ditch effort to distract that person while at the point of surrender to Christ and reception of eternal life. The devil will manipulate and utilize anything and everything that he can as the god of this world to keep people from responding to the gospel.

Satan's effort to stop the spread and reception of the gospel is spiritual warfare in evangelism, which Christians must be aware of to experience victory over their enemy. While this is true, a word of caution should be made here. Although Satan is real and spiritual warfare in evangelism is real, believers should not be overly fascinated with spiritual warfare or overly fearful of Satan himself. The reality is that believers tend toward two extremes when it comes to spiritual warfare. They either overemphasize it or underemphasize it.[10] The same is true with Satan. When underemphasizing Satan, believers make the mistake of ignoring him, which allows him to "carry out his work undetected"[11] or they give him too much attention and see the devil "behind every bush."[12] What is needed when dealing with Satan and spiritual warfare is biblical balance, which keeps the subjects in perspective. The reality is that the devil is a defeated foe and Christ's death on the cross and resurrection from the grave has already won the victory over Satan![13] But Satan is like a snake that is "venomous and vengeful in his defeat, lashing out at whoever is in range."[14] Although the church ultimately will be victorious over Satan in this spiritual war, battles must still be fought for the eternal souls of human beings. The first step for the church to fulfill the Great Commission, and to prepare for spiritual warfare in order to win the world to Christ, is to accept and be aware of the reality of spiritual warfare in evangelism.

BE ARMED WITH THE WEAPONS OF
SPIRITUAL WARFARE FOR EVANGELISM

Satan has "blinded the minds of the unbelieving so that they might not see the light of the Gospel" (2 Cor 4:4). He deceives unbelievers by lying to them and by "stealing" the truth of the saving gospel of Jesus Christ from their hearts.[15] As a result, those apart from Christ are "held captive by him [Satan] to do his will" (2 Tim 2:26). The lost are Satan's "prisoners

---

10. Dean Sherman, *Spiritual Warfare for Every Christian* (Seattle: YWAM, 1990), 20.

11. Paul Gittiebent, *Anthropological Reflections on Missiological Issues* (Grand Rapids: Baker, 1994), 213.

12. Lawless, *Discipled Warriors*, 16. Cf. C. S. Lewis, *The Screwtape Letters* (New York: Macmillan, 1961), 3.

13. See Heb 2:14 and Col 2:15.

14. Taylor, *Victory Over the Devil*, 6.

15. See Rev 12:9, 2 Cor 11:14, Matt 13:19, and Luke 8:12.

of war" in the cosmic conflict for the souls of humanity. Ultimately, Satan wants to take them to hell. In order to find freedom from Satan and sin, and escape the fires of hell, unbelievers must respond to the truth of the gospel. Because Satan is a powerful supernatural being and the lost are under his control, believers who are mere weak physical beings must be armed with the divine weapons of spiritual warfare in order to win the battle for the souls of men and women, boys and girls who desperately need salvation. This is the next step in preparing for spiritual warfare in evangelism. To win souls to Christ, the primary weapons in the arsenal of the believer are the authority of Christ, the armor of God, and the assistance of the Holy Spirit.

Authority of Christ

The first major weapon in the arsenal of the believer to win souls is the authority of the Lord Jesus Christ. When asked how the Great Commission begins, most believers will respond with "Go and make disciples," which is not accurate. The Great Commission actually begins with Jesus boldly declaring that "All authority has been given to Me in heaven and on earth" (Matt 28:18).[16] Following the assertion of his absolute sovereign authority over the universe, Jesus then commanded his followers to "Go and make disciples." The Great Commission begins with the authority of Christ and—by his authority—the Great Commission will be accomplished. Jesus declared, "I will build my church, and the gates of hell shall not prevail against it" (Matt 16:18, KJV). Under his divine authority, the church attacks the gates of hell and advances the kingdom of God by fulfilling the Great Commission: go and make disciples of all nations.

When the seventy disciples returned from their successful evangelistic mission to which they had been commissioned by Jesus, they joyfully declared, "Lord, even the demons are subject to us in Your name" (Luke 10:17).[17] The Apostle John revealed in the book of Revelation how believers will be victorious over the evil one when he recorded, "And they overcame him because of the blood of the Lamb and because of the word of their testimony, and they did not love their life even when faced with death" (Rev 12:11). These last two verses provide insight as to how to appropriate the authority of the Lord Jesus Christ in waging spiritual

---

16. A description of the absolute authority of Christ is provided in Eph 1:20–23.

17. See also Acts 16:18.

warfare for effective witness and the fulfillment of the Great Commission. Specifically, the authority of Christ that the believer possesses for effective evangelism is found in the name of Jesus, the blood of Jesus, the word of Jesus, and the life of Jesus.

The Name of Jesus

The name of Jesus possesses great power. Through the name of Jesus, people are saved. "Whoever will call on the name of the Lord will be saved" (Rom 10:13). The Lord's name is Jesus and "there is no other name under heaven . . . by which one must be saved" (Acts 4:12). God has "bestowed on Him the name which is above every name, so that at the name of Jesus every knee will bow . . . and that every tongue will confess that Jesus Christ is Lord, to the glory of God the Father" (Phil 2:9–11). Jesus' name represents "Who He is." His name stands for his perfect character and his divine authority. The name of Jesus gives believers authority to share the gospel with powerful results.

The Blood of Jesus

As the name of Jesus represents "Who He is," the blood of Jesus speaks of what he has done. Through the shed blood of Jesus on the cross of Calvary, salvation was purchased and forgiveness of sin was made possible.[18] The cross and the shed blood of Jesus canceled all the claims that Satan had on the human soul.[19] As a result, once a person is saved Satan no longer has authority over him. The believer now has authority over Satan and can overcome him with a powerful witness "by the blood of the Lamb" (Rev 12:11).

The Word of Jesus

The word of Jesus is what Jesus said, as recorded in Holy Scripture. The word of Jesus is also the word about Jesus as inspired by the Holy Spirit which is the word of God.[20] The word of God is alive and powerful and able to defeat the devil.[21] When Jesus was tempted by Satan in the wilderness, Jesus demonstrated the power of the word to overcome Satan. Each

---

18. See Acts 20:28, Eph 1:7, Heb 9:11–12, 14; 13:12, 1 Pet 1:18–19, 1 John 1:7, and Rev 5:9.

19. See Col 2:13–15 and Heb 2:14–15.

20. See John 5:39.

21. See Heb 4:12.

time Satan tempted Jesus, the Lord Jesus countered Satan's attack by quoting the holy word of God. The liar Satan was defeated when confronted with the truth of the word.[22] According to Revelation 12:11, believers overcame Satan by the "word of their testimony," which they possessed because the word of Jesus changed their lives. The word of God and the testimony of the believers proceeding from the word wield authority over the devil. The word shared in witness to the lost overcomes the lies of the devil and leads them to salvation.

The Life of Jesus

In the believer, the life of Jesus has the power to overcome Satan for evangelism. That life is the presence of the Holy Spirit, within the one who has been born again and indwelt by the Spirit of God. The Holy Spirit within believers provides them power to take a stand against the forces of evil and overcome the evil one himself, even when threatened with death.[23] The Apostle John categorically stated that the life of Jesus within the believer provides authority to defeat the devil. "You are from God, little children, and have overcome them; because greater is He who is in you than he who is in the world" (1 John 4:4). The life of Jesus displayed in the believer, and the declaration of the source of that life with absolute confidence, provides a powerful witness to a lost world.

Armor of God

The next major weapon in the arsenal of the believer is the full armor of God. The spiritual armor the believer should be outfitted to live the victorious Christian life, as well as to win souls to Christ, is described by the Apostle Paul in his letter to the Ephesians.

> Put on the full armor of God, so that you will be able to stand firm against the schemes of the devil. For our struggle is not against flesh and blood, but against the rulers, against the powers, against the world forces of this darkness, against the spiritual forces of wickedness in the heavenly places. Therefore, take up the full armor of God, so that you will be able to resist in the evil day, and having done everything, to stand firm. Stand firm therefore, having girded your loins with truth, and having put on the breastplate of righteousness, *and having* shod your feet with the preparation

22. See Matt 4:1–11.
23. See Rev 12:11.

of the Gospel of peace; in addition to all, taking up the *shield of faith with which you will be able to extinguish all the flaming arrows of the evil one. And take the helmet of salvation*, and the sword of the Spirit, which is the word of God.[24]

Much has been written concerning the full armor of God.[25] Putting on the armor of God is both a daily prayer exercise and a commitment to personal spiritual disciplines. The believer can "pray on" the pieces of the armor each day, but he must live out the meaning of each piece of the armor in order to be armed and ready for spiritual battle. Believers should be intentional and consistent about putting on the armor of God realizing that the "essence of 'putting on the armor' . . . is about daily living in truth, righteousness, faith , and hope, while always being ready to proclaim the gospel of peace found in the Word."[26]

Space does not allow for a comprehensive exegetical examination of the Ephesian passage on the believer "taking up the full armor of God." However, a few explanatory comments should prove to provide a better understanding of the meaning of the various pieces of the spiritual armor. Application can then be made as to how the armor can be employed in victorious Christian living, as well as effective Christian witnessing.

Through the Apostle Paul, the Lord commanded the believer to outfit himself with God's armor in order to wage spiritual warfare and win spiritual victories. W. Curtis Vaughan writes:

We are therefore urged to "put on" the whole armor of God in order that we "may be able to stand against the wiles of the devil" (v.11). The tense of the verb "put on" denotes urgent and decisive action. . . . "To stand" in this context means not only to stand ready

24. Eph 6:11–17. Italics mine.

25. The classic work on the subject of the armor of God in spiritual warfare, written originally in 1655, is still in print today. See William Gurnall, *The Christian in Complete Armor*, 3 vols. (Carlisle, PA: Banner of Truth Trust, 2009). A more recent treatment of the subject was written by Chuck Lawless, *Putting on the Armor: Equipped and Deployed for Spiritual Warfare* (Nashville: LifeWay Press, 2006). Several other works include sections on the armor of God in the broader discussion of spiritual warfare such as Chip Ingram, *The Invisible War* (Grand Rapids: Baker Books, 2006); Sammy Tippit, *Fit for Battle* (Chicago: Moody Press, 1994); and David Jeremiah, *Spiritual Warfare* (Atlanta: Walk Thru the Bible Ministries, 1995).

26. Chuck Lawless, "Spiritual Warfare: Reaching People by Taking on the Enemy," in *The Complete Evangelism Guidebook*, by Scott Dawson, ed. (Grand Rapids: Baker Books, 2006), 106. For an insightful discussion concerning the wearing of the armor as a lifestyle for the believer, see Lawless, *Discipled Warriors*, 54–57.

to fight but to hold one's ground. The "wiles of the devil" are his strategies, the many and subtle ways by which he assails God's people. . . . In verse 13 . . . instead of "put on" Paul here writes "take up" (ASV), the more common military expression for arming one's self. . . . The tense is again such as to denote urgency. . . . The word rendered by "to withstand" means to resist successfully. . . . "Having done all" is a particularly strong expression meaning "having thoroughly done everything." The reference is not the preparation for the conflict but to the end of the conflict; when the enemy has been thoroughly vanquished. "To stand," speaks of the stance of victory.[27]

The Apostle Paul employed the imagery of a Roman soldier "fully equipped for heavy battle."[28] He identified six different pieces of equipment that comprise the "full armor of God" in Ephesians 6:14–17. Each literal piece of weaponry utilized by the Roman soldier represents a corresponding spiritual weapon the believer has at his disposal for spiritual warfare. The first five of these comprise defensive armor while the last identified is the only offensive weapon.

Belt of Truth

The first piece of armor is the belt of truth. The belt was usually a thick leather band which served to hold the soldier's tunic in place and to which the scabbard for his sword was attached. The "girding of the loins" carries the idea of preparedness while "truth" indicates sincerity and genuineness. The modern day Christian soldier is prepared for spiritual battle by trusting and obeying the truth of God's word.

Breastplate of Righteousness

The second piece of armor is the breastplate of righteousness. Normally made of leather with metal rings, although sometimes a full piece of metal, the breastplate protected the soldier's vital organs of the chest and abdomen. Righteousness here can be understood as both the righteousness of God, which is the righteousness of justification as well as the personal righteousness of the believer. The righteousness imputed to the believer at conversion and the righteousness practiced by the believer guard his heart in the spiritual conflict.

27. W. Curtis Vaughan, *The Letter to the Ephesians* (Nashville: Convention Press, 1963), 132–33.

28. Ibid., 131–32.

Sandals of Peace

The shoes of the soldier comprise the third piece of armor; they were absolutely essential for battle. These leather sandals had soles that were studded with nails for surefootedness. Because ancient warfare was primarily conducted by hand-to-hand combat, footwear that allowed for stability, as well as swiftness of movement, was essential. Having "the preparation of the gospel of peace" on his feet means the believer stands in readiness to quickly and to boldly share the gospel message, which brings peace between sinful man and holy God.

Shield of Faith

Another weapon of warfare used by the Roman soldier was his shield. The reference Paul made was not to a small round shield but to the large oblong wooden shield behind which the soldier was protected. The wooden shield covered by thick leather could stop the "flaming arrows" which were some of the most dangerous weapons of ancient warfare. As the flaming arrows would sink into the wooden shield and be extinguished, through faith, utter dependence, and total reliance upon God, the believer is able to thwart the most victorious attacks of Satan.

Helmet of Salvation

A vital piece of armor for the soldier was the metal or leather helmet equipped with cheek coverings that protected the entire head. Nothing short of a direct blow from an axe could penetrate the sturdily built helmet. The helmet of salvation protects the mind of the believer so that he thinks clearly and acts decisively as a disciple and a witness.

The Sword of the Spirit

The final piece of the armor, the sword, was the only offensive weapon employed by the soldier. The Roman sword was not a long medieval sword but a shorter, wider dagger for close hand-to-hand combat with the enemy. Paul indicated that the believer should use the sword supplied by God's Holy Spirit which is the holy word of God. The truth of the word of God spoken by the believer and lived out by the believer can stop Satan's strategies. The Scripture shared and received can shatter the bonds of sin and save the soul of the sinner.[29]

29. See Rom 10:17, John 8:32, 34–36, and Eph 5:26.

Assistance of the

The final major weapon in the believer's arsenal for fulfilling the Great Commission is the assistance of the Holy Spirit. Before his ascension to heaven following the Resurrection, Jesus declared to his disciples, "But you will receive power when the Holy Spirit has come upon you; and you shall be My witnesses both in Jerusalem, and in all Judea and Samaria, and even to the remotest part of the earth" (Acts 1:8). The Holy Spirit empowers the believer to carry out the Great Commission. Without the assistance of the Holy Spirit of God, evangelism of lost persons cannot be accomplished. The Holy Spirit assists the believer in evangelism in several ways but two are specifically highlighted in Ephesians 6 in reference to evangelism and spiritual warfare. This passage reveals that the Holy Spirit assists the believer in fervent intercessory prayer and bold gospel witness.

Fervent Intercessory Prayer

Paul concluded the passage in Ephesians 6 with an appeal for prayer. He directed the saints in Ephesus to pray "in the Spirit" with vigilance and perseverance for "fellow soldiers" in the spiritual battle as well as for himself. Specifically, he requested that they pray for him to proclaim with boldness the message of the gospel. In like manner, the believer today should pray for fellow believers who will endeavor to lead people to faith in Christ. As Jesus observed, "The harvest is plentiful, but the workers are few. Therefore beseech the Lord of the harvest to send out workers into His harvest" (Matt 9:37–38). The believer must pray for the needed laborers in the fields for a harvest of lost souls.

Because it is God's stated will in his word that all people be saved, the believer should intercede as well for the salvation of all lost persons.[30] When the believer prays for the salvation of the lost, he is waging spiritual warfare. God uses the fervent prayers of his people to remove barriers that keep people from knowing Christ.[31] "We are to pray 'in the Spirit'—under His influence and with His gracious assistance."[32] With the assistance of

---

30. See 1 Tim 2:4, 2 Pet 3:9, and Rom 10:1.

31. See James 5:16. For resources in praying for unbelievers, see Lee E. Thomas, *Praying Effectively for the Lost* (Milford, OH: John the Baptist Printing Ministry), 2003 and *Praying Your Friends to Christ* (Alpharetta, GA: North American Mission Board), 1998.

32. Vaughan, *Letter to the Ephesians*, 137. See Rom 8:26 and Jude 20.

the Holy Spirit, the prayers of the believer result in more saints being soul winners and more sinners being saved.

Bold Gospel Witness

The object of prayer requested by the Apostle Paul in verses 18–20 of Ephesians chapter 6 was the bold proclamation of the gospel to the lost without Christ. He desired to communicate the message of salvation with clarity and confidence. Paul knew that for his witness to be effective, he needed the empowerment of the Holy Spirit. This truth was dramatically evidenced in the book of Acts in the ministry of the apostles and members of the early church. Following their imprisonment and release from the Jewish authorities, Peter and John prayed for confidence to speak God's word. The result was that they were "all filled with the Holy Spirit and began to speak the Word of God with boldness" (Acts 4:29, 31). As well, the believer today should seek to witness with boldness. That boldness will come only from the assistance of the Holy Spirit of God. God has chosen to use the Spirit-empowered, bold witness of believers to communicate the life changing message of the gospel so that those who have been held prisoner by Satan might be delivered from the kingdom of darkness into the Kingdom of light.

CONCLUSION

Because of the battle raging for the souls of men and women, believers must be willing to engage the enemy in spiritual warfare in order to fulfill the Great Commission and win the lost souls to faith in Christ. Preparing for spiritual warfare in evangelism necessitates awareness of the reality of spiritual warfare, as well as being armed with the weapons of spiritual warfare. Both awareness and arms are needed to engage and overcome the enemy of the human soul. It is significant that the context of the most informative and instructive passage on spiritual warfare in the Bible, Ephesians 6:10–20, is evangelism. The Apostle Paul wanted the "Christian soldier" to be outfitted with the armor of God in order to proclaim boldly the message of the gospel. As Lawless observed, "Evangelism demands obedient believers, undergirded in prayer and empowered by the Holy Spirit, going into a pagan world and announcing the good news of Christ."[33] When believers are aware of the reality of spiritual warfare

---

33. Lawless, "Spiritual Warfare and Evangelism," 39.

in evangelism and armed with the necessary weapons to wage spiritual warfare for evangelism, the church will be prepared to fulfill the task of the Great Commission by storming the gates of hell with the gospel and setting the prisoners free!

13

Practical Principles for Perennial
Personal Evangelism

J. D. Payne

Personal evangelism is practical by nature. Like the game of golf, each witnessing encounter is unique, requiring the use of different approaches to communicate the never-changing message that Jesus is Lord. Such approaches are called *methods*. While evangelism methods abound, and are necessary for mobilizing a Great Commission Church for the harvest fields, there are important, never-changing, biblical principles that establish the foundation on which our important, ever-changing methods are constructed. Using Jesus and the Apostolic Church as the example, there are at least eight principles that provide a foundation for developing a Great Commission Church.

WE MUST SHARE THE EXCLUSIVE MESSAGE

The Scriptures attest that the message of the good news is an exclusive message, which is a major hindrance for people coming to faith in Christ. Jesus stated that "I am the way, and the truth, and the life. No one comes to the Father except through me" (John 14:6, ESV).[1] Such a truth is the antithesis to a number of other soteriological perspectives. The words of Jesus speak against universalism: The claim that if there is a heaven, then

---

1. Bible quotations in this chapter are from the ESV translation.

everyone ultimately will be there. His words push against pluralism: The claim that all sincere followers of any faith system will make it to heaven (or their understanding of paradise). And Jesus also contradicts the inclusivist's view: the claim that all sincere followers of any faith will come to God, because Jesus' atoning sacrifice is behind the differing faiths of the world.

While supporting the exclusive message, Peter and John made it very clear that explicit faith in Jesus is necessary for someone to come to the Father. Luke records their words: "And there is salvation in no one else, for there is no other name under heaven given among men by which we must be saved" (Acts 4:12). Those who come to faith must do so through the person and work of Jesus. There is no such thing as an "anonymous" Christian, following another faith system and remaining ignorant of the gospel.

From Genesis to Revelation, the message of the good news is an exclusive message. Exclusivity is established in the three major parts of the Old Testament. In the Torah, the other faiths of the world are viewed as false and inadequate to measure up to the standards of the holy God. Abraham, Moses, and the Israelites are called to follow the one true and living God in a pluralistic world. In the Writings, the religion of hedonism is not seen as a legitimate way of life. Again, other religions are acknowledged but they are misleading and an abomination. Other gods are acknowledged, but are false gods. Throughout the Prophets, the lifestyle of following other gods results in destruction and death. The only hope for any restoration is through repentance and covenantal faithfulness. The Gospels portray Jesus as Messiah, with John the Baptist calling people to repentance. Jesus calls the religious leaders to repentance (Luke 13:3; John 3:16); he calls followers of the Samaritan faith to himself (John 4). The Gospels make it clear that not everyone will be saved (Matt 7:21–23, 25). The disciples are told to go throughout all the world and make disciples of all peoples (Matt 28:19). In Acts, the gospel is preached to all nations, Jewish religious leaders, Samaritans, god-fearers, polytheistic Lystrians, Athenians, and animistic Ephesians. (Acts 1:8; 4:12; 8:5; 10:33; 14:14; 17:22; 18:24–25). The Pauline and General Epistles point out that the message of the gospel, though foolishness and a stumbling block to some, is the only hope of salvation (1 Cor 1:18), and that the doctrines of this world are actually doctrines of demons (1 Tim 4:1). Finally, Revelation is not reserved when pointing out that the exclusive message is to be proclaimed throughout the world, and those who reject Jesus are cast into the lake of fire (Rev 20:15).

WE MUST BE INTENTIONAL IN SHARING THE GOSPEL

Throughout the Bible, Jesus and the Apostolic Church modeled intentionality in their evangelism. They did not simply leave the preaching of the gospel of the highways and hedges to happenstance. There was a focus to their communication of the truth. They had eyes to see the fields from a divine perspective.

In John 4, Jesus departed from the Jewish norm of travel during his day. Leaving Judea for Galilee, he ventured through the region of Samaria, a deviation against the mores of the day for a Jewish man. John, anticipating that the readers of his Gospel would be shocked to read that Jesus did not circumvent that region of "half-breed" Samarians, simply included, "And he had to pass through Samaria" (John 4:4), revealing Jesus' evangelistic intentionality. For the only event that was recorded as happening in Samaria was the conversion of the Samaritan village.

A reading of any of Paul's missionary journeys reveals the intentionality in his evangelistic work. Even after being persecuted in one city, he would depart to another city to repeat the message (Acts 14:19–21). Throughout his letters, Paul noted his evangelistic intentionality (Eph 6:19).

Of all the spiritual disciplines in the life of the believer, evangelism is usually the first to be neglected. Rather than understanding evangelism to be a program or an event, the disciple must recognize that evangelism is a part of his or her entire being. To be a follower of Jesus means that the person is a witness for Jesus. Paul writes, "Therefore, as you received Christ Jesus the Lord, so walk in him" (Col 2:6). Intentionality includes asking the Lord of the harvest to provide you with a supernatural perspective of everyone you meet. Several years ago, I heard of a great evangelist viewing everyone he encountered with an *L* or an *S* on their foreheads. The *L* stood for *lost* and the *S* for *saved*. This man went on to say that he assumed that everyone had an *L* until he knew otherwise.

WE MUST BE SPIRIT-LED IN OUR EVANGELISM.

Again, throughout the Scriptures this principle is encountered time and again. It was the Spirit that led Philip to the chariot of the Ethiopian (Acts 8:29). The Spirit enabled Peter to overcome his racism and guided him to the house of Cornelius (Acts 10:19). It was the Spirit that called out Paul and Barnabas on the first missionary journey (Acts 13:1–3). And it was the same Spirit that interrupted the evangelistic intentionality of the church planting team, preventing them from sharing Jesus in Asia Minor (Acts 16:6) and Bithynia (Acts 16:7). Rather, this same Spirit had other plans for Paul's missionary team.

Without the Spirit, people will not come to faith in Jesus. As followers of Jesus we are called to live life everyday in the power of the Holy Spirit. A failure to do so is a failure to walk in the light as he is in the light (1 John 1:5–7). A failure to be led by the Spirit through daily life means that the believer is grieving and quenching the Spirit (Eph 4:30; 1 Thess 5:19).

WE MUST KNOW THE IMPORTANCE OF CULTURE

An examination of several scriptural passages reveals that Jesus and the Apostolic Church understood the importance of culture when communicating the truth of God's love. Yet they also realized that the kingdom ethic sometimes required the preacher to break some social mores and taboos of the day. For example, Jesus demonstrated such acts by touching those who were labeled unclean (Luke 5:13) and allowing "sinners" to touch him (Luke 7:36–39). He shockingly engaged a Samaritan woman in conversation, even asking for a drink of water (John 4:7). In just the right time (Gal 4:4) and location, the Word incarnated himself and walked within a culture (John 1:1, 14). Jesus communicated the truth to men, women, boys, and girls in a culturally appropriate way that connected with them.

When we examine the ministry of the Apostle Paul, we see evidence that he understood the cultures of the day; this understanding enabled him to communicate the good news to the peoples more effectively. The classic example of such wisdom in action is found in his address at Mars Hill (Acts 17). Knowing that the Athenians greatly appreciated compliments regarding their religious pluralism, Paul began by complimenting them (Acts 17:22). He did not condone such behavior, for he was highly grieved at the presence of the numerous idols (Acts 17:16). This compliment immediately caused Paul's listeners to connect with him. The second significant element in his presentation, because he knew their culture well enough, was quotes of the theology of their pagan poets. Again, Paul was able to establish a connection with the people and then take them to the cross.

God also works supernaturally within a cultural context. He is at work through general revelation (Psalm 19:1; Rom 1:20), pressing on the consciences (Rom 2:15) of people. Meanwhile, there are many false teachers in the world, and corresponding demonic activity. Those in the kingdom of darkness are under the influence of the evil one, the flesh, and the world. Those doing the work of an evangelist must understand the people to whom they speak the message. They need to walk in the footprints of the sons of Issachar, understand the times and know what to do (1 Chr 12:32) to communicate the never-changing message of "Jesus is Lord" to ever-changing societies.

As we go making disciples, we must make certain that we are receptor-oriented in our communication.[2] In other words, it is important to constantly ask ourselves how the person interprets what we are saying. Listening and understanding are two different matters. Paul noted, "And how are they to hear without someone preaching" (Rom 10:14). The Christian must preach. But as we preach, we must make certain that our listeners understand what we are communicating.

I once heard of a pastor who was working in a foreign country. He was approached by a young boy desiring to be saved. The minister asked him, "Son, are you a sinner?" To which the child replied, "Oh, no, preacher! I'm not a sinner!" The pastor's response was to smile and send the child away, assuming the child had not grasped his separation from a holy God. While in reality, the pastor's question may have only revealed that the young mind did not know the definition of the English word "sinner." Upon hearing this story, I could not help but wonder if the pastor had been asked if he personally had committed, for example, *hamartia*, would he have denied it like the child, perhaps not knowing that *hamartia* is a Greek word used in the New Testament for sin.

Knowing the culture of the people to whom we share the good news of Jesus will help us communicate more clearly the truth of the gospel. The offense of the cross is to be the only stumbling block (Rom 9:30–33) that we set before others. I fear many times we forget to understand the worldview and way of life of others, and we make our personal evangelism methods the stumbling block. Unbelievers never get to understand

2. I first learned the importance of being receptor-oriented when communicating with others from David J. Hesselgrave. For more information on this topic, see his excellent book *Communicating Christ Cross-Culturally*, 2nd ed. (Grand Rapids: Zondervan, 1991).

the message Christians desire to communicate to them because they erect cultural obstacles before them on the way to the cross.

WE MUST REMAIN FLEXIBLE

As a child, I remember one of my friends having a pet ferret. This furry creature was the epitome of flexibility. My friend enjoyed putting this weasel-like creature on display, doing harmless parlor tricks. For example, without harming the animal, he could roll the creature into a ball. However, the most impressive feat involved sending this pet headfirst into a long cylindrical Pringle's potato chip can, only to have the animal turn around inside the can and crawl out headfirst. This amazing creature was able to adapt quickly to the shape of his context, without getting trapped.

The preaching of the gospel in a post-Christianized North American context requires that believers enter into dialogue with those to whom we preach. This approach shows love and respect (1 Pet 3:15) during evangelistic engagement, and this approach requires that we remain flexible to the context as we introduce others to Jesus. While there is great value in learning different models of personal evangelism (e.g., Roman Road, Continual Witness Training, Evangelism Explosion, F.A.I.T.H., Share Jesus Without Fear), we must make certain that we do not get locked into a model. Try not to become "trapped" in the witnessing conversation and fail to follow the Spirit's leading, being so concerned that we must get through our model's form of the gospel presentation. Witnesses must keep in mind that models are good and necessary for learning how to share the gospel, but we must make certain that we do not become dependent on a model (or train others to be dependent on a model).

I have been in a conversation with someone, when the person asked me a question to which no model equipped an adequate response. For example, I was once asked about what the Bible says concerning life on other planets. In such situations, the Lord always provided grace to know how to respond with sincerity, integrity, and knowledge of how to make the connection between the topic of discussion and the cross of Christ (though I'm not certain that I always did the greatest job). The important matter is to remain flexible throughout the dialogue and always look for ways to take the person from the question of the moment to the cross of Christ.

WE MUST BEGIN WHERE THE PEOPLE ARE
IN THEIR JOURNEYS

I find it amazing that as followers of Jesus, we can get locked into one way of doing something for the Lord, to the exclusion of other biblical ways. For example, why as evangelicals do we talk to people about being "born again," but not about "drinking living water?" We are quick to place emphasis on Jesus' account with Nicodemus (John 3), and make it paradigmatic for all witnessing encounters. Yet, Jesus also had an encounter with the Samaritan woman, shortly after the Nicodemus account (John 4).

Jesus told Nicodemus he had to be born again, because Nicodemus had placed his eternal security in the fact that he had been born of the correct bloodline (i.e., child of Abraham). Jesus used this moment to cause the religious leader to recognize that it was only through a regenerative work of the Holy Spirit that one can avoid perishing (John 3:16). At Jacob's well in Samaria, Jesus met a woman whose need was to satisfy her physical desire for water. Without it, death was quick and inevitable in the Middle Eastern heat. She was at her point of need on the highway of life and Jesus revealed to her that his living water would not only satisfy her for the present but sanctify and secure her for eternity (John 4:13–14).

Beginning where people are in their journeys requires a recognition that people are created in the image of God (Gen 1:27) and are spiritual beings (Acts 17:26–29). Such an approach to personal evangelism requires that, though we have the truth to proclaim, we look for the best way to communicate it to this particular person, at this particular moment, in this particular place. Like the pilot who circles the city waiting for clearance to land the plane at the proper time and in the proper location, we must be sensitive to where people are in their spiritual journeys, always looking for the appropriate way to communicate the gospel. If we truly believe that God has been at work in the lives of people long before our encounter with them (e.g., Cornelius in Acts 10; Acts 17:26–27), then we must remember Paul's words to "Walk in wisdom toward outsiders, making the best use of the time. Let your speech always be gracious, seasoned with salt, so that you may know how you ought to answer each person" (Col 4:5–6).

WE MUST BE SENSITIVE TO THE FEARS, HURTS, AND CONCERNS OF OTHERS WHILE SPEAKING THE TRUTH IN LOVE

Knowing the culture of people, knowing how to effectively communicate the gospel, and beginning where people are in their spiritual journeys does not mean that we are to compromise the message we preach. We are still to declare repentance toward God and faith in the Lord Jesus Christ (Acts 20:21). While Jesus and the Apostolic Church never vacillated from the message of abundant and eternal life, they were sensitive to the fears, hurts, and concerns of others. Though there are examples (Luke 13:3) of Jesus and the Apostolic Church speaking harsh and condemning words to the self-righteous, indignant, and recalcitrant (and we should also follow their example in similar situations), they used a more sensitive approach with those who were interested in hearing more about the good news.

Jesus did not relegate the Samaritan woman's adultery and fornication to a place of insignificance, but he did not chide her over her known wickedness. Jesus confronted the rich young ruler with his idolatry, yet loved him (Mark 10:17–22). Zacchaeus and Matthew were in all likelihood thieves who worked under the auspices of their governmental jobs. Yet, Jesus called them to follow him, and he became known as a friend to tax collectors and sinners (Matt 11:19).

Peter reminds us in general to respond to others with gentleness and respect (1 Pet 3:15–16). The preaching of the good news requires us to call people to repentance but to do so out of a heart of love. Forsaking all to follow Jesus is a radical change. For many people it means a loss of lifestyles, families, homes, friends, lovers, money, careers, and possibly a loss of their very lives. Jesus recognized that following him was not a matter into which people should enter flippantly but gave stern warnings about counting the cost (Luke 14:25–33). Those doing the work of evangelists *must* keep these matters in mind when calling someone to follow Jesus. Failure to consider the fears, concerns, and emotions of the unbeliever, who is counting the cost during our witnessing, is insensitive and ungodly. Such is evangelism done without gentleness and respect.

WE MUST BE FOLLOW-UP ORIENTED

Because the Great Commission involves the church making disciples, one should not be satisfied with converts. Though the *first* step in the process of seeing people come out of the kingdom of darkness and into the kingdom of light is conversion; the sanctification process is also a lifelong journey. Anyone who assumes that the work of an evangelist is only to see someone come to faith, without any regard for that new believer's growth in Christ, does not have the Great Commission on his or her heart.

It is has been said that the largest part of an iceberg is the portion that rests submerged beneath the ocean's surface. In a similar fashion, when it comes to the Great Commission, evangelism is just the tip of the iceberg. Teaching new believers to obey all that Christ commanded (Matt 28:20) is the remainder of the iceberg.

Jesus and the Apostolic Church were very much concerned with the post-conversion aspects of people's lives. Jesus sent the delivered demoniac immediately back to his people with the good news (Mark 5:19). He noted that only those who do the will of the Father are those who enter into the kingdom (Matt 7:21). Philip made certain that the Ethiopian was baptized (Acts 8:38–39). The book of Acts notes that after evangelism occurred in various cities, the new believers were gathered together as churches (Acts 14:21–23). After the birth of the church in Antioch, the Jerusalem church sent Barnabas to follow up with them (Acts 11:22-26). Upon hearing of the conversion of the Samaritans, Peter and John went to investigate and minister to the new believers (Acts 8:14–17). Paul returned to visit, sent other messengers, and wrote letters to follow up with new believers.

CONCLUSION

Following after the pattern of Jesus and the Apostolic Church, the contemporary church is able to be better prepared for mobilizing and sending laborers into the harvest fields. While understanding different methods for personal evangelism is very important, it is even more significant that our methods be built upon a healthy foundation of biblical principles. Preaching the never-changing message requires different methods depending on the situation. And while methods will differ, the foundation for personal evangelism must come from the biblical principles. Without biblical principles, it is not possible to have healthy perennial personal evangelism.

14

Apologetics:
The Key to Revitalizing Personal Evangelism

Adam W. Greenway

ONE MIGHT WELL DESCRIBE the challenge facing contemporary ministry practitioners by simply acknowledging that, indeed, the times are a-changing. In their relationship to contemporary ministry practices, concepts such as postmodernism, moral and ethical relativism, pluralism, and inclusivism were mostly unheard of just a generation ago. Evangelistic strategies are increasingly less effective with each passing year, and it seems with each new day another survey or statistic appears that generates great discussion, but produces little in tangible change. There can be little doubt that lost people are starting from a position further and further away from God, but what are we doing to actually reach such persons with the Gospel?

The situation is complicated in that a mainstay of modern evangelical evangelism—local church witness training for door-to-door "visitation"—seems to be inadequate to meet all the challenges this new century has brought. Lest I be misunderstood, I'm not calling for an immediate cease and desist order to organized outreach, nor am I arguing that traditional evangelism is hopelessly irreparable. Rather, I am advocating for another sort of approach called Apologetics—a method/way of thinking/ way of reasoning that reaches out to people with relevance and credibility. This method not only guides the evangelism process, but focuses on meaningful life change following conversion. Let me offer a personal illustration to better frame this issue.

I was raised in a wonderful little community in central Florida named Frostproof (and yes, it really is most of the time!). When I was growing up in the 1980s, there were only Protestant churches in my hometown—First Baptist, First United Methodist, and the Church of Christ were all built right next to each other, with the Associate Reformed Presbyterian (ARP) Church just down the street, and the Church of God and Assembly of God not too terribly far away from all the above. During the summertime, each of these churches would hold a weeklong "Vacation Bible School," but all on different weeks! Parents could get their kids out of the house for six weeks if they chose to—not a bad deal! Even the atheist in my hometown was a "Christian" atheist, because the God he rejected was merely the God of the Bible

But around the late 1980s and early 1990s, things began to change in my hometown. A Muslim presence was established in the community, and an openly atheist science teacher became employed at the local high school. No longer was it a fairly safe assumption that the only options for every child growing up in Frostproof would be to make the "VBS circuit" each summer and learn the Bible's people and places. Moreover, this trend would expose some unexpected weaknesses in how evangelism had traditionally been practiced, and not just in places like my hometown.

My home church had been involved in *Evangelism Explosion*, a popular outreach training program designed by the late Presbyterian pastor and author D. James Kennedy. Its focus was on getting into spiritual conversations with lost persons by asking two diagnostic questions: (1) "May I ask you a spiritual question?" and (2) "If you were to die tonight, and you were to stand before God, and he were to ask you, 'Why should I let you into my heaven?' what would you say?" Of course, there was only one right answer—a personal acknowledgement of repentance toward God and faith in the Lord Jesus Christ. There were wrong answers like living a good life or going to church. If someone gave a wrong answer, we were taught to transition the conversation by asking another question, "May I share with you how the Bible answers this question?" A scripted gospel presentation would then follow, and if favorably received, a sinner's prayer would hopefully be uttered in response to conclude.

While programs like *Evangelism Explosion* have been greatly used by God to mobilize believers for personal evangelism, the assumption that every lost person is uniform in terms of background and worldview and, therefore, can be given one of a few script answers to the diagnostic questions, underlies these approaches. In asking someone about how he or she would respond to a question from God himself at the judgment in heaven, the evangelist is in effect *presupposing* that this person *believes* in (among other things) a literal heaven, a judgment after death, and a personal God to whom there is accountability. Should the evangelist follow-up with a request to share the gospel message from the Bible, the uniqueness, authority, and accuracy of the Scriptures is likewise being presupposed. Now in the hometown of my youth, that supposition was a fairly safe one to make, because of the overarching Judeo-Christian ethos that permeated the culture.

But what if that assumption turns out to be inaccurate? What if you have a little different scenario unfold, like the one recalled by prominent philosopher and prolific author Norman Geisler in his book *I Don't Have Enough Faith to be an Atheist*:

> Knock, Knock.
> "Who's there?" (A man came to the door.)
> I stuck out my hand and said, "Hi! My name is Norm Geisler, this is my partner, Ron, and we're from the church at the end of the street."
> "I'm Don," the man replied, his eyes quickly sizing us up.
> Immediately I jumped into action with question one: "Don, do you mind if we ask you a spiritual question?"
> "No, go ahead," Don said boldly, apparently eager to have a Bible-thumper for dessert.
> I laid question two on him: "Don, if you were to die tonight and stand before God, and God were to ask you, 'Why should I let you into my heaven?' what would you say?"
> Don snapped back, "I'd say to God, 'Why *shouldn't* you let me into your heaven?'"
> Gulp . . . he wasn't supposed to say that! I mean, that answer wasn't in the book![1]

For many believers, the conversation would be over before it really even began—thwarted by this off-script response. This dialogue should serve to remind us that real evangelism is indeed *personal*, and thus cannot be accurately scripted to cover every conceivable response. Moreover,

---

1. Norman L. Geisler and Frank Turek, *I Don't Have Enough Faith to be an Atheist* (Wheaton: Crossway, 2004), 42; emphasis original.

the diagnostic questions themselves are revealed to be rather ineffective if the person being witnessed to does not share the same Christian theistic worldview of the evangelist.

One might be tempted to label the above encounter as an extreme example, but in actuality it is far more common than might appear at first glance. It is indeed a sobering reality to consider the fact that in North America today, lost people are starting further away from God than perhaps at any time in our history. Traditional evangelism strategies designed for a culture and context that assumes much pre-Christian knowledge on the part of the unregenerate must be reexamined and revised to meet the challenges of our so-called postmodern age. Presupposing concepts such as heaven, hell, sin, God, and even a subliminal knowledge of the cross must be reexamined in a post-Christian context.

It is precisely this post-Christian reality that I believe presents a great opportunity to see personal evangelism revitalized! Evangelicals through the years have done a fairly solid job of being able to tell someone *how* to become a Christian, but given today's atheistic and multi-religious context, that's not always enough. We must also be equipped and ready to tell persons *why* they should become Christians, and it is here where the necessity and value of apologetics can be more clearly seen.

The term *apologetics* comes from the Greek word *apology*, usually translated as either *answer* or *defense*, as in 1 Peter 3:15: "[B]ut honor the Messiah as Lord in your hearts. Always be ready to give a defense to anyone who asks you for a reason for the hope that is in you."[2] The language here is that of the courtroom; the place where arguments and evidence are offered in support of one's case with the goal of proving or disproving allegations of guilt. Christian apologetics has two primary functions:

1. To respond to criticisms or attacks against the faith.
2. To provide positive evidence supporting the truthfulness of faith claims.

Both of these tasks are vitally important given the challenges presented by today's cultural context.

But why is apologetics the key to revitalizing personal evangelism? Let's revisit that witnessing encounter from earlier to get the rest of the story and see Geisler's response:

2. Scripture quotations in this chapter are from the Holman Christian Standard Bible (HCSB).

After a split second of panic, I offered up a quick prayer and replied, "Don, if we knocked on your door seeking to come into your house, and you said to us, 'Why should I let you into my house?' and we responded, 'Why *shouldn't* you let us in?' what would you say?"

Don pointed his finger at my chest and sternly replied, "I would tell you where to go!"

I immediately shot back, "That's exactly what God is going to say to you!"

Don looked stunned for a second but then narrowed his eyes and said, "To tell you the truth: I don't believe in God. I'm an atheist."

"You're an atheist?"

"That's right!"

"Well, are you absolutely sure there is no God?" I asked him.

He paused, and said, "Well, no, I'm not *absolutely* sure. I guess it's possible there might be a God."

"So you're not really an atheist, then—you're an agnostic," I informed him, "because an atheist says, 'I know there is no God,' and an agnostic says, 'I don't know whether there is a God.'"

"Yeah . . . alright; so I guess I'm an agnostic then," he admitted.

Now this was real progress. With just one question we moved from atheism to agnosticism! But I still had to figure out what kind of agnostic Don was.

So I asked him, "Don, what kind of agnostic are you?"

He laughed as he asked, "What do you mean?" (He was probably thinking, "A minute ago, I was an atheist—I have no idea what kind of agnostic I am now!")

"Well, Don, there are two kinds of agnostics," I explained. "There's the *ordinary* agnostic who says he *doesn't* know anything for sure, and then there's the *ornery* agnostic who says he *can't* know anything for sure."

Don was sure about this. He said, "I'm the ornery kind. You can't know anything for sure."

Recognizing the self-defeating nature of his claim, I . . . [asked] him, "Don, if you say that you can't know anything for sure, then how do you know *that* for sure?"

Looking puzzled, he said, "What do you mean?"

Explaining it another way, I said, "How do you *know* for sure that you can't *know* anything for sure?"

I could see the light bulb coming on but decided to add one more point: "Besides, Don, you can't be a skeptic about everything because that would mean you'd have to doubt skepticism; but the more you doubt skepticism the more sure you become."

He relented. "Okay, I guess I really *can* know something for sure. I must be an *ordinary* agnostic."

Now we were really getting somewhere. With just a few questions, Don had moved from atheism through *ornery* agnosticism to *ordinary* agnosticism.

I continued, "Since you admit now that you *can* know, why *don't* you know that God exists?"

Shrugging his shoulders, he said, "Because nobody has shown me any evidence, I guess."

Now I launched the million-dollar question: "Would you be willing to look at some evidence?"

"Sure," he replied.[3]

Geisler, in response, gave Don a book,[4] and subsequently returned for a visit a little while later. Don would accept Jesus Christ as his personal Savior and Lord just a few short weeks thereafter.[5]

So did apologetics make a difference? Absolutely! How? Simply stated, apologetics allowed the *conversation to continue*. Rather than Don "checkmating" the visitation team with his supposed atheism, for example, Geisler used apologetic reasoning to overcome Don's answer of unbelief and continue the conversation, ultimately getting to the gospel itself. The goal was not to merely win an argument, nor to arrogantly display mental and verbal prowess for pride's sake, but rather to remove any supposed intellectual obstacles that would otherwise have kept Don from seriously considering the claims of Christ. Increasingly, evangelistic dialogues today will inevitably touch upon issues such as biblical authenticity and accuracy, the existence and nature of God, the reality of heaven and hell, and the deity and resurrection of Jesus Christ, because these truths are no

---

3. Geisler and Turek, *I Don't Have Enough Faith*, 42–43.

4. Frank Morison, *Who Moved the Stone?* (Grand Rapids: Zondervan, 1977).

5. Geisler and Turek, *I Don't Have Enough Faith*, 44. Geisler adds in conclusion, "Today Don is a deacon in a Baptist church near St. Louis, Missouri. Every Sunday morning, for years, he's driven the church bus through the local neighborhood to pick up those kids whose parents wouldn't come to church. His ministry has special meaning to me (Norm) because two men like Don (Mr. Costie and Mr. Sweetland) picked me up with a church bus more than 400 times—every Sunday from when I was nine until I was seventeen. I was in a position to accept Christ at seventeen largely because of that bus ministry. I guess it's true what they say, 'What goes around comes around,' even if it's just the Sunday school bus."

longer taken to be self-evident. For that matter, a portion of the population today even denies the existence of objective and absolute truth (a self-defeating claim, as already noted by Geisler)! Since, as Christians, we are committed to proclaiming the message of the One who is indeed *"the way, the truth,* and *the life"* (John 14:6), it may at times require us to share why we believe in a personal creator God before being able to tell someone that "God loves you and has a wonderful plan for your life."[6]

In light of the importance of apologetic training for personal evangelism, pastors should consider training their members (especially students) in areas such as:

1. Reliability of the Bible. Study the Bible's background, origins, development, canonicity, and historical accuracy. Study the reliability of its manuscripts and the care taken in preserving and translating its message. Compare that to the other ancient writings like Homer, Plato, and Aristotle.

2. Common objections to the gospel. Consider the universality of the gospel's message versus "it's just for you and it's not for me." Address the gospel's uniqueness in the face of today's subjectivity, as well as it's individuality in light of today's collectivism. Emphasize the reality of sin in light of today's self-justification.

3. The beliefs of different faith groups and cults, and the biblical basis of the church's doctrinal commitments. It is important for those who evangelize to understand other belief systems that differ so radically from biblical Christianity. It is helpful for those who evangelize to understand the teachings of the Church of Jesus Christ of Latter-day Saints (Mormons) and Jehovah's Witnesses. They should understand the foundational tenets of Catholicism, Judaism, and Islam. Given today's cultural context, a familiarity with Eastern religions like Buddhism and Hinduism also should be encouraged.

4. Studies on atheism, agnosticism, and secularism. Perhaps the trickiest, most complex, and closest to home challenge in contemporary evangelism is the impact of these worldviews. Their impact has been greatly seen in our educational systems, and many second generation Christians have been led into spiritual

6. See *The Four Spiritual Laws* tract, developed by the late Bill Bright, founder of Campus Crusade for Christ.

apathy as a result. Understanding these systems and how to reach people caught in their grip would be a great benefit to the New Testament evangelist.

Determine specific belief patterns in the area of your church. There may be the predominance of a cult or religious group which needs special attention. Customize your training to the needs of your church and its surroundings. This type of training provides a dual blessing for church members: it establishes them in their faith and allows them to be better equipped to reach others for Christ.

The times may indeed be a-changing, but our mission and mandate have not been altered. The challenges are great, but the opportunity is even greater. We need to have a passion and priority for doing not only the work of an evangelist, but also that of an apologist, if we are serious about reaching our Jerusalem and beyond for Christ in this present age. I believe this commitment is the key to seeing individual believers and local New Testament churches be truly mobilized for effective Great Commission outreach.

15

Servanthood Evangelism as a Bridge
to the Gospel

David Wheeler

WASHING FEET AND SHARING CHRIST

Learning the Power of the Towel and Basin

NEXT TO THE HOLY Spirit, the Bible, and the gospel message, there is nothing more powerful or useful in the call of evangelism than the towel and the basin. As demonstrated by Jesus in John 13, the example of washing the disciple's feet serves as a reminder of Christlike humility and surrender that should be manifested in the lives of all true believers. One thing is for sure, it is a life-changing concept in evangelism when put into daily practice.

An Agnostic is Saved

While I was in college, a young man named Steve began attending a weekly prayer group that was hosted in our dorm. When asked about his faith, he quickly responded that he was an agnostic in search of the truth.

After several weeks spent building a relationship, Steve was invited to stay after one of the meetings in order to discuss his questions related to Christianity. He seemed intrigued and even stated that he wanted to "believe," but he "just couldn't *see* it." At that point, one of the co-workers in the prayer group stood up and quickly left the room, only to return a few minutes later with a couple towels and a basin of water. After setting the basin at my feet, he then turned to Steve and said, "If you can't see what faith in Christ is all about, we will show you." He proceeded to wash my feet, allowing me to return the privilege. Afterwards, we prayed and sang a few worship songs; it was evident that the Holy Spirit was present.

Steve later explained that when he returned to his dorm room that evening, he was confused about what he believed and vowed never to return to the prayer group. However, all of this changed early the next morning. After laying in bed from midnight until about 3:30 a.m., desperately trying to forget what he had "seen and heard" (see Acts 4:18–20), all he could think about was Christ and especially the humble demonstration of washing feet. After hours of feeling God's conviction for sin and being unable to rest, he slipped to his knees and told Christ, "If you are there and if you are real as I saw and experienced tonight, I need you Lord Jesus to save me, I surrender everything . . . please come into my life!"

Steve's life radically changed through the power of genuine faith as demonstrated through washing feet and proclaiming the saving message of Christ. For lack of a better description, we call this biblical approach *servanthood evangelism*.

SO . . . WHAT IS SERVANTHOOD EVANGELISM?

Servanthood Evangelism Defined

Servanthood evangelism involves intentionally sharing Christ by modeling biblical servanthood. It is the simplest, most transferable and, yes, most fun approach for moving believers closer to a lifestyle marked by consistent witnessing. With that said, servanthood evangelism is also the most biblical approach: *intentionally* demonstrating Christ's love and message to an unsaved world.

Servanthood Evangelism Described

Servanthood evangelism is a combination of simple acts of kindness and intentional personal evangelism. The concept is as old as the New Testament. Like many profound truths, this one is so simple it is easily missed: Get a group of believers, for instance at a local church, and begin practicing simple acts of kindness with an *intentional* aim toward evangelism. In many cases, such acts of kindness open the door for the greatest expression of kindness a Christian can give: the gospel.

Note: The aspect of *intentionally* connecting the verbal message of Christ through acts of service is what differentiates servanthood evangelism from the negative connotations of the Social Gospel movement that became popular with liberal theologians over the past century.

Servanthood Evangelism Delivered

It is essential that Christians understand what kindness means; it does not mean telling people what they want to hear so they will feel good about themselves. It also does not mean doing mere acts of kindness with no intended purpose towards evangelism. Granted, there are valuable ministries, such as taking a loaf of bread to newcomers, and others, which are helpful, but they are not explicitly evangelistic. While servanthood evangelism acknowledges that this kind of ministry does not always result in evangelistic conversations—it is by nature *intentionally evangelistic.*

However, by no means does servant evangelism seek to coerce. When doing an act of kindness, the witness may say, "I am doing this to show the love of Jesus in a practical way." Then, as the Holy Spirit opens the door, usually through the individual responding, "Why are you doing this?" the one performing the act of servanthood has a captive audience and proceeds to share their conversion testimony coupled with a simple gospel presentation. If the other person is not open to having a discussion, the witness goes no further, except to offer quality evangelistic literature and a brief time of prayer.

You will want to note, however, that years of pastoral experience reveals that servanthood evangelism leads to a full presentation of Christ much more often if the concept of servanthood is not ignored. It all depends on the leadership of the Holy Spirit and the boldness of the witness to verbalize their faith.

HOW DO YOU APPROACH SERVANTHOOD EVANGELISM?

Personally/Individually

It is not by accident that we are discussing how to do servanthood evangelism on a personal/individual level before explaining how it is manifested in a corporate setting. Unless it first becomes a lifestyle that is practiced by individual Christians in their daily lives, it will certainly not take hold in a congregational setting.

So, how can the individual develop a lifestyle of evangelism marked by intentional service?

Learn to identify needs

The first step in developing an evangelistic lifestyle is very simple. *Learn how to identify the needs of the people.* Police officers are trained to analyze situations immediately. If there is a problem or something suspicious, a good officer should be able to handle the situation in a professional and effective manner. Much in the same way, we as Christians need to train ourselves to spot the needs of hurting people.

Matthew 6:32–33 states plainly that while the unsaved spend their lives chasing after their own needs, Christians ought to first seek after the kingdom of God and his righteousness. In other words, as Christ followers, we must first be concerned with advancing God's kingdom and not our own. That means taking the focus from ourselves and aiming it towards those around us who are in desperate need of an encounter with Christ.

Jesus modeled this attitude in John 4 when he and is disciples traveled through Samaria, (this went against Jewish religious tradition). Verse 4 states that "it was necessary" that Jesus went through Samaria. This was undoubtedly confusing for his disciples, because as good Jews they would never intentionally travel through Samaria. It is not until verse 7 and Jesus' encounter with the woman at the well that we are given a glimpse of why he chooses to go against Jewish tradition. As the story progresses, it becomes obvious that his genuine concern for the woman's spiritual condition far outweighed his desire for adhering to religious traditions.

Go where needs are

The next step to developing an evangelistic lifestyle is to *go where the needs are.* Returning to the example of Jesus in John 4; we can see that Jesus not only identified the needs of the people, but he went *to* them regardless of how it was perceived by others. As his followers, we need to have the same attitude when it comes to evangelism.

Christians must indentify needs and be willing to go where they exist, even if it means going into an unpleasant or unfamiliar setting. Too many Christians play it safe by avoiding hurting areas in favor of focusing their witnessing efforts on less abrasive and less challenging locations. *This was not the approach of Christ!*

Case in point, the woman at the well was not the type of person who would have been accepted by religious leaders in the temple. Not only was she a "half-breed," according to the Jews, but she was an adulterous woman, maybe even a harlot. In the typical Jewish mind at that time, this made her less than human, not deserving of their attention or God's grace. Samaritans were the offspring of Jews that had intermarried with people of other faiths, and eventually mixed pagan traditions and teachings of Judaism. With that in mind, it is not hard to see why the Samaritans were viewed so lowly by the Jews. Not only were they not full-blooded Jews, but they had compromised their theology and had abandoned the precious faith of their fathers.

This makes the events of John 4 even more spectacular. While the disciples were disconnected from the woman's needs and appeared extremely uncomfortable, Jesus was not hindered in his desire to impact the woman and the people of the surrounding community.

Initiate a plan

The third step is to develop a life that is characterized by evangelism. When Jesus went to the woman at the well, he had a proven strategy. He listened to her politely and spoke to her in a non-aggressive tone. Eventually, he confronted her with the truth without embarrassment or manipulation. Only then, when she was ready, did he offer the ultimate solution to her problem.

Once we identify the needs of people, we must initiate a plan to serve and meet that need. This is where the fun of servanthood evangelism comes into play. For example, let's say your neighbor's yard is full of leaves. According to the size of the job, the obvious response is to secure willing helpers from the church to assist in the servant opportunity. If you are sensitive and willing, hundreds of possibilities will soon arise.

This step centers on doing intentional acts of kindness for other people, simply because they are loved by God and made in his image. Isn't this what Christ's sacrifice was all about? Did he not come to us while we were yet sinners and die even for the ones who were hurling insults at him while he hung on the cross?

Indeed, the incarnation of Jesus should be seen as the ultimate expression of servanthood evangelism. While he identified the world's need for forgiveness and a restored relationship with the Father, he didn't stop there. Jesus was willing to *GO* where the need existed, namely to earth; and so he wrapped himself in human flesh and came as one of us. He initiated a plan to meet the desperate need of humanity: to die on the cross in our place in order to make restoration to the Father possible for all people. He didn't give up on us and leave us to our own devices to figure out how to live the Christian life. Christ sent "another," the Holy Spirit who is our comforter and sustainer. This leads us to the last step to developing a lifestyle of evangelism.

Be willing to stay

Once we initiate a plan to meet the needs of the people, we need to be willing to stay and invest our lives through servanthood. In John 4, after Jesus had ministered to the people from Sychar, he stayed with them for two days. He stayed with them longer because he cared for them and wanted to develop lasting relationships.

This is exactly what we need to do as we try to develop lives that are characterized by evangelism and service. We need to be willing to forge relationships with people in our spheres of influence. They need to know that they are not just numbers and that we are not simply marking off *evangelism* on our own personal list of things to do. Once this happens, people will realize that we care about them individually. This is one of the best illustrations of Christ's love for humanity.

Corporately

Where does Servanthood Evangelism fit into your Congregation's strategic plan for outreach?

After working in a church consultation role for over fifteen years, and having met with literally hundreds of congregations, new and old, of various sizes, and from numerous regions across North America, it is obvious that we have lost sight of the basic biblical principles that create genuine growth and lasting expansion of the Kingdom. Sadly, the concept of *servanthood* and meeting needs is rarely mentioned

When contacted, I almost always hear the same requests for the latest programs or "silver bullets" that will bring instantaneous growth! In reality, while most programs will work for a season, this kind of reasoning does not deal with the heart of the problem, nor will it lead to strategic thinking. This type of logic tends to lead congregations to develop an attitude of entitlement and that it is the clergy's responsibility to accomplish evangelism and church growth.

At this point, I usually ask the church leader to back up and take a long look at the overall ministries of his congregation. After more in-depth study and honest appraisal of the situation, it is normal to find a church calendar filled with countless activities and unconnected evangelism events spread throughout the year. After further probing, it is also usual to find a church budget, overall structure, and prayer list (if one exists) that are heavily focused on meeting the inward needs of the congregation.

After reality sets in, the church leader will normally begin searching for solutions. It is here that I usually introduce the *three basic biblical principles* to moving the congregation in a strategic direction, especially in relation to their evangelism ministry.

The *first* basic principle is the need to plow the fields through prayer. As Psalm 126:5 says, "Those who sow in tears will reap with joyful shouting" (NASB). It is shocking how few congregations have an ongoing prayer ministry that includes consistent intercession for the unsaved. In most cases, prayer lists are filled with local church needs of all kinds, especially physical and emotional. Unfortunately, for some reason, the unsaved are completely ignored. As Minette Drumwright, the former director of the International Prayer Strategy for the International Mission Board of the Southern Baptist Convention once observed, "Someone said, in our churches we spend more time praying to keep sick saints out of heaven than we do praying lost people into heaven."[1]

So, what is the solution? To begin with, a congregation needs to keep an ongoing list of unsaved people and begin daily to pray for each person by name. This should also be done in a public manner every time the church comes together for worship services or Bible study.

It is then that the prayer ministry of the church should go mobile through the regular activity of *prayer-walking*. There is no greater pre-evangelism activity for a congregation to practice, than regular prayer-walking, especially when it is united with simple servanthood evangelism projects.

For instance, imagine delivering packages of cookies to neighbors as you walk and pray. You can even attach a note that says, "If you

1. Minette Drumwright, *The Life that Prays: Reflections on Prayer as a Strategy* (Birmingham: Women's Missionary Union, 2001).

think these cookies are sweet, then you need to taste the fellowship at _____ church." Always be on the lookout to share a verbal witness.

This leads to the *second* basic principle: consistently plant the gospel seed. The unfortunate truth is that most congregations are so harvest/results driven that they ignore the vital importance of consistently planting seeds. In most cases, it is popular to blame the culture for declining results. The truth is, the greatest way to kill the harvest is to ignore the plowing and planting. Once again, look back at Psalm 126. It says in verse 6, "He who goes to and fro weeping, carrying his bag of seed, Shall indeed come again with a shout of joy, bringing his sheaves with him" (NASB).

This is why servanthood evangelism is so important to a strategic plan for outreach. While most congregations will admit that only 5 to 10 percent of the people will ever participate in an outreach activity, it doesn't have to be this way! Because of our over-dependence upon multiple programs—that require memorization and tend to be time constraining, among other things—*we have unintentionally made evangelism too difficult for the average church member to feel like they can participate.*

So, what is the remedy? Servanthood evangelism is a very effective mobilization and pre-evangelism tool, especially for the large percentage of people who are presently inactive in sharing their faith. In many cases servanthood evangelism will serve as a first step to drawing people into more in-depth evangelism approaches. Regardless, by serving others as Christ's ambassadors it is a tremendous way to spread the gospel seed, and in doing so, to discover prospects for *intentional* evangelism efforts.

In a strategic sense, it is worth noting that servanthood evangelism does not compete with existing approaches in outreach. Rather, it compliments every approach to evangelism. Imagine for a moment the possible number of seeds that can be sown in a three-hour period spent wrapping Christmas presents for free at the local mall in December or washing cars for free in June. What about giving out free soft drinks in the parking lot of a grocery store, washing windshields in the same parking lot, or as mentioned earlier, going door-to-door in a new community with a small package of cookies and a note?

Agriculturally

Let's review the biblical (agricultural) principles. In order to expand the kingdom, people have to consistently do the *plowing* and *planting*. In turn, this leads to the *third* principle, which is to *harvest*, as God blesses the efforts. According to 1 Corinthians 3:6, while others may "plant" and "water," it is God, and him only, who gives the "increase" (KJV). This means our call as believers is to be faithful in plowing and planting, always ready to share when the Father draws the net for the harvest.

This is the beauty of servanthood evangelism. It is an effective lifestyle approach, regardless if one is *plowing, planting,* or *harvesting.* Considering the notion that much of the non-religious world has preconceived objections related to Christianity, servanthood is a powerful tool when applied through the life of a genuine believer. In most cases, it is realistic to assume that people will not believe the truth of the gospel until it is manifested in the actions and attitudes of professing born-again Christians. *The attraction of a servant life that is connected back to Christ and his message as a "bridge" in effective evangelism cannot be overstated!*

HOW DO YOU "APPLY" SERVANTHOOD EVANGELISM IN YOUR CHURCH?

The following is an acrostic representing a process that will assist you and your church as you seek to implement servanthood evangelism:

S: Seek the Father's Power and Presence

Prayer is essential to effective evangelism. Pray for those who will be participating in the servanthood evangelism projects, as well as those who will be reached.

Planning regular prayer-walks or similar activities in the areas you seek to saturate is also advisable. By mapping out target areas, church members can begin to pray over particular streets and houses, neighborhoods, and shopping centers before the servanthood evangelism activities. Earnest prayer is essential to every evangelistic opportunity or approach.

E: Enlist the People

Make sure trained witnesses will be involved. These people will be your team leaders.

Always provide opportunities for training. Suggestions include a training clinic on Saturday morning, a banquet on Friday evening, a discipleship class, or a presentation on servanthood evangelism from a biblical perspective during Sunday morning worship, in Sunday School, and so forth. Have a time of open commitment where everyone (including children, youth, senior adults) can sign up. Team leaders can use the list of volunteers to recruit participants for specific projects. It is strongly advised to couple the training with immediate opportunities for involvement through a variety of servanthood evangelism projects.

Providing opportunities to experience servanthood evangelism is always the best approach to ongoing enlistment. Skeptical church members can quickly and easily be swayed after experiencing the joy and fellowship of personal involvement.

Note: Do not use sign-up sheets to the exclusion of personal enlistment. A sign-up sheet without a personal face-to-face invitation makes it too easy for church members to pass-the-buck of evangelistic responsibility. *All Christians need to be held personally accountable to participate in serving others and sharing their faith.*

R: Resources

One of the strengths of servanthood evangelism is that many of the projects usually do not require a large amount of financial resources. Nevertheless, there is the necessity to gather resources for specific projects.

Some congregations have chosen to dedicate a room or small area of the church as a supply pantry for materials needed for servanthood evangelism projects. Church members are encouraged to provide various materials (i.e., boxes of microwave popcorn, glass cleaner, cases of sodas, light bulbs, packaged foods, nine-volt batteries, rakes, and shovels) to be used by the teams as they plan projects. Although it is advisable to eventually include servanthood evangelism as a line item in the church budget to pay for cards and other incidentals, it is not required.

By keeping the regular needs and activities in front of the church on a consistent basis, most of the projects are usually completed through the generosity of interested church members who are enthusiastic about the process. In some cases, community business leaders are willing to donate needed supplies as a way of participating in public service projects. For instance, an Indiana church informed a local popcorn distributor of their plans of saturating their area with microwave bags. As a result, the distributor voluntarily agreed to provide all the needed supplies. As always, God rewards commitment and faithfulness.

V: Vacate the church

After mapping out your community and targeting specific areas for saturation through servanthood evangelism, it is time to "vacate" the church walls and "invade" the community to share the wonderful love of Jesus.

One scenario has been to send out several evangelism teams during the worship hour Sunday morning or every evening during revival services. With recent statistics revealing that more people are at home from 9:00 a.m. to noon Sunday than at any other time of the week, the potential is endless. Admittedly, this approach may not be for everyone. However, such options have been very effective.

You may choose to set up larger projects that target the participation of the entire church body or simply allow the servanthood evangelism teams to complete community projects at least once a month or every six weeks. It is usually advisable to do both.

The larger projects are a good time to enlist new participants. The team approach allows greater flexibility. You will also want to meet with the team leaders at least once a month as a time of encouragement, accountability, and planning; the meeting can take place at any time of the day or week. This is part of the flexibility of servanthood evangelism.

E: Evaluate

After a time of participation, always plan to have a reporting period for evaluation. Undoubtedly, this time will encourage participants through sharing stories and experiences. Most important, this time provides the opportunity to report names of prospects and those who prayed to receive Christ. Be sure to immediately follow-up on individuals who have made salvation decisions. Participants can also share their "best practices," and what they might do differently the next time.

Always encourage creativity relating to new ideas. Before dismissing in prayer, the pastor and team leaders should share about upcoming projects so the excitement and commitment continues. It is imperative to keep the vision alive.

FOUNDATIONAL PRINCIPLES FOR
SERVANTHOOD EVANGELISM

It stands to reason that anything with so much potential for good also has the potential for misuse and even harm. Therefore, three foundational principles must be expressed:

Those Participating Must Be Intentionally Evangelistic

Servanthood without evangelism is social ministry without a biblical purpose. For years, the legacy of theological liberalism has been the emphasis on changing societal taboos and meeting physical needs. Sadly, these acts of kindness are often done to the exclusion of verbalizing the message of Christ.

This must not be the case with servanthood evangelism. Participants should always be *intentional* in verbalizing their faith. A person may ask, "Why are you doing this?" Your response should be, "to share a personal testimony and seek to present the gospel." While it is true that you may not get the opportunity to witness on every occasion, if you remain intentional and biblical, God will give the increase.

Those Participating Must Genuinely Care about the Needs of People

In our success-driven society, the church and its leaders can become more motivated by the increases in baptisms, church membership, and offerings than by the potential transformation of human life by the saving message of the gospel. Eventually, people will recognize if you are not genuine in your concern for their well-being.

In Matthew 9:35–38, Jesus is described as having compassion for the multitudes because "they were distressed and downcast like sheep without a shepherd." He then moves immediately to the subject of the harvest and the need for disciples who could work in his harvest fields. If, indeed, Christ is the example for ministry, it seems logical that he expects the same genuine compassion and love from his disciples as they serve and work in his fields. Servanthood evangelism done without genuine compassion for people is nothing more than a Christianized version of the old bait and switch. A caring and compassionate attitude is always a necessity.

Eventually, Those Participating Must Be Equipped as Personal Witnesses

One of the beauties of servanthood evangelism is that it does not require one to be a witnessing expert. In fact, because it is such a great entry-level approach to personal evangelism, a person can participate on a servanthood evangelism team without having been an active witness in the past. Nevertheless, to remain intentionally focused on pure evangelism, it is imperative that each group has someone who is experienced at leading people to Christ. This also provides a mentoring opportunity, as the inexperienced participants can learn how to witness through watching and listening to others.

Eventually, it is suggested that every active participant receive witness training that includes the use of their personal testimony and a simple presentation of the gospel.

WHY SERVANTHOOD EVANGELISM IS EFFECTIVE AND ESSENTIAL

To *ignore* evangelism is, of course, not acceptable, as proclaimed through the words of Christ in Acts 1:8, where he states, "You will be My witnesses."

One approach to evangelism is to merely provide the right *information* through various presentations of the gospel. While this is essential, by itself it does not properly represent the whole picture of evangelism as an *incarnational* expression of both the message and the lifestyle of a redeemed individual.

Biblical evangelism is the *intentional* mixture of the *informational* message and the *incarnational* expression through one's lifestyle. This is why servanthood evangelism is effective and essential to any outreach strategy. Consider the following explanations:

1. *Servanthood evangelism demonstrates the heart of Christ.* It is impossible to divorce Jesus' message of redemption from the man he represented to the world. He was not a hypocrite. It is safe to say that his behavior matched his beliefs!

2. *Servanthood evangelism addresses the sin of isolation.* In a day when personal contact is avoided through the use of technology, the concept of *intentional* and *consistent* servanthood forces Christians to engage with hurting humanity in their spheres of daily influence. Christians are never off duty.

3.   *Servanthood evangelism addresses the fallacy of the "I do not know enough to share Christ" syndrome.* The traditional programmatic approach to training people for evangelism can be stifling when it comes to application. In most cases people are educated and then mobilized into the field. However, this was not the approach of Christ. The Bible indicates that Jesus sent the disciples out as "sheep unto wolves" (Matt 10;16) and promised he would "give them the words to speak" (Matt 10:19) when the time came. Servanthood evangelism encourages the immediate mobilization of Christians into the fields *as* they are being trained in order to tear down the walls of hesitation that may arise.

4.   *Servanthood evangelism encourages a "missional" lifestyle.* Properly understood, Servanthood evangelism is not a *program*, rather it is a *process*. It is not something one does only at the church building. On the contrary, it is a lifestyle that *invades* everything one does on a daily basis. The ultimate goal is for every Christian to see their neighborhood, workplace, school, and so on, as their "Jerusalem" to be evangelized.

5.   *Servanthood evangelism speaks the language of contemporary culture.* The old saying, "actions speak louder than words" is especially true when addressing a postmodern culture. There is a very real sense today that one has to earn the right to be heard. *While biblical truth is constant, it can be compromised in the eyes of an unsaved world if one's behavior is not consistent with one's Christian beliefs.*

FIVE SERVANTHOOD EVANGELISM PROJECTS THAT WORK

1.   1. Gas "buy-down." Secure a local gas station and buy-down every gallon of gas that is sold from 11:00 a.m. to 1:00 p.m. by twenty-five cents per gallon, up to twenty gallons. If the gas is $3.00 per gallon, it would be sold for $2.75 per gallon and the church will make up the difference. Church members will pump the gas and clean windshields.

2.   Adopt local public schools. Take fresh donuts to the teacher's lounge each week. Volunteer to take up tickets for sporting events or feed the teachers for free on in-service days.

3. Have church members adopt their surrounding community by mapping out their neighborhood and praying for at least twenty *unchurched* families. Encourage them to cook a meal or dessert for one or more of the families each week and utilize the delivery as an opportunity to ask for prayer requests and to get acquainted. Use good dishes so that they will have additional contact when they are returned. One can also shovel snow, rake leaves, mow yards, provide free babysitting, and so on. Acknowledging birthdays, graduations, and anniversaries can also be effective.

4. Adopt special days. For instance, give away chocolate on Valentine's Day or carnations on Mother's Day. Cookies work well throughout the year, especially at Christmas. As for Halloween, do reverse trick or treating by going out to neighbors and delivering small gifts of appreciation. Be on the lookout for servant projects at each of the houses you visit and be willing to offer assistance.

5. Use "intentional connection cards." The cards can say something as simple as, "We just want you to know that we care." On the back might be a small map to the church and other pertinent information. The cards are good for any servant evangelism activity, but when used by Christians—in cases like anonymously paying someone's bill in a restaurant, or paying for the drive-through meal of the passengers behind you—it is an effective way to plant seeds. For instance, a pastor in Richmond, Virginia, recently paid the check for the car behind him at a fast-food drive-through. He also tipped the worker and gave the person a connection card. When he returned to the same drive-through the next week, he was pleasantly surprised to find out that his act of service created a small movement. It seems that the next fourteen cars after him repeated his kind deed and also paid the check for the car behind them. Never underestimate the power of servanthood![2]

I call on Christians everywhere to mobilize their church to outreach by holding a towel and taking a basin, just as Jesus did when he washed the disciples' feet, and intentionally serve others for the sake of sharing the gospel.

---

2. For further information, go to www.servantevangelism.com. Also see the *Servanthood Evangelism Manual* by Alvin Reid and David Wheeler (Atlanta, GA: North American Mission Board of the Southern Baptist Convention, SS 1998, 2009).

16

Effective Outreach through Sports Evangelism

Josef Solc

ONE OF THE GREATEST problems the church is facing in the twenty-first century is the lack of interest among secular people to listen to the gospel message. Ninety-five percent of them do not visit a church of their own volition. When Christians visit them in their houses, they encounter a cold reception. The loss of Christendom in the Western world is undeniable. Unless we find new ways to attract the secular people around us, we will not fulfill the Great Commission that Christ gave us.

I want to prove that Christianity can find a way to open the door to secular people by joining them in sports activities. This is an indirect approach that can build a foundation for relationships with non-Christians. Sports provide a language that is understood all over the world. Such a communication is available in spite of cultural, social, political, religious, and linguistic barriers. Sports can open the door to individual encounters that are so important for Christians who desire to share their faith. These encounters are limitless. Two skiers can meet on the chair lift and spend the rest of the day skiing together and enjoying the day of healthy activity. A group of ice hockey players can play for fun and after the game go to relax over a meal in the restaurant with an opportunity to discuss their scoring chances and future plans. And who would challenge the fact that some people play golf just to socialize with others in a beautiful environment of a well-groomed golf course. These examples could go on and on, but it will suffice to say that in a world that is as impersonal as ours, sports bring individuals together.

Sports also engage nearly all nations of the world in a unified sports experience we call the Olympic Games. The world stops for two weeks every other year when all sports-minded people, about 95 percent of all people living in our world, are interested in the results of worldwide competition. They cheer the athletes from their respective countries and are elated when they win medals or are saddened when they lose. Yet, in spite of the joy of victory and the despair of defeat, the world gets together over and over again to compete in sports. This achievement is unparalleled in relationships among people and nations.

There is a yearning in the hearts of Christians to bring the world together through faith in Jesus Christ who is the Savior of the world and who is capable of improving the life here on earth and who offers eternal life with him in heaven. But the truth of the matter is that some nations will not even allow Christians to present the good news in their lands. This is also true of secular individuals who reject or are not interested in anything Christians do or say. This fact looms as an enormous obstacle for the evangelization of the world. Our traditional ways of doing evangelism have not been producing desired results; therefore, we must discover ways that open the doors for renewed efforts to reach all nations.

One way to influence people around us is through sports. Many people either play sports or love to watch them. Christians can join them in a non-threatening way and can establish relationships with them. An invitation to attend a church service may go unheeded, but an offer to play sports will be joyfully accepted. Strangers will speak the same language. They can engage in an activity that is good for their physical and emotional wellness. Before long they are not strangers, but friends. The sport they love will provide a common ground that will facilitate opportunities that did not even exist before.

As a pastor, I did my share of outreach in the community around my church. I knocked on thousands of doors, but only seldom did I feel welcome. As if I were an intruder who encroached on people's time, they didn't want to give. I was convinced of the urgency to proclaim the gospel and at the same time I questioned the way I went about it. When our church moved to a new location, we bought a racquet club with twelve tennis courts, a large swimming pool, a soccer field, and a clubhouse. We invited the people of our community to enjoy our facility. We organized tennis clinics and offered swimming lessons. Non-Christians, who would have never thought of rubbing shoulders with Christians before, participated gladly. I remember especially one tennis player who loved to play tennis but showed no interest in spiritual things. First, I just played tennis with him, but later on he started asking questions about things concerning God and heaven. I was able to answer some questions he had, and then he was willing to hear more. Eventually, I presented the gospel to him and he became a Christian. I baptized him and taught him in a Sunday school class while we continued playing tennis as well. A similar scenario happened with others who came to swim or to play tennis.

CHRISTIANITY AND SPORTS

Sports and religion have existed together from the ancient times. The Egyptians worshipped the goddess Sehet as the goddess of sport. The Greeks held the ancient Olympic Games for the first time in 776 BC on Olympia, known for its magnificent temple to Zeus. They honored Zeus through the Olympic Games every four years. These games were so important that the Greeks counted their time in Olympiads rather than by years. Olympia became the very center of the religious, sporting, and cultural events in ancient Greece. Those who participated in the Olympic Games did so as unto their gods. The religious element could not be denied. Since these events became a celebration of pagan religiosity, the emperor Theodosius ordered the end of the Olympic Games in AD 393. He considered the games to be in competition with Christianity. He would not tolerate other activities that would challenge the supreme position of the official Christian religion of the Roman Empire. Here was the very first conflict between sports and Christianity. Theodosius's defense of Christianity was alien to the approach the apostle Paul would have taken. Paul had no problem comparing athletes to Christians, since both were examples of striving to win a race. He wrote:

> Do you not know that in a race all the runners run, but only one gets the prize? Run in such a way as to get the prize. Everyone who competes in the games goes into strict training. They do it to get a crown that will not last; but we do it to get a crown that will last forever. Therefore do not run like a man running aimlessly; I do not fight like a man beating the air. No, I beat my body and make it my slave so that after I have preached to others, I myself will not be disqualified for the prize. (1 Cor 9:24–27)

Paul probably watched the Isthmus games in Corinth while he stayed there and was sufficiently impressed with those athletes to make comparisons between their effort and that of Christians. He realized that in order to reach the masses of the first century, he could not overlook the appeal of sports. He familiarized himself with sports and contextualized his approach so that he would reach all people.

Early Christian leaders did not follow Paul's example. They did not catch up with the masses, as is evident in Chrysostom's statement, "If you ask Christians who is Amos or Obadiah, how many apostles there were or prophets, they stand mute; but if you ask them about the horses or drivers they answer with more solemnity than rhetors."[1] No matter how much the Christian leaders disliked sports; they did not prevent Christians from being enchanted by them. And when the idolatrous elements of sports were removed, the tide could not be stopped. When Christianity became the empire's religion, Christians participated in their culture and embraced sports, but they did not forget to be constantly critical of possible abuses connected with sports. Their involvement was not overwhelming, because of the lack of leisure time. People in general did not have much time left after working each day to provide for the basic necessities of life. The military provided more leisure for soldiers in time of peace to engage in sports like fencing and archery. These sports became part of the festivities enjoyed by many spectators.

Moving on to the Reformation period, some reduction of the Roman Catholic influence opened the door to secularization and more activity in sports. The Puritans objected to playing sports on Sundays in spite of the permission spelled out in the Book of Sports in 1617 that allowed games to be played after worship services. This decision only increased the friction between sports and Christianity. Sports then flourished on their own, offering a new variety of sports such as boxing, soccer, and cricket. But it was not until the Industrial Revolution that sports grew in numbers and that spectators were willing and capable to pay for watching their favorite teams.

The church tried to regain its position in the progressively secularized world. The eighteenth and nineteenth century's revivals, both in England and America, propelled the church on the stage of the cultural environment that included sports. Some Christians seized this oppor-

---

1. Gregory Baum and John Coleman, *Concilium: Religion in the Eighties: Sport* (Edinburgh: T&T Clark, 1989), 93.

tunity to reconsider the relationship between Christianity and sports. They introduced sports into Christian schools as part of a permanent curriculum, and they promoted sports as preparation for life. They believed that sports would enhance discipline, teamwork, courage, and determination. The positive outcome of this approach resulted in graduates who lived the Christian principles at home and on the foreign mission field. They showed Christian perseverance and skills that made a difference in the world.

The next period of significant progress in sports relating to Christianity was "muscular Christianity." The term appeared first in a review of Charles Kingsley's book *Two Years Ago* in the February 21, 1857, issue of Saturday Review. Thomas Hughes, a personal friend of Kingsley's, developed the concept of "muscular Christianity." He compared muscular Christians in 1860 with the "musclemen" in his book *Tom Brown at Oxford*. He wrote, "The only point in common between the two being, that both hold it to be a good thing to have strong and well-exercised bodies. . . . Here all likeness ends. . . . The least of the muscular Christians has hold of the old chivalrous and Christian belief, that a man's body is given to be trained and brought into subjection, and then used for the protection of the weak, the advancement of all righteous causes, and the subduing of the earth which God has given to the children of men."[2] Kingsley and Hughes provided impetus for other scholars, such as Gerald Redmont, Peter McIntosh, Andrew Miracle, Roger Rees, and Michael Oriard, to pursue the theme of muscular Christianity. Their definitions varied, but the four main characteristics could be summed up as "manliness, health, morality, and patriotism."[3] This core ideology was not always interpreted unanimously. It meant different things to different evangelical Christians like Amos Alfonso Stagg, Dwight L. Moody, Charles T. Studd, and Luther Gulick. These small variations did not keep them, however, from affecting significantly the relationship of sports and Christianity within the larger context of society.

Here we have to make a point that could be easily overlooked. Muscular Christianity did not originate in a vacuum. There were societal changes in progress that could have been ignored by Christians and not used for affecting the society. First, industrialization opened the door for

2. Thomas Hughes, *Tom Brown at Oxford* (London: Macmillan, 1861), 83.

3. Tony Ladd and James A. Mathisen, *Muscular Christianity: Evangelical Protestants and the Development of American Sport* (Grand Rapids: Baker, 1999), 16.

new means of production and consumption. More leisure time resulted for workers in major cities where teams found fans to support professional sports. Second, fourteen million immigrants came to the United States between 1865 and 1900. The increase in population meant more spectators in stadiums and more revenues for sports. Third, educational facilities were built and students participated in competitive sports. Fourth, with increased productivity, there was more money for capital development. Owners and managers of teams provided structures for building sports facilities and formed leagues that would declare through elimination the ultimate winner. All of this could have gone unnoticed by Christians. They could have gone on doing church in their sanctuaries, as it is done quite often even in our day. But the proponents of muscular Christianity saw a unique opportunity to be right in the midst of these major changes. They knew they could serve as catalysts in this new era. A contextualized Christian movement was born first in England and later on in America. But this linkage was not to continue without problems. There were periods of engagement and disengagement between muscular Christianity and sports due to strong critical forces in the evangelical community. Billy Sunday, an exceptional baseball player, who became a famous evangelist, saw the benefits of linking Christianity with sports. He used baseball illustrations in his preaching, won many people for Christ, but turned against sports later in his ministry. The next great evangelist, Billy Graham, was instrumental in a new engagement with sports by asking major professional athletes to testify about their faith during his crusades. He also held his meetings in the biggest stadiums throughout the world. People came to hear him and felt at home in familiar surroundings. This helped him gain important credibility among nominal Christians and sports minded people in general. Graham reintroduced the church and sports to each other and so overcame, to a certain degree, the cultural isolation of Christianity in an increasingly secular society of the twentieth century.

Parachurch organizations discovered the field of sports as a new way to connect with the unchurched. New organizations came into existence, such as Sports Ambassadors, the Fellowship of Christian Athletes, Athletes in Action, the International Sports Coalition, and Sports Outreach America. Because these organizations were created for the purpose of engaging Christians in the field of sports, the continuation of Christian ministries among sports-minded people was not only guaranteed but mushroomed. Sports, education, and evangelical churches invented networks and programs of mutual cooperation that flourished and are with us in the twenty-first century. The question remains whether this progress will continue or not.

The flux of change in our postmodern world is in constant motion like a runaway train. We must figure out how to climb into this train and let our presence known because the people inside of the train face a grave danger, at least from the Christian perspective of God's judgment. There might be many ways to do it, but I will limit my suggestion to our present topic of outreach through sports evangelism. Sports are conquering the Western culture and receiving more attention than anything and anybody else. Millions of people would rather go to a football game than to read a scientific book. Millions of parents would rather take their kids to a baseball practice than to have them play a musical instrument. Millions of people, and not just men, would rather read the sports section in the daily newspaper than to digest the editorial on an important issue. Millions of people will pay much more money individually to experience the highly emotional atmosphere of car racing on Sunday than to go to church and pay their tithe. They are living the postmodern craving for an authentic experience and the church, as a whole, has barely entered the competition. That is the reason why Christians are looked upon as the past and predominantly insignificant. Yet not all is lost. Christians still gather in their churches. They still try to follow the teachings of Jesus Christ. But they must enter the world as Jesus did. They must and can be the salt and the light of the world. There is no better place than to join the sport-minded people where they enjoy themselves. Recreational facilities are waiting for us, but I am not talking just about family life centers where Christians segregate themselves from the sports culture. Clubs are open to new members. Christians can invite their non-Christian friends to watch a game. This can be the most natural way to penetrate the secular culture at home and in the rest of the world.

I visited Bangladesh with the goal of witnessing to some people there. During my stops in restaurants, shops, hotels, and universities, I was able to talk to men and women on a superficial level. Then I visited a local tennis club where I introduced myself as a former professional tennis player. An invitation to play with the best player in the club followed immediately. Then I played a doubles match with three other players who desired to hit the ball with me. I was exhausted because of the high temperature and humidity there, but those players would not let me leave. They begged me to teach their young people to play tennis. I did that for three days. At first I had fifteen students, the next day there were thirty-five youngsters listening to my instruction, and on the third day there were more than fifty beginners eager to learn from me. When the president of the club saw the interest of those young players, he offered me a job as a professional tennis teacher in his club. My students of three days asked me to stay as well. When I said I had to go back to the States to teach in a Christian university, they gave me their pictures and addresses so that I would not forget them. I could not have done anything like this had I not been capable and willing to use sports to befriend those young people.

We can benefit from this relationship of Christianity with sports, but we must enter the sports world with determination to build upon our similarities while upholding our differences. Representing Christ well should convince the postmodern people about the beauty, sacredness, validity, and the possibility of a personal relationship with the Almighty God.

THEOLOGICAL REFLECTIONS ON INVOLVEMENT IN SPORTS EVANGELISM

Theology should not be relegated to theoretical thinking only. Knowing the mind of God concerning the evangelization of the world must produce innovating thinking and practice so that we make progress in achieving the goal set before us by Christ himself. The question is, "How can we improve our witness to secular people around us?" We must find a way to approach sports people with the gospel. They are all around us and most of them will not go to church on their own. They play or watch sports on Sunday. While we might gather one thousand believers in a sanctuary, there are more than one hundred thousand sports-minded people in a stadium watching a car race and additional millions of fans sitting in front of their TV sets cheering their favorite drivers. There is no single verse in the Bible giving instructions about sports evangelism. So we need to look for a general principle that could be our guiding light.

Paul faced a similar problem. He was determined to fulfill the command of Christ to go and to carry the name of Christ "before the Gentiles and their kings and before the people of Israel" (Acts 9:15). His method was to use synagogues as the starting point to meet the Jews of a particular region. He presented the gospel among them and some of them became followers of Christ. But his assignment was much larger than just his countrymen. He had to reach the Gentiles and their kings. Visiting the local synagogue did not fit this enormous task. So he devised a new plan, as we read about in 1 Cor. 9:22–23: "To the weak I became weak, to win the weak. I have become all things to all men so that by all possible means I might save some. I do all this for the sake of the gospel, that I might share in its blessings."

We can follow Paul's example and establish a principle that would be biblical and practical. The words of Maclaren will help us here: "The great principle incumbent on all Christians, with a view to the salvation of others, is to go as far as one can without untruthfulness in the direction of finding points of resemblance and contact with those to whom we would commend the Gospel."[4] We must determine at the very beginning how far we can go in assimilating our lives into the lives of sports people. There is no question in my mind that they will ask us to accept their secular ways. They do not know any better. They think that their behavior is the norm. They live like they do and do not see much beauty in Christ and his followers. In fact, most of them think that Christians have very little fun in life.

Sports evangelism can change this preconceived idea. My son and I joined an amateur ice hockey club so that we could witness to those players who were not Christians. We played well and helped the team to win the league. Playing ice hockey with the team week after week enabled us to witness and to demonstrate the Christian life to them. They noticed our different lifestyle but were not turned off by it. On the contrary, they respected our convictions and were open to our proclamation of our faith in Christ. Some of them admitted that we were the first people to take the time to tell them about Jesus Christ.

Knowing the mind of God should help us embrace the theory of sports evangelism. It will open the doors into the hearts of people all over the world. The worldwide sport of soccer is probably the best sport to use. Soccer is played in rich and poor countries. A sports evangelist needs only one soccer ball, the ability to kick it, and a desire to share Christ through this ministry. We can use other sports on a smaller scale while determining the best opportunity in a given country. The possibilities are enormous.

---

4. Alexander Maclaren, *Expositions of Holy Scripture: Corinthians* (Grand Rapids: Baker, 1982), 142.

THE FUTURE OF THE RELATIONSHIP OF
SPORTS AND CHRISTIANITY

Christians have been pioneering the possibility of a mutual and beneficial relationship with sports, especially in the past two hundred years. Most Christians are willing to overlook differences arising from moral and ethical problems in two different worlds. They try to emphasize the positive aspects of sports, like spiritual growth through overcoming difficulties, the development of strong character, perseverance to win, building a strong body, and the provision of a common ground to share the Christian faith.

The future of Christianity is guaranteed by the promise of Jesus in Matthew 28:20: "And surely I am with you always, to the very end of the age." And the future of sports seems quite bright, at least for now. Power and performance sports, especially, will continue to dominate in our culture. They appeal to the athletes who like to prove their superiority by intimidating and defeating their opponents. The fans rejoice and applaud their players when they are winning and they are saddened when they are losing. But fans are forgiving, at least for a short period of time, because they will be back to cheer their warriors again. They are even ready to pay a lot of money to see the battle. They think that their presence brings about the desired win. Then, there are the sponsors who want to be associated with the winners who help them promote their products. They are helping sports' clubs to continue competing, and creating celebrities who are highly marketable. This phenomenon is happening on a worldwide scale, even in countries that are not as rich as America.

I need to mention another sports model that emphasizes pleasure and participation. These sports are more about personal enjoyment and expression, without the burden of having to defeat the opponent. They connect people who want to play for the sake of good health, relieving stress, and the joy of physical activity. Pleasure and participation sports do not generate willing sponsors, so the growth will be slow. But with the graying of America, we might see more institutions providing funds, space, and coaching for sports where winning is not everything.

Christians should understand these two models in order to adjust their methodology of penetrating both of them. Former professional, college, and high school athletes are well equipped to reach out to those who are immersed in power and performance sports. Christians with no competitive background in sports can easily associate with athletes who play sports for the fun of participating in a playful activity. The future of these ministries rests with us Christians. As we represent Christ in the midst of a secular sports culture, we can claim the presence and blessings of God.

There is no doubt in my mind that our involvement in sports evangelism is a gift of God to us in the twenty-first century. Jesus is aware of the increasing difficulty we face in order to connect with people who are being influenced by secularization. Our efforts have not been strong enough to slow down the growth of the secular population. We can no longer afford doing ministries that are not effective. We need to proclaim the same gospel and be missional in our approach to non-Christians. Here is the test. Are they going to see us as different from them, yet loving, understanding, and helpful? Are they going to see the reflection of the real Christ in us as we join them in their stadiums, parks, and gymnasiums? Are we convinced that we have something exceptional to offer that cannot be found anywhere else? If we pass this test, we are ready to go out and communicate the good news of Jesus Christ on the playing fields of the whole world and be winners in the kingdom of God.

17

Get Real:
Mobilizing Students to Witness

Alvin L. Reid

W HEN I WAS A child my family actively attended a small, young
church (we would call it a church plant today) just outside
Birmingham, Alabama. As an eleven-year-old in 1970, I would have been
described as a typical church kid—I had never done anything terribly
pernicious, but I needed Christ. This was the age of Woodstock, rock and
roll, and youthful protests, so plenty of young people were involved in all
sorts of vice. But not every young adult sought to smoke pot and take over
a college admin building. For example, at this same time of renowned
youthful rebellion, a group of hippie-types came to Christ and became a
part of our church, radically changing the culture there. In fact, our little
church was the fastest growing small Southern Baptist Church east of the
Mississippi that year because so many young people's lives were changed.

When I met Jesus, I saw the radical change he could make. While
my conversion at one level illustrated just another church kid "getting it"
and following Christ, at another level I witnessed a passion for the gospel
like I have rarely seen since. I knew Jesus could save—he saved me, and
he saved some really lost young people!

During my youth, we had a revolving door of youth pastors, but
an overall healthy student ministry. We did choir tours, retreats, revival
meetings, and saw many come to Christ. Those were exciting days. I

became a leader in my student ministry, serving as president of the student group my senior year. At my high school a friend and I started a Fellowship of Christian Athletes (FCA), and another Christian club soon followed. By my senior year we saw quite an impact at our public school. We even sponsored a youth retreat my senior year—at a public school! I led a devotional at awards day as well. We saw a strong impact made for Christ. There was only one problem.

The problem? I could organize a group. I could lead people. I could invite friends to church services. But I did not know how to share my faith. No one helped me there.

Then, in my freshman year in college, a new student pastor came to our church. He had such a passion for souls. He took a group of us through simple witness training, showing us how to use the gospel tract The Four Spiritual Laws. Within two weeks I led my first person to Christ! From then until now I have been passionate about sharing Christ and helping other believers do the same. I have given my life to this.

I share this autobiographical account to make a point: Had I been taught how to share my faith as a freshman in high school instead of college, I have no doubt that I could have led many friends to Jesus. I needed someone to train me and to show me. In college a man named Curtis Tanner mentored me along with a couple of other guys. He had us memorize Scripture, and he took us to the University of Alabama in Birmingham to share our faith. What a blessing that was in my early years!

From then until now I have been burdened about the need to enlist, equip, and engage students in the work of evangelism. I have taught literally thousands of young people to share their faith and have myriad testimonies of salvation from them. But as I travel and speak at DiscipleshipNow events (DNows), camps, and youth conferences, I am still grieved to see how many churches focus on a youth group that is inward-looking rather than a student *ministry*, interested in helping churched students become followers of Jesus who yearn to see others come to Christ. Other churches do in fact reach lost students, but do so at occasional big events, rarely, if ever, taking time to help believing students develop both a biblical mind-set and the tools to share the good news with their peers.

The church in America needs a makeover: it's overweight and under-challenged spiritually; this is especially true with students. Try building a big enough roller coaster to scare students away from riding it. You cannot build one that big! These Millennials want a cause, to seek something real, and are weary of the institutional church, which they often perceive as simply a form of organized religion. As I write this, our high school daughter has just asked us to move her from private to public school because of her great burden for students who do not know Christ. I speak to thousands of students every year and talk weekly to scores of them via Facebook, Twitter, and other forms of social media. There is a generation begging to be challenged to do something big for God. The church has nothing more magnificent to offer students than to be a part of the amazing work of the Great Commission!

PRINCIPLES FOR MOBILIZING STUDENTS

First, examine your perspective. The church has a tendency to see youth more as children finishing childhood than young adults entering adulthood. The Millennial Generation (born between 1982 and 2002) is the largest group of young people in history. They lead the way in social networking. They win gold medals in Olympics. One of their own, a seventeen-year-old named Zac Sunderland, recently sailed around the world by himself. In Scripture we read of a seventeen-year-old named Joseph living for God when his own brothers sold him into slavery; a teenager named David, too young to be a soldier in the military, killed a giant; a youth named Jeremiah was called to be a prophet; a young leader named Josiah led a revival; and a young lady in her teens gave birth to Jesus. Study the Scriptures and see what we can learn from the Bible and other cultures around the world—other than the West in recent years. In these other cultures young adults are both capable of and expected to behave like young adults, not like goofballs.

Look at the work of students in history involved in great spiritual movements. Young adults have been instrumental in some of the greatest work of the church. Jonathan Edwards observed that the First Great Awakening was essentially a youth movement. The Jesus movement mobilized a small army of youth, passionate for the gospel in the early 1970s. As a result, my tradition, the Southern Baptist Convention, witnessed her greatest years of evangelistic effectiveness in the early 1970s, and primarily because of the youth coming to Christ through the Jesus Movement.

Students can handle theology in church—they are learning trigonometry in high school! Even the Mormons get this better than Evangelicals, calling their young people to save money to go on a two year mission while about college aged. What if we in the church began to see youth as the greatest missionary force of our time, capable of going to the nations and to their neighbors with the gospel? I constantly challenge parents not to let their children finish high school without first getting out of the country on mission. Our children went to Central America, Europe, and Asia before starting college.

Teach them the gospel. Pastors and youth workers must help young people while they are young understand two fundamental aspects about the gospel. First, the gospel is the greatest idea, truth; in fact it is the most amazing message they will ever know. We fail youth when we celebrate the gospel at a rally for lost students but fail to remind believing youth of its wonder in believers' lives as well. I have witnessed too often a tendency, no doubt unintended, for ministries to focus on the gospel for unsaved students only, but not as the center of the Christian life for saved students. We, by our practice, push the gospel to the edge of our ministries, minimizing its glory. We also have a tendency to give them as little of the message of the gospel as is needed, when we should be giving them all the gospel we can in its wonder.

As I preach to students all over the nation, I constantly remind them of the great drama of redemption: that God created everything, and made everything amazing and beautiful, with people created in his very image. But the fall broke everything, so that even creation groans for redemption. Thus we have disease, and calamity, for all has been tainted by the fall. That is why Jesus came, not to teach a drill on "do this and don't do this," but to rectify what has been broken in the fall, namely our relationship with God. Thus through his death and resurrection by repentance and faith, we can have life in his name! And, one day he will consummate this age, ushering in a new creation with a new heaven and earth. This is a glorious message to be made much of with students!

Second, therefore, the gospel is not just a focus at a youth rally, it is the centerpiece of all history, all creation, all of Scripture. And thus we must teach students that the gospel is the center of all our lives. Tim Keller said it so well:

> 'The gospel' is not just a way to be saved from the penalty of sin, but is the fundamental dynamic for living the whole Christian life—individually and corporately, privately and publicly. In other words, the gospel is not just for non-Christians, but also for Christians. This means the gospel is not just the A-B-C's but the

> A to Z of the Christian life. It is not accurate to think 'the gospel' is what saves non-Christians, and then, what matures Christians is trying hard to live according to Biblical principles. It is more accurate to say that we are saved by believing the gospel, and then we are transformed in every part of our mind, heart, and life by believing the gospel more and more deeply as life goes on.[1]

Before we mobilize students to witness, we must help them to see the wonder of the gospel.

Show them the way—take them out. Teach them how to share and then take them with you to do it. As I write this I am about to take a large group of students out to share their faith this afternoon. I love seeing the enthusiasm of students involved in something that matters!

We ought to teach youth to love Jesus so much that if a mosquito flew up and bit them, it would fly away singing "Power in the Blood!" Okay, that's a bit facetious, for mosquitoes cannot tell our love for God. But people can. There are many tools to train students to share their faith. I like to use gospel booklets. You can find great tools today, or you can simply create your own. The tool matters, but the gospel is the point.

> "Some people want to live in the sound of chapel bells. But I want to run a rescue shop yard from the gates of hell." C. T. Studd.

Imagine a new football coach at the local high school who began fall season two-a-day practices with great zeal, working the students to exhaustion daily. After weeks of such practice, he told the team, "I decided that we will not have any games this year. Instead, we are only going to practice the entire season."

Having played football, I can tell you such a statement would demoralize the team. You practice so you can *play*. But this is precisely how we often treat youth. We give them our teaching, and even teach them to share their faith. But do we let them in the game? Do we take them out into the world to put their training to the test?

I learned something over the past several years. As I began to speak more and more at youth events, I made a commitment that if we had a youth weekend, such as a DiscipleshipNow event (DNow), we would give strong emphasis to prayer, to worship, to biblical preaching and teach-

---

1. Tim Keller, accessed August 28, 2008, "Keller on Preaching in a Post-Modern City," accessed April 19, 2010, http://www.westerfunk.net/archives/theology/Tim%20Keller%20on%20Preaching%20in%20a%20Post-Modern%20City%20-%201/.

ing, and to evangelism. We always have students go out witnessing on Saturdays. Many of these youth, who go for their first time ever, do not want to stop witnessing when the time is up. I have received dozens of e-mails from young people on fire for the Lord and who are leading their peers to Christ because they learned to witness by witnessing.

Kelly Green has capitalized on this emerging generation's desire to change their world by organizing Frontliners, a ministry that includes about four thousand youth in various locations spending an entire week of their summer street witnessing. Greg Stier's "Dare to Share" conferences include taking students out to share Christ.

There is a lot of talk about Christian clubs at public schools these days, and I applaud this. In the 1970s I helped start a Christian club at my school. It became the largest organization on campus. Unfortunately, most *youth groups* are merely ingrown Christian clubs. Does anyone have a burden to reach the teeming masses of teenagers? From my experience in speaking to youth, some do—Christian young people. May God raise up a generation of students with a passion for souls. I totally agree with the following quote by Len Taylor and Richard Ross: "By mobilizing [students'] efforts and empowering them to be missionaries, they can be Great Commission Christians, accomplishing the work of ministry. Sometimes we sell short the capabilities of these youths and fail to equip them for ministry. The church needs youth ministry built on new principles. Drawing a crowd is not enough. We have been good at drawing crowds of youth. But, if pizza gets them to church, what will take them out?"[2]

Christian band Audio Adrenaline wrote a great song years ago called "A.K.A. Public School." In it they sing, "They pay to put you in the classes, it's your chance to reach the masses." The greatest mission field in America is the public school classroom, where youth can reach their peers.

Perhaps it is time to train and commission Christians who teach in public schools as missionaries. Perhaps it is time to do the same with students who love Jesus.

Taylor and Ross make the point well: "Do you know where 95% of all youth can be found 7 hours a day, 5 days a week, 9 months a year for seven years of their life? And no, it's not their bed. It's their school campus. . . . We must go where they are.

2. Len Taylor and Richard Ross, "Leading an Evangelical Youth Ministry" (Nashville: LifeWay Press, 1999) 14.

"Let's face it, youth are not breaking down the doors of our churches to get there. As the teenage population continues to rise, we continue to fall further and further behind in reaching youth. Could it be that we are trying to reach them where the majority cannot be found?"[3]

Teach them a missional lifestyle. The United States now has the distinction of being the fourth largest nation on earth in terms of the number of unbelievers. We must begin thinking like and living like missionaries in an increasingly unchurched world. This starts with raising a generation to think like missionaries. Help students think about how their future careers can be lived out in a missional manner. Help them to see that witnessing means much more than occasional outreach events or community blitzes, but that it means a lifestyle of living, being, and telling the gospel in the course of our daily lives.

THE VITAL ROLE OF THE STUDENT LEADER

If you are a student pastor, a parent, or a student leader, you will never be neutral with those you lead. You either lead people to know Jesus better, or you nudge them away from him. The stakes are simply too high for us to be indifferent toward evangelism.

The passion that youth bring to witnessing can affect a whole church. I have seen this on a number of occasions. So has Greg Stier. "A handful of students in one dead church can remind the adults of what this Christianity thing is all about," he writes. "Passionate evangelism burning in the hearts of on-fire teens can set a whole congregation ablaze."[4]

George Barna notes that youth "crave unique and fun experiences."[5] I agree, and this is a great advantage for the church if we would wake up. For example, you don't have to teach teenagers how to have fun. They are quite good at having fun. They are quite good at laughing, pulling pranks, telling jokes, and so on. What we can do, however, is to coach them, to show them how to *redefine fun.* For example, on the numerous occasions when I have taken teenagers out to share their faith, their hearts race, and their knees knock. They are terrified! It is definitely an experience to remember. But, over and over and over again after these students have

---

3. Ibid., 89.

4. Stier, *Outbreak: Creating a contagious youth ministry through viral evangelism* (Chicago: Moody, 2006), 63.

5. Barna, *Real Teens* (Ventura, CA: Regal, 2001), 44.

gone out to show their faith, they've come back with such an adrenaline rush, such excitement—giving each other high fives, hugging each other, not wanting to stop, excited about the next time they get an opportunity to do that. One weekend I was out with several churches and, because of bad weather, one church was not allowed to let the teenagers go out witnessing because parents were concerned about the safety of the children. The young people who were forbidden to go out witnessing were terribly disgusted and disappointed . . . they were ready to go.

I heard about a group of teenagers in Wisconsin who were taught for one year about sharing their faith. When the classes were over they asked, "Now that we have learned this, why don't we go out and practice it?" The students encouraged the adults that led them, and they went out to share the gospel and had an incredible time. We do not need to teach young people how to have fun, we need to coach them that how living for Jesus is the greatest ride you can ever take, and that whenever you step out of your comfort zone into new, exciting, and even frightening situations where you have to depend on the Lord, there is a level of fun not of this world.

If you haven't noticed, young people *love* to talk about spiritual things. Saved youth do. Lost youth do. You don't have to have a slick salesman-like technique to get into a gospel conversation. You don't have to be clever. Just be real.

Here are some practical ways to do this:

- Mission trip: By mission trip I do not mean a glorified vacation under the banner of a church. I mean trips focused on the gospel, and in particular helping to plant churches in areas where they are lacking. I constantly challenge parents not to let their children finish high school without getting out of the country on a mission trip. I think you should do three trips a year and make them available to students: global—going to another nation; national—going to a great American city; local—doing missionary work in your own community.

- DNow: Use a Saturday afternoon for a time of outreach.

- Camp: During your summer youth camp, take an afternoon to lead an outreach project.

- Regular outreach: The church where my family serves has a ministry called G:local, which is for students involved in regular outreach into the community and preparation for annual global trips.
- In schools: Be involved in parachurch ministries like FCA or other Christian clubs.

Take an honest assessment. Is your student ministry reaching lost teens? Does your church really care about the lost youth in your community? What about you as a leader—are you committed both to sharing Christ and to mobilizing students to do the same?

Whether you are a student leader or a student reading this chapter, let me ask you a question—how is your witnessing? Evangelism is caught far more than taught, so one of the best ways to mobilize students to witness is to put them around youth workers who constantly share their faith!

If you are a student leader who has not led your students in witnessing because *you* are afraid or feel unprepared, here is some advice:

1. *Be honest.* Tell your students you are learning. They want a real person, not superman.

2. *Be a learner.* Learn to share your faith. Check out Greg Stier's book *Outbreak* for starters.

3. *Be a grower.* Let them see you are willing to grow and be changed.

Over 80 percent of professions of faith occur before age twenty. Barna found that about half of the youth who call themselves Christians and participate in youth groups in a typical month are not actually believers. That means around seven million unsaved youth are in church regularly![6]

Share the gospel in your youth meetings. Teach the word, but include the gospel in your teaching. Charles Haddon Spurgeon, the prince of preachers, said to explain the text, expound the Scriptures, and plow a furrow to the cross. How sad would it be for a student to bring a lost friend to the youth meeting and then for the speaker not to offer the gospel?

Also, teach your youth not only to invite their lost friends, but to be patient with them. There is a tremendous need in youth groups to teach young ladies biblical modesty in their dress, for example. But a lost young lady need not be singled out for her attire if she doesn't know any better. Note: Christian young ladies should! Teach guys to behave like gentle-

6. George Barna, *Third Millennium*, (Ventura, CA: Barna Research, 1999), 59.

men, but exercise gentleness if an unruly student shows up who has no idea how to act in church.

Douglas Hyde notes how Communists appealed to the idealism of youth: "The Communists' appeal to idealism is direct and audacious. They say that if you make mean little demands upon people, you will get a mean little response which is all you deserve, but, if you make big demands on them, you will get a heroic response."[7]

I recently began utilizing an idea I got from Greg Stier's *Dare 2 Share Training*. When youth return from witnessing encounters, inevitably some were slammed (slammed means to have a door slammed in your face). So, Stier applauds those teams as graduates of "Persecution University." After all, Jesus said we are blessed when we are persecuted (Matthew 5). So, I keep a tally at report time not only of how many times the gospel was shared, but also how many had doors slammed in their faces, or got chased by a dog, or got cursed for the sake of the gospel.

Persecution is a good thing. It binds people together like nothing else. Let a band of teens get radical for the gospel and face ridicule. They will bind together. Want to find a group of believers who really understand fellowship? Find a group facing persecution—they *need* each other.

Greg Stier's *Dare 2 Share* approach is another excellent way to involve youth in witnessing. His approach includes: *Prayer* (praying for lost friends), *Dare* (challenge lost friends to come to church to hear the gospel), and *Share* (unleash youth to witness to their peers). The approach *Dare 2 Share* uses in witnessing follows the acrostic GOSPEL:[8]

1.   God created us to be with Him.
2.   Our sins separate us from God.
3.   Sins cannot be removed by good deeds.
4.   Paying the price for sin, Jesus died and rose again.
5.   Everyone who trusts in Him alone has eternal life.
6.   Life that is eternal can never be lost.

Stier, who has spent much more time than I have with youth pastors, asks a series of sobering questions to youth pastors. I paraphrase below:

1.   When is the last time you shared your faith?

---

7. Douglas Hyde, *Rededication and Leadership*, (South Bend: University of Notre Dame Press, 1996), 17, in Stier, *Outbreak*, 58.

8. Stier, *Outbreak*, 195.

2. Do you talk about evangelism more than you do it?

3. Are you so busy doing good things you cannot do great things (like witnessing)?

4. Are you so busy studying the latest youth fad or technology that you fail to study the Scriptures to get a word from God?

5. Do you burn with a passion to reach every lost youth in your area for Christ?[9]

During one youth weekend, I had two ninth-grade girls on my team as we went door-to-door to share Christ. I took the two most frightened students in the youth group, because I like to do the talking! We were dropped off on one side of the street while another team took the other side. We had an uneventful afternoon, and then came to a home where we were greeted by a big, elderly gentleman. When I introduced us and named the church, he retorted angrily, "I don't like that church!" Well, I have done this a lot, and I had a hunch he was just having a good time with us.

"I bet you are a member of that church, aren't you?" I asked.

He laughed, and said, "Yes, I am." While we chuckled, I turned and saw two young ladies with faces as white as sheets. They didn't get it! They thought this man was Satan incarnate and was going to cut off their ears or worse! We had a good time laughing once they figured out he was only kidding.

Several months later, one of those young ladies e-mailed me. She thanked me for teaching her how to witness. And then she added that because of what she learned, she had led two of her friends to Christ!

Evangelism is caught more than it is taught. You can mobilize students to witness. Why not start now?[10]

---

9. Ibid., 238.

10. Much of this chapter is taken from *Raising the Bar: Ministry to Youth in the New Millennium* by Alvin L. Reid (Grand Rapids, MI: Kregel, 2004). Used by permission of the publisher. All rights reserved. Suggestions for further reading: Alvin Reid, *Raising the Bar: Ministry to Students in the New Millennium* (Grand Rapids: Kregel, 2004); Alvin Reid, *Join the Movement: God Is Calling You to Change the World* (Grand Rapids: Kregel, 2007), and Greg Stier, *Outbreak* (Chicago: Moody, 1997).

18

Effective Methods for Reaching College Students

Edward Pearson

P ETER DRUCKER SAYS, "EFFICIENCY is doing things right, effectiveness is doing the right things."[1] Enough has been written concerning postmodernists and their religious views, so the focus of this chapter
will be to consider how to effectively reach today's college students.
First, let us look at a brief overview of collegiate ministry overseas and
in North America to understand the significance of this people group,
their effectiveness in Christian work over the centuries, and why we
ought to reach them today and how.

Throughout the world's history, creative religious ideas have been
the achievement of the intellectual and spiritual insight of young men. In
literature, the arts, and the sciences, many of the most revolutionary ideas
have been worked out by young men under thirty and frequently by youths
between eighteen and twenty-five years of age.[2] The achievements are evidenced by the following names: St Francis of Assisi, Savonarola, Loyola,
Huss, Luther, Erasmus, Wesley, Mott, and Hugo. In addition, Charles
Spurgeon was a successful pastor at eighteen; Alexander Hamilton commanded the attention of his country at eighteen; George Stevenson had
the steam engine in his head at nineteen, Washington Irving and William

1. Harold Bullock, "Building a Value Shaping Ministry," unpublished DMin seminar
notes, Midwestern Baptist Theological Seminary, Spring 2004.

2. Clarence P. Shedd, *Two Centuries of Student Christian Movements: Their Origin
and Intercollegiate Life* (New York: Association, 1934), xix.

Jennings Bryan were both excellent writers at nineteen. Also at nineteen, George Washington ranked as a major and Ulrich Zwingli had read the New Testament until he doubted the authority of the church; Alexander the Great mounted the throne at twenty-one years of age and at twenty-one William Wilberforce became a member of Parliament.

Historically, students congregated in urban centers. The oldest universities date from the late twelfth century, yet the thirteenth century witnessed the university blossom as main study centers.[3] The activation of student evangelism arguably is found in Germany in the seventeenth century. Gustav Warneck writes of seven law students from Paris who committed to carry the gospel overseas. Three of those students left for Africa, yet today only information on one student remains. The student, Peter Heiling went to Egypt for two years and into Abyssinia in 1634. Heiling invested his life in the Abyssinians for twenty years and translated the Bible in the language of the people. David Howard notes, "The original impetus to leave his own land and carry the gospel to another part of the world came when he banded with fellow students to pray and work for the extension of the Church overseas."[4]

Count Nicolaus Ludwig von Zinzendorf, key leader in the Moravian movement, started a club while studying in Halle, Germany, called the "Order of the Grain of Mustard Seed." One of the club's purposes was to take the gospel overseas, and the Moravian missionaries did send out two for service in 1732. Missiologists trace the modern worldwide missionary movement's inception with this group of young men praying for world evangelism in Halle, Germany.

In 1726 Charles Wesley created the Holy Club while in college at Oxford, England. John Wesley, Charles older brother, joined the club and helped develop the methods of Christian growth, which led them to be known as Methodists, and a denomination bears the name today. A priest challenged John by saying, "The world is not your parish," and Wesley countered by saying, "The world is my parish."[5] God set a desire in the heart of John to reach the American Indians and that desire began

3. Justo Gonzales, *The Story of Christianity: The Early Church to the Present Day* (Peabody: Prince, 2005), 315.

4. David M. Howard, "Student Power in Missions," in Ralph Winter and Steven C. Hawthorne, eds., *Perspectives on the World Christian Movement: Student Power in World Missions*, 3rd ed. (Pasadena: Carey, 2004), 277.

5. John Mark Terry, *Evangelism: A Concise History* (Nashville: Broadman, 1994), 104.

as a member of the Holy Club at Christ Church College. I have viewed the University of Arizona as my parish, or mission field, and believe that campus ministers can lead students to see the college community as their field of Christian service.

Charles Simeon, minister in England at the end of the eighteenth century and beginning of the nineteenth century, opened his life to college students and made a tremendous difference. Five students in 1827 started the Jesus Lane Sunday School to reach children for Christ. These students became skilled in biblical scholarship, and the InterVarsity Fellowship of England shares that its origins are tied to the work of Simeon. Worthy of note, Charles Simeon stayed fifty-four years in the same place and influenced many students toward the gospel.

In 1882 seven young men, named the Cambridge Seven, had means, intellect, and athletic ability. Because of the influence of D. L. Moody, three of the seven placed their faith in Christ at Cambridge University and committed to service in China. C. T. Studd, one of the Cambridge Seven, helped keep the church progress going forward for world evangelism.

NORTH AMERICAN STUDENT MOVEMENTS[6]

Harvard College

Student religious societies date from 1706 at Harvard College and the earliest document with regard to a student religious club is dated January 10, 1723.[7] W. F. Howard mentions that the societies met for theological dialogues, expositions, and debates. Howard stated that there existed no campus-wide Christian student organization committed to total campus outreach in America at this period of history.[8]

---

6. Clarence P. Shedd, *Two Centuries of Student Christian Movements: Their Origin and Intercollegiate Life* (New York: Association Press, 1934) provides a wealth of information and historical documentation concerning the Student Christian Movement. Appendix 3 documents some extant works he found in his research from 1934.

7. Charles Ashby, *31 Great Years of Texas BSU Happenings: W. F. Howard-"Mr. BSU" 1943-1974* (Ft. Worth: BACA, 1978), 1.

8. W. F. Howard, "Christian Student Movements," unpublished class notes, Southwestern Baptist Theological Seminary, Fall 1987. Professor Howard taught student ministry courses at SWBTS in Ft. Worth, Texas. I am privileged to have some of Dr. Howard's hand written notes concerning student ministry, which he gave during a private meeting in his office.

The Haystack Prayer Meeting

Overseas evangelism had its launch due to the influence of one student, Samuel Mills. Mills was a preacher's son who learned to pray and lead others to do the same. Attending Williams College in Massachusetts, Mills helped to develop the pattern of praying twice a week with other students down by the Hoosack River. The Haystack Prayer Meeting happened in the fall of 1806. Led by Samuel Mills, this group of five young men went to prayer by the Hoosack River on Wednesday and Saturday afternoons. One day, lightning and thunder flashed and sounded as they ran to the college for shelter. The shower passed over them and the sun came back out again. The students dropped by a haystack and continued their time of prayer.

Mills turned the prayer time to missionary service in foreign lands. He proposed that they challenge the American church in relation to missions to other lands outside the United States. At this time, there were no American foreign missionary societies, and the British missionary societies were few. He said, "We can do this if we will," which meant that Mills and the other young men could become missionaries. Mills mentioned that they all should be prepared to serve overseas and these were the first American student volunteers for foreign missions who willed their lives to God's service wherever he needed them. The dedication of the Haystack group gave birth to the first student missionary society in America! The Williams College young men officially formed a Society of the Brethren in 1808 for the purpose of recruitment and to target missions to heathen lands. W. F. Howard quotes Kenneth Scott Latourette as saying that the "Haystack meeting provided the impetus for mission involvement for the United States."[9]

The society had a focus to advance the gospel to the world. By 1810, the Haystack Prayer Meeting emphasis about foreign missions spread to the other campuses and awakened the churches to their foreign missionary responsibility, which resulted in the creation of the first American foreign missionary society. The year 1810 also saw Samuel Mills as a theology student at Andover Seminary and, along with Adoniram Judson, requested the organization to send out foreign missionaries. They both helped to persuade Baptists of North America to develop a foreign mission emphasis. Two years later in 1812 the first five missionaries were

9. Howard, "Student Power in World Missions," 280.

appointed. Samuel Newell, Adoniram Judson, Gordon Hall, Samuel Nott and Luther Rice all sailed for Calcutta, India.

Collegiate ministries can learn from the pattern of prayer set through these college students led by Mills and The Haystack Prayer Meeting, which spawned the North American mission society and missionaries into service.

Young Men's Christian Association

The Young Men's Christian Association (YMCA) came into existence in 1844. The YMCA offered evangelism, prayer, and Bible study, and the first collegiate YMCA began in January 1858 at the University of Michigan in Ann Arbor.

The YMCA absorbed much of the collegiate religious life into its organization and functioned under the strength of evangelistic leadership like D. L. Moody's. Moody invited 251 students to Mount Hermon, Massachusetts, for a four-week Bible conference in August 1886. One hundred students out of the 251 volunteered for overseas mission work. These one hundred students made a key contribution to the church as foreign missions thrust itself to the forefront of the church. Moody's conference marks the genesis of one of the greatest mission movements in history of Christianity.[10]

Student Volunteer Movement

The Student Volunteer Movement (SVM) had the greatest influence of the time. The watchword, "The evangelization of the world in this generation," packed a powerful vision. The movement organized in 1888 with John Mott as chairman. Notably, the SVM developed a pledge card that read, "It is my purpose, if God permit, to become a foreign missionary."[11] What stands out is that the pledge places the onus upon the student signer to pray and seek the Lord about mission involvement. Students who signed the card had to deal with their commitment and the challenge of missions, or explain God's leadership not to go into missions. Accountability with peers is a good thing, but accountability should not take the role of the Holy Spirit's guidance. The SVM grew substantially for three decades and had its best year statistically in 1920. In 1920 close to

10. Charles Ashby, *31 Great Years of Texas BSU*, 9.

11. Howard, "Student Power in World Missions," 283.

6,890 attended their convention, 2,800 students signed the pledge card, and 637 students served overseas.

The year 1920 also brought the demise of the SVM. For an extensive and intensive scholarly overview, read the work of Arthur Johnston's *World Evangelism and the Word of God.* He carefully examines the International Missionary Council (I.M.C.) from 1921 until its development into the World Council of Churches in 1961. Johnston examines methodically the growth of separation between evangelical and ecumenical thought. Evangelism is far more a theological problem than one of methods. Methods change, yet principles undergirding the methods of evangelism are far more important.[12]

The SVM broke apart because of the ecumenical influences of biblical higher criticism, the social gospel, and weak leadership. The watchword, "The evangelization of the world in this generation" transitioned to "Provide an ecumenical instrument for following the church and university world to speak to each other, to encourage Christian response on campuses to human issues, and to act as an agent through which sponsors could provide resources and services to campus life."[13] Verbal proclamation of the gospel took a backseat and brought to an end the great Student Volunteer Movement officially in March 1969.

Denominational Student Ministries

Denominational ministries abound today through the following titles: Bible Chair (Church of Christ), Westminster Foundation (Presbyterian), Reformed University Fellowship, or RUF, (Presbyterian Church), Chi Alpha (Assemblies of God), Canterbury House (Episcopal Church), Newman Center (Catholic Church), Wesley Foundation (Methodist Church), Lutheran and Evangelical Lutheran Campus Ministry (Lutheran Church), Roger Williams Foundation (American Baptist), and the Baptist Student Union, or BSU, of the Southern Baptist Convention.

Baptist Collegiate Work and Some Statistics

The largest collegiate ministry throughout North America currently is the Baptist Collegiate Ministry (BCM). Baptist Collegiate Ministry, histori-

12. Arthur P. Johnston, *World Evangelism and the Word of God* (Minneapolis: Bethany, 1974), 14.

13. Howard, "Student Power in World Missions," 284.

cally called Baptist Student Union (BSU), began under the leadership of Frank Leavell in 1922.[14] Leavell viewed his work from a missionary perspective. The campus is the field of service and the missionaries consist of the BSU leaders and volunteer collegiate workers.[15] Leavell saw collegiate workers as on-field missionaries reaching a particular people group. The National Collegiate Ministry (NCM) 2007–2008 statistics show the following: 271,590 students were involved in BCM for the 2007–2008 school year; 9,050 Baptist students received evangelism training; 102,105 evangelistic contacts were made resulting in 8,685 decisions for Jesus Christ!

Why continue to reach college students? College students provided the impetus for international missions and world evangelism. Those who work with college students then and now understand they have no fear and most are ready to take the world by the tail and go forward. College workers on campus and through the local church have a great responsibility to equip and train this powerful mission force to effectively take the gospel to their peers locally and globally throughout the twenty-first century and thus emulate their historical peers.

INSIGHTS TO REACH STUDENTS IN THE TWENTY-FIRST CENTURY

I personally believe that disciplining someone is incomplete unless I have worked with the individual to develop their personal evangelism skills. I use the term disciplining because the word is biblical and connotes a relationship that potentially lasts through a lifetime. So, as we discuss the idea of effectively reaching students today, consider four works that you can pass on to your students.

First, you ought to familiarize yourself with the Higher Education Research Institute (HERI) report from UCLA released in the spring of 2005. HERI provides us all with rich insights into the spiritual interests and practices of today's North American students and can give us insights

14. The Baptist Student Union (BSU) name wears many different titles today yet are the same organization. For example, Baptist Collegiate Ministry (BCM), Baptist Student Ministry (BSM), Christian Challenge (CC is found primarily in the western United States), Student Venture, and Priority are all the same organization.

15. Frank Leavell, *The Master's Minority* (Nashville: Broadman, 1949), 96. Anyone who studies Baptist Collegiate work knows that Leavell was disciplined in the art of personal evangelism and that he modeled the evangelistic discipline to leaders and students alike.

as we reach the next generation with the good news of Jesus. For example, some of the findings include:

- 80% are interested in spirituality
- 76% are searching for meaning/purpose in life
- 74% have discussions about the meaning of life with friends
- 81% attend religious services
- 80% discuss religion or spirituality with friends
- 79% believe in God
- 69% pray

Despite the fact that considerable numbers of students are "searching for meaning and purpose in life" (76%) and discussing spirituality with friends (74%), more than half (56%) say that their professors *never* provide opportunities to discuss the meaning and purpose of life. Similarly, nearly two-thirds of the students say professors *never* encourage discussions of spiritual or religious matters (62%).[16] I believe a simple way to enter into a conversation with postmodernists is to ask the question, "Do you have any interest in spiritual matters?" We have found that HERI is correct, because (80%) of the students encountered indicate affirmatively their interests in spiritual matters and enter into conversation where the gospel can be shared. Personal involvement in the discipline of evangelism for the past twenty years leads me to believe that students appreciate an honest conversation about the gospel and spiritual matters over a rehearsed monologue presentation.

Second, read Dave Geisler's apologetic work *Conversational Evangelism*. Geisler has developed an effective practical model to evangelize in our postmodern culture. The forward by Ravi Zacharias posits an excellent definition of evangelism and reminds us that evangelism connects the mind to the real questions of the heart. He reminds us that evangelism without apologetics is like setting down your weapons in the heat of a battle.

Dave Geisler spent over ten years on staff with Campus Crusade for Christ, and he began to see that the presentational approach using

16. The HERI report, Spirituality In Higher Education: A National Study of College Students' Search for Meaning and Purpose Summary of Selected Findings (2000–2003); accessed November 5, 2009, http://www.spirituality.ucla.edu/docs/reports/Findings_Summary_Pilot.pdf.

the Four Spiritual Laws did not have the effectiveness that it once did thirty to forty years ago when many baby boomers were won to Christ. He believes that our models of evangelism need an overhaul, because while proclaiming the gospel may be simple, getting to the proclamation is not, at least on the university campus.[17] What stands out with Geisler is that his work in East Asia shows that the presentational model is not as effective as it once was in the East or the West. Not only has the presentational model waned in effectiveness, but the world we live in has changed. Students worldwide question moral absolutes and this has led to an indifference toward the truth and an intolerance toward those who believe there is absolute truth.[18] Students on today's campuses are not interested in a monologue; but if approached appropriately they may be open to a dialogue or conversation about spiritual issues. Truth imposed on others may not get beyond the eardrums, but truth surfaced conversationally is like tilling the soil of a mind or heart as a person realizes that what they believe has consequences. As Christians we would agree that mankind's ultimate problem of sin can only be taken care of through Jesus Christ who suffered, died, and rose again from the dead. The typical nonbelieving collegiate just read in the above sentence that the Christian viewpoint is intolerant, narrow, and arrogant, because we believe Jesus is the only way. I believe that Geisler offers us an approach to ponder as we grow deeper into the worldview where there is no meta-narrative, the overarching story that unites us all.

We have to remember that learning apologetics may bring the horse to water, but only the Spirit of God can make them drink. What *Conversational Evangelism* (CE) posits is that we live in a world where people are reluctant to be told what is true but are willing in some cases

17. Geisler, 17. Dave is an evangelism practitioner, he works at the discipline of evangelism. Growing up under one the leading apologists of our time, Norman Geisler, and friends with Ravi Zacharias, worldwide apologist, he teaches students the art of asking questions to help their peers drop defenses and converse about the gospel. Readers will enjoy the appendixes provided by the Geisler's. To learn more, go to his website: http://www.meeknessandtruth.org; accessed November 11, 2009.

18. The readers should take note that even in fundamental Muslim countries the students are questioning what they have been told is truth. My experience is that Muslim students appreciate a respectful approach and will engage you in conversation about spiritual matters where you may share the gospel. Accessed November 10, 2009, http://www.nydailynews.com/news/world/2009/11/05/2009-11-05_student_stuns_iran_by_criticizing_supreme_leader_.html.

to see for themselves (as in a mirror) the inconsistencies of what they believe. The CE model is a good way to supplement what your ministry leans on currently to get the gospel on campus. Geisler would say that apologetic evangelism is a tool that the Holy Spirit can use to draw students to Christ. The CE approach is really a pre-evangelism thrust to get us to the proclamation of the good news. Those of us working on today's university campuses know we need to be prepared to answer the difficult questions and ask the Holy Spirit to enable us to ask thought provoking questions that make a difference in a student's belief system.

Third, Don Everts and Doug Schaupp cowrote *I Once Was Lost* and have witnessed over two thousand college students repent and place their faith in Jesus.[19] The experiences of these men and their cohorts have led them to what they term "thresholds to cross." They feel that there are five thresholds that students cross before they become Christians. The thresholds are as follows:

1. Distrust to trust of Christians
2. From complacency to curiosity about Jesus
3. From being closed to change to being open to change
4. To move from meandering to seeking
5. To cross the threshold into the kingdom through a personal relationship with Jesus

You will find these two men living in the land of the lost, and they work at evangelism. While not systematic theologians, what I like about their idea is that they present the visual of the thresholds. Much like the Rainer Scale or Engel Scale, the five thresholds allow us to see the faith stages that student's stand at currently. Schaupp tells us that he began his evangelism ministry by singing Christian songs at the top of his lungs in the middle of the UC Berkeley campus. He has moved from a leader that repelled students, to observing five thresholds in which over two thousand students have walked across since 1996 on their way to a saving faith in Christ. I believe that this is a book worth reading, because these men are involved in the harvest of collegiate souls.

Next, to piggy back on Everts and Schaupp, I would encourage the readers to consider the evangelism strategy of Hope Community Church

---

19. Don Everts and Doug Schaupp, *I Once Was Lost: What Postmodern Skeptics Taught Us About Their Path to Jesus* (Downers Grove, IL: InterVarsity, 2008).

in the Dallas Fort Worth metro area called *Evangelism the Process*.[20] Hope Church grows primarily by conversion. Harold Bullock developed this evangelism strategy for his church congregants, not specifically for the college community, yet the strategy will work equally well in both areas. The major problems in evangelism are efficiency versus effectiveness. He suggests that Christians in Western culture used to approach people at random, or door to door, and saw many more first-time decisions for Christ than we observe today. Consequently, when an Evangelism Explosion, Continuing Witness Training, or FAITH Team visits a door today, Bullock suggests that people respond because of those prior relationships they have had with Christian friends.

In viewing evangelism as a process, Bullock posits that evangelistic fruit grows on a relationship tree in Western culture. The gospel is more like agriculture than it is industry. The more you plant and tend, the more you harvest. Hence, I see that the five thresholds found in *I Once Was Lost* and *Evangelism-The Process* provide a winning combination to effectively reach college students. In addition, Geisler, Bullock, Evert, and Schaupp are all evangelism practitioners and live and work in the trenches of non-Christians. Since these men live and breathe to be biblical, effective, committed, and evangelistic, I believe we ought to consider what they posit because their methods bear lasting fruit. Additionally, students are more open to a team approach in evangelism and working together side by side in the harvest.

Last, to plant and tend anything is hard work. Prayerfully positioning within a mission field and into another's life is not easy. Whatever method your ministry utilizes to equip attendees to share the gospel, remember that the gospel is the power to your ministry bearing fruit, not the method. Romans 1:16, "For I am not ashamed of the gospel, for it is the power of God for salvation to everyone who believes, to the Jew first and also to the Greek."[21]

Some common phrases and words used within collegiate ministry circles today are: ooze into the cracks and crevices of society; doing life together; convert to community; help people belong so they can come to

---

20. Harold Bullock, *Evangelism_The Process* [lecture online], http://discipleshiplibrary.com/search.php?a=1&e=1&m=0&p=0&n=0&s=message_title&t=NAME&ss=Bullock&st=speaker_exact&ssf=Harold,, accessed September 29, 2007.

21. *New American Standard Bible:1995 Update* (LaHabra, CA: The Lockman Foundation, 1995).

believe; students need to connect before they commit; morph; engage; incarnational; and so on. My question to the collegiate fellowship across denominational lines is when you have oozed, morphed, connected, engaged, and done life together, and you have an opportunity to share the gospel, what are you going to say? The gospel is what we market, and getting the good news to the group we seek to reach is our mindset.

Each gospel writer has their version of and focus concerning the Great Commission.[22] I suggest that the commission text found in Luke's gospel, Luke 24:46–47, contains the contents of the gospel. Jesus suffered and died on the cross and rose from the dead on the third day. Repentance for forgiveness of sins must be proclaimed in his name to all the nations. College students are keen to the suffering plight of humanity today due to instant data through online resources, and younger evangelicals view social justice issues as gospel imperatives.[23] They need to know that the suffering servant, Jesus, identifies with humanities' pain and suffering today. Jesus died for their sins and rose again from the grave to break the power of sin and death and they must repent and turn from their way of live and place their faith and trust in Jesus, and he will offer forgiveness of sins and a new life.[24]

Consistently and strategically position yourself for evangelistic opportunities on campus. Our campus ministry club has positioned itself

22. Thomas P. Johnston, *Charts for a Theology of Evangelism*, 12th ed. (Liberty, MO: Evangelism Unlimited, 2005), 13–19. Read these charts for a thorough scope and academic overview on the Great Commission texts.

23. Social justice issues are prevalent today within collegiate ministry, and rightly so. Yet, leaders of these ministries ought to seek the balance between Matthew 25 and Matthew 28 or they may end up like the Student Volunteer Movement led by J. R. Mott. The Associated Baptist Press makes a point in their article, http://www.abpnews.com/index.php?option=com_content&task=view&id=4077&Itemid=53, accessed November 11, 2009.

24. *The Art of Sharing Your Faith*, Joel D. Heck, ed. contains a chapter entitled, *The Art of Speaking the Gospel* by the evangelist Roy Fish. Fish mentions that 87 percent of a person's decision making process is based upon the sense of sight. To draw an illustration for someone could influence their decision process, and readers are encouraged to learn the bridge (sin barrier) or another gospel illustration for use when a witnessing opportunity calls. Hence, two graphs at the end of this chapter summarize Luke's Great Commission text. I start gospel conversations by saying that Jesus identifies with our pain and suffering, because he is the suffering servant. He knows and understands your pain and offers help. A Christian charter school had me speak in an assembly about the gospels contents. After my talk, I asked if everyone understood that Jesus is the suffering servant. A little first-grade girl said, "I get it, Jesus knows my ouchies."

every Wednesday from 10 a.m. to 2 p.m. with a fair booth on the campus for over a decade. Just by having a consistent presence we have had substantive conversations where the gospel is shared weekly, and four hours allows a multitude of our students to participate. In addition, a quality large group meeting is a help in collegiate ministry. I suggest having your large group meetings on campus because students who normally would not show up at a Christian facility off campus will attend a Christian event on their campus. Share the gospel at your meetings and in your small group Bible studies. A good way to end the semester's small group studies is to have them all meet together for a party and share testimonies and the gospel.[25]

Christ has called us to proclaim the gospel to a culture wrestling with postmodernism. We need to be like the men of Issachar and understand the times and what to do. First Chronicles 12:32, "Of the sons of Issachar, men who understood the times, with knowledge of what Israel should do, their chiefs *were* two hundred; and all their kinsmen *were* at their command."[26]

My prayer is that students will view evangelism as a regular discipline of the Christian life. Also, my prayer is that they will be equipped and ready to share the gospel within relational and non-relational contexts and that collegiate tribes will effectively keep up with the twenty-first century university harvest field.[27]

25. The first time we hosted a complete Bible study fellowship approximately one hundred students attended a big ice cream sundae party. We shared some testimonies along with the gospel and five students trusted in Jesus.

26. *NASB 1995 Update*. Italics mine.

27. I will posit two visuals for further consideration. The first is pillars holding up Jesus' person, work, and man's responsibility to proclaim the message. The second, entitled *The Center Holds*, illustrates the bridge to eternal life that Jesus provides and can be used to share the gospel in today's world (including both the drawing and the explanation).

The Center Holds

Humanity

Repentance

We must repent (turn) from our sins and place our faith in Jesus. {Have you?}

Forgiveness

Only God's forgiveness of our sin makes us right with him. {Have you been forgiven through Jesus Christ?}

Transformed Life

You can live a new life of strength and hope through Jesus' resurrection and become his witness to share the Good News with others!

Jesus Christ

Only Jesus Can Connect People to God

Sin Barrier Overcome by the Cross

God

Jesus Christ, God the Son, loves us and shows us how much because he

Suffered

Jesus willingly suffered for our sins and he identifies with humanity's pain and suffering.

Died

Jesus died for our sins on a cruel Roman cross.

Rose Again

Jesus arose from the dead after three days in the grave, defeating sin's power and DEATH!

And he said to them, "Thus it is written, that the Christ would suffer and rise again from the dead the third day, and that repentance for forgiveness of sins would be proclaimed in His name to all the nations, beginning from Jerusalem. You are witnesses of these things." Luke 24:46-48

The Center Holds

Each of us has a center — something we hold onto as true and right. Some hold to authoritative sources, like the sciences or the arts. Some hold to their personal experiences in life.

What's your center, and how's that working for you? In Christianity, Jesus Christ is the center. Luke's Gospel Chapter 24:46-48 explains how Jesus holds the center.

JESUS' WORK

Jesus Suffered: Luke 24:46 "Thus it is written that the Christ would suffer ..." Jesus suffered before he died, and he understands our pain and suffering. We may not know why things happen, but we can know for certain that Jesus, God the Son, knows our pain and suffers with us all.

Jesus Died: Jesus suffered and died for our sin. Why? Sin separates us and creates a barrier between humanity and God. Jesus substitutes his perfect life for our sinful life because he loves us. He BRIDGES the sin barrier and connects us to God.

Jesus Arose from the Dead: Luke 24:46 "and rise again from the dead on the third day ..." Sin brings death, but Jesus rose from the dead to defeat sin and death. Imagine the power that he holds as he stares down death and hell and says, "You are both defeated." The resurrection guarantees that your sin can be forgiven only through the Messiah, Jesus. Christ Jesus has the power to run and guide your life — better than you could ever imagine.

MAN'S RESPONSIBILITY

Repentance for Forgiveness: Luke 24:47 "and that repentance for forgiveness of sins would be proclaimed in his name to all the nations, beginning from Jerusalem." Repent means to turn from your sins. You realize the path of self-rule that you are on in life is the wrong path.

Sin is not a matter of quantity, but reality. The issue is not "Have I sinned less than others?" Instead ask, "Is sin existent in my life?" Sin is a reality, and we all sin. Each of us must ask forgiveness and call out to Jesus, who died for our sin. Then, your sin is nailed to the cross and Jesus declares that you are right with God.

Transformed Life: Luke 24:48 "You are witnesses of these things." Those who turn from their sins, ask for forgiveness and place their faith in the hands of Jesus Christ receive a new beginning, a new life. They are transformed.

Faith saves people, not good works. You cannot please God without living a life of faith in Jesus Christ. Trust in the finished work of Jesus Christ who suffered, died and rose from the dead after three days. Turn now from sin and trust Jesus to forgive and declare that you are right with God.

How are you holding up? Jesus can hold the center of your life, and he will become your greatest joy!

Pray: Dear Lord Jesus, I know that I have sinned and need your forgiveness. I believe that you suffered for sin, died for sin, and arose from the dead victoriously. Forgive my sins and take control of my life. Teach me to trust and follow you as Lord and Savior. In Jesus' name. Amen.

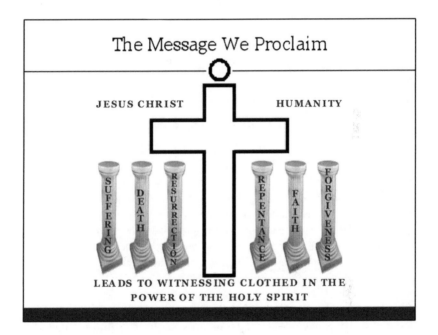

19

Disciplemaking:
Preserving the Fruit of Evangelism

Timothy K. Beougher

And Jesus came up and spoke to them, saying, "All authority has
been given to Me in heaven and on earth. Go therefore and make
disciples of all the nations, baptizing them in the name of the
Father and the Son and the Holy Spirit, teaching them to observe
all that I commanded you; and lo, I am with you always, even to
the end of the age." (Matt 28:18–20, NASB)[1]

JESUS' COMMAND IN THE Great Commission is clear. He does not command us to "make *decisions*," or to "make *converts*," but to "make *disciples*." We are instructed not simply to help lead people to faith in Jesus
Christ as Lord and Savior, but to instruct them in how to follow him in a
lifelong process of discipleship.

So how do we do that? How do we make disciples? In this chapter, I
want to follow a very basic outline. First, we will clarify the "what"—what
is a disciple? Second, we will examine the "why"—why should we make
disciples? Finally, we will look at the "how"—how can we go about making disciples?

---

1. Scripture quotes in this chapter are from the New American Standard Bible.

WHAT IS A DISCIPLE?

If we are to make disciples, we must first be clear on the definition of disciple. The noted theologian Humpty Dumpty, in the classic theological treatise *Alice in Wonderland* says, "When I use a word, it means exactly what I want it to mean—nothing more and nothing less." So when one speaks of a disciple, what does that word mean? The word means different things to different people. Put one hundred people in a room and ask them to define a disciple and you are likely to get two hundred different definitions.

At its root, the word *disciple* means a learner or a follower. Therefore, a Christian disciple is one who is following Christ, one who is learning from him. A disciple is a person in process, one who is growing in the love for and obedience to Christ. There are several verses in Scripture that add specifics to this basic definition. Matthew 10:24 emphasizes a disciple's humility and desire to learn. Luke 6:40 highlights how a disciple will become more Christlike. Luke 14:26–27 speaks to the need for a disciple to forsake all for the sake of Christ. John 8:31 focuses on abiding in Christ's word, while John 15:8 speaks of bearing fruit. John 13:34–35 illustrates that a disciple is one who unselfishly loves other believers. To summarize them all, a disciple is a person who has a supreme love for, loyalty to, and obedience to Christ.

When our youngest daughter, Karisa, was at her kindergarten orientation, the teacher, Mrs. Carter, presented a "shoebox biography" of herself. She took different items one by one out of a shoebox to help the students and parents learn more about her. For example, she took a small porcelain cat out of the shoebox and talked about how much she loved cats. To conclude, she pulled out a picture of her husband and said, "This is my husband Steve—he is my best friend."

Without warning, our daughter Karisa jumped to her feet and asked, "EVEN MORE THAN JESUS?" Mrs. Carter looked dumbfounded at our daughter, but then smiled and said, "No, sweetheart, not more than Jesus." Our daughter said "okay" and promptly sat back down. Sharon and I have a lot of failings as parents, but in this instance, by God's grace, one of our lessons had gotten through to our five-year-old daughter: no one, not even a spouse, should have a higher priority in your life than Jesus. That is a mark of being a disciple of Jesus Christ. A disciple is one who responds to the question, "Do you love me more than these?" by affirming, "Yes, Lord, you know that I love you—I will follow you."

WHY MAKE DISCIPLES?

Motivation is vitally important. When we are motivated to do something, we will make it happen even if it involves challenges. When we lack motivation, little if anything gets accomplished. What is our motivation to make disciples? Let me suggest five reasons why we should make disciples.

The Command of Christ (Matt 28:18–20)

This chapter began by citing Matthew 28:18–20, where Jesus *commands* us to make disciples. But here is a key question: do we *believe* commandments or do we *act on* them? The issue is not *agreement* but *obedience*! I am convinced if we were to ask for a show of hands in the typical evangelical church in response to the question, "How many of you believe in the Great Commission?" virtually every hand in the auditorium would be raised, many of them enthusiastically. But if we were to ask, "How many of you are actively involved in making disciples at this point in your life?" the number of hands raised would be strikingly few in comparison.

In Matthew 28:18–20, the only imperative in the passage is the command to "make disciples." The main verb phrase (make disciples) tells *what* is to be done, and the participles (going [or "as you go"], baptizing, teaching) tell *how* it is to be done. That means as a Christian, I have to be consumed with making disciples, not just decisions. I need a burden for evangelism *and* discipleship. What God has joined together, let not man put asunder. Billy Graham has often noted that the decision is five percent of the work, while the following up on the decision is ninety-five percent.

The Example of Christ and the Early Church
(Mark 3:14; Acts 14:21–22; Acts 15:36)

Jesus poured his life into the twelve disciples. Mark 3:14 records, "And He appointed twelve, so that they would be with Him and that He could send them out to preach." Jesus modeled disciplemaking in his training of the twelve.

The early church followed his example. Acts 14:21–22, referencing Paul and Barnabas, says, "And after they had preached the Gospel to that city and had made many disciples, they returned to Lystra and Iconium and Antioch strengthening the souls of the disciples, encouraging them to continue in the faith." We see Paul's burden for making disciples, not merely decisions, in Acts 15:36: "And after some days Paul said to

Barnabas, 'Let us return and visit the brethren in every city in which we proclaimed the word of the Lord, and see how they are.'"

In Colossians 1:28–29, Paul gives us his mission statement, his purpose in ministry: "And we proclaim him, admonishing every man and teaching every man with all wisdom, that we may present every man complete in Christ. And for this purpose also I labor, striving according to his power, which mightily works within me." What was his objective? It was to present every person *complete* or *mature* in Christ. Paul was preoccupied with making disciples. He was not satisfied simply with seeing people come to faith in Christ—he wanted them to grow to the point in their Christian life where they would bear fruit and could begin to help others!

The Vulnerability of New Believers (1 Pet 5:8)

First Peter 5:8 reminds us that we have an adversary and that Satan prowls about as a roaring lion, seeking whom he may devour. The devil is out to destroy us! Christianity is not a game—it's a battle. New believers are especially vulnerable to temptation as they do not yet fully know the word of God and the power of the Spirit. New believers have experienced a new birth, but it is only a birth.

In the physical realm, as parents we understand our responsibility is not over when a baby is born. We are to nurture that young life so he or she grows and develops. New babies need a lot of help and training as they grow, and spiritual babies need the same. The new believer is very vulnerable and needs help and instruction.

The Stewardship of Life (James 4:14)

Romans 14:12 reminds us that each one of us will have to give an account of the stewardship of our life. James 4:14 tells us that our life is like a "vapor" that appears for a short time and then vanishes away. Life at its longest is brief; therefore, we need to be good stewards of our opportunities.

What is our greatest stewardship? To "lay up treasures in heaven and not on earth" (Matt 6:19–21). As the philosopher William James observed, "The greatest use of life is to spend it on that which will outlast it." What is eternal? The Bible notes that only three things are eternal, only three things will last forever.

The first, of course, is God himself. Psalm 90:2 exclaims that "from everlasting to everlasting, You are God." God is eternal. Second, God's word is eternal. Isaiah 40:8 instructs us: "The grass withers, the flower fades, But the word of our God stands forever."

A third thing that is eternal is people. *Everyone* is going to live forever, either in heaven with God or in hell separated from him. People are eternal! If we are going to invest in eternity, if we are going to lay up our treasures in heaven, we must be involved in evangelizing unbelievers and in establishing new believers. As the saying goes, One life to live, t'will soon be past. Only what's done for Christ will last.

To Advance the Kingdom of God (2 Tim 2:2)

Paul gives us a concrete example of spiritual multiplication in his relationship with Timothy: "The things which you have heard from me in the presence of many witnesses, entrust these to faithful men who will be able to teach others also" (2 Tim 2:2). Within this verse we see four generations of disciplemaking: Paul, Timothy, faithful men, and others.

Multiplication is the best strategy to reach the world for Christ. We are all here because of physical multiplication. The first command of the Bible is, "Be fruitful and multiply, and fill the earth . . ." (Gen 1:28). That is perhaps the only commandment of God that humanity has consistently obeyed! Should any one generation cease having offspring, life would die out within a matter of some one hundred years. Each generation must reproduce itself to perpetuate the next.

Look at the spiritual realm. How did you become a Christian? Someone shared Christ with you. How did that person become a Christian? Someone shared with them, and the process goes back to the early Christians. *Spiritual multiplication* involves leading a person to Christ and then helping that person grow to spiritual maturity so that he or she can then in turn lead others to Christ; they can then grow and reproduce more spiritual lives. It involves not being content with merely *adding* them to the kingdom, but helping them to become a *laborer* in the harvest field.

To illustrate this truth, imagine that you have three different individuals in your Sunday school class. The first person, Fred, is a lawyer. After a challenging lesson on evangelism, Fred begins to share his faith. He is so burdened and passionate that he talks to everyone he meets. By God's grace, he begins to lead a person to faith in Christ every week. Each Sunday he is bringing a new believer to the Sunday school class. If Fred were to lead one person to faith in Christ every week for sixteen years, he would see 832 people saved. Not bad!

A second person in your Sunday school class is Mary, a real estate agent. She sees Fred involved in witnessing and thinks, "If he can do it, so can I." Mary has a lot of contact with people, and through her faithfulness in witnessing, she sees *one person a day* trust Christ as Lord and Savior. Each Sunday, Mary pulls up in her real estate van and seven new believers pile out to head to the Sunday school class. If Mary were to continue seeing one person come to faith in Christ every day, after sixteen years she would see 5,840 people saved and brought into the Sunday school class. That's a big Sunday school class even in Texas!

A third person in your Sunday school class is Bill, a plumber. Bill is challenged by Fred and Mary's example, and so he begins witnessing also. He leads a fellow plumber, John, to faith in Christ. But instead of just adding John to the kingdom, Bill begins to disciple him, seeking to multiply his life. After six months, there are just the two of them, but John is now trained in how to share his faith with others. Both Bill and John each reach someone else with the gospel and then train those persons in walking with Christ and sharing him with others. At the end of the first year, there are only four of them (whereas Fred has "added" twenty-six and Mary has "added" one hundred and eighty-two). But if Bill and John were to continue this strategy of multiplication versus a strategy of addition, at the end of sixteen years they would have reached 4,294,967,296 people! That is over four billion persons!

Billy Graham summarized:

> One of the first verses of Scripture that Dawson Trotman, founder of the Navigators, made me memorize was, "The things that thou hast heard of me among many witnesses, the same commit thou to faithful men, who shall be able to teach others also" (2 Tim 2:2, KJV). This is a little like a mathematical formula for spreading the gospel and enlarging the Church. Paul taught Timothy; Timothy shared what he knew with faithful men; these faithful men would then teach others also. And so the process goes on and on. If every believer followed this pattern, the Church could reach the entire world with the gospel in one generation! Mass crusades, in which I believe and to which I have committed my life, will never finish the Great Commission; but a one-by-one ministry will.[2]

2. Billy Graham, *The Holy Spirit* (Waco, TX: Word, 1978), 147.

The immediate question arises, "If this strategy is correct, then why haven't Christians seen it fulfilled?" It is *not* because the strategy is not sound. The breakdown occurs with people. We have settled for making decisions, not making disciples. But even if the strategy is only 10 percent effective, the sheer numbers of people reached with the Gospel is staggering. We must not settle for a strategy of addition, but we must emphasize multiplication. This illustration is in no way intended to discourage people from being involved in witnessing—far from it! We must witness to every single person we can. But we must remember our goal is not simply to lead people to make decisions, but to help them become disciples. We want those new believers deployed as kingdom workers in the harvest fields of the world.

Having seen the "what" and the "why," let me conclude with a few practical suggestions on the "how."

DO WE MAKE DISCIPLES?

Understand the Process

Perhaps the best way to understand the process of discipleship is to set forth a biblical sequence:

- *Evangelizing* (Acts 1:8)
- *Establishing* (Col 2:6–7)
- *Equipping* (Eph 4:11–12)

Evangelizing is sharing the gospel with an unbeliever, resulting in a new believer. *Establishing* is helping new believers become rooted and grounded in Christ, where they are in the process of becoming maturing believers. *Equipping* is helping a maturing believer become a ministering believer, one who reproduces his or her life in others.

In implementing the process of establishing and equipping, it is also helpful to reflect on the four means of disciplemaking utilized by the Apostle Paul. First, we observe that Paul discipled through *personal contact*. In 1 Thessalonians 2:8, Paul testifies, "Having so fond an affection for you, we were well-pleased to impart to you not only the gospel of God but also our own lives, because you had become very dear to us."

Second, we see that Paul utilized *follow-up materials*. What were these follow-up materials? Letters! The majority of the New Testament is composed of Paul's follow-up letters to new believers and/or new churches. While unlike Paul (we do not write inspired Holy Scripture), we can utilize the principle of supplying materials that will answer common questions that new believers have, and give them instruction on Christian growth.

Third, we notice that Paul utilized *trained representatives*. Notice the progression of events in 1 Thessalonians 3:1–6:

- Therefore when we could endure it no longer, we thought it best to be left behind at Athens alone,

- And we sent Timothy, our brother and God's fellow worker in the gospel of Christ, to strengthen and encourage you as to your faith,

- So that no one would be disturbed by these afflictions; for you yourselves know that we have been destined for this.

- For indeed when we were with you, we kept telling you in advance that we were going to suffer affliction; and so it came to pass, as you know.

- For this reason, when I could endure it no longer, I also sent to find out about your faith, for fear that the tempter might have tempted you, and our labor would be in vain.

- But now that Timothy has come to us from you, and has brought us good news of your faith and love, and that you always think kindly of us, longing to see us just as we also long to see you.

Paul was unable to minister to them personally, but he was able to ensure that a trained representative (in this case, Timothy) was there to encourage and guide them.

Fourth, we observe that Paul utilized what may be the supreme method of disciplemaking: *prayer*. Paul writes to the Thessalonian believers, "We give thanks to God always for all of you, making mention of you in our prayers" (1 Thess 1:2). Paul may not have been able to be with these new believers in person, but he could personally pray for them and ask God to be at work in their lives in a powerful way.

Understanding all four of these means is important, as some people only view disciplemaking as being done through personal contact. While that approach is important, at times circumstances will warrant the use of follow-up materials or trained representatives. And of course prayer should always be the foundation for the disciple-making process.

Follow Key Principles

It has been noted that methods are many; principles are few. Methods often change; principles never do. Following are some key principles to apply in the disciplemaking process.

Focus on the basics

New believers need to be taught *doctrine*, to help them become doctrinally grounded and scripturally oriented. They also need to be instructed in *devotion*, how to walk with God on a daily basis through reading the word and prayer. If babies do not eat, they do not grow. Spiritual "babes in Christ" need to feed on the word of God for their spiritual growth. They also need to be trained in *ministry*, especially in how to share their new-found faith with others. New believers have great potential in witnessing, because they usually know many unbelievers. What a shame to wait until they are years old in the faith to train them in how to share Christ with others! Finally, new believers need to grow in *character*, to learn how to cultivate their strengths and strengthen their weaknesses.

Tell them why

While initially it is fine to encourage a new believer to practice the spiritual disciplines "because they are helpful to growth," at some point the discipler needs to help the new believer develop his or her own convictions about spiritual matters. If they are doing something simply because it is *our* conviction, what happens when we are no longer around? They must develop their own convictions. As Paul said to Timothy, "You, however, continue in the things you have learned and become convinced of . . ." (2 Tim 3:14).

Show them how

The discipler must model what he or she wants others to do. Paul expressed it well, "Follow me, as I follow Christ" (1 Cor 11:1).Or as Robert Coleman has asserted, "One living sermon is worth one hundred explanations." Disciples cannot be mass produced. The process must be modeled by someone. If you cannot disciple someone personally, help them connect with someone who can disciple them.

Keep them going

New believers need encouragement! At times we forget how frustrating the process of learning and growth can be. Hebrews 3:13 provides a practical exhortation: "But encourage one another day after day, as long as it is still called 'Today', so that none of you will be hardened by the deceitfulness of sin." Provide regular and abundant doses of encouragement to new believers.

Point them to Christ

The discipler's objective is to help a person become a disciple of Jesus Christ, not of you or me. We must always point the person to Christ, not to ourselves (1 Cor 11:1). We will at times not live up to the truth we profess; we will be a hypocrite before others. But there is one who never fails—the Lord Jesus Christ. He is our perfect example. He will never leave us or forsake us.

TWO CLOSING THOUGHTS

First, we need to always remember that kingdom work is a spiritual enterprise. As Paul reminds us in Ephesians 6:12, "For our struggle is not against flesh and blood, but against the rulers, against the powers, against the world forces of this darkness, against the spiritual forces of wickedness in the heavenly places." We must follow the example of the Apostle Paul as he was constantly praying for new believers that they would come to maturity in Christ.

Second, the most common excuse I hear from individuals as to why they cannot disciple someone else is that "I have never been discipled." Do you know the definition of an excuse? It has been said that an excuse is "the skin of a reason stuffed with a lie." When persons say, "I haven't been discipled," they may be right—if they are referring to a formal, structured process. But all of us have been discipled in many ways: by family members, friends, and other believers. Other people have helped us in our walk with Christ, even if it was informally. We simply need to begin to be more intentional about the disciplemaking process in our lives and in our churches.

Also, even if you have not been formally discipled, that does not mean you cannot help someone else grow. The key principle is that you only need a short head start. I enjoy the game of golf (even though I'm not that good at it). If I were to see Phil Mickelson on a driving range, it would be the height of audacity for me to presume to give him tips on his swing. And he would be absolutely crazy to listen to anything I have to say about golf. But suppose I'm at a golf driving range and I see a beginning golfer holding the club by the wrong end, holding the head of the club in his hands and attempting to hit the ball with the grip end of the handle. Would it be arrogant of me to help him turn the club around? Of course not! I may not be able to help him become a PGA Professional, but I can help him hold the club by the right end.

I don't have to know everything before I can help someone with the disciplemaking basics:

- Do you know how to have a daily quiet time? Then you can help someone else.

- Do you know the basics of prayer? Then you can help a new believer with his or her prayer life.

- Do you know how to communicate the gospel message to an unbeliever? Then you can help a new Christian learn how to share.

You only need a short head start.

Jesus did not command us to make decisions, but make disciples. Let's start obeying our Lord and Master!